BLESSED

AND

OBSESSED

Official Autobiography
of Mick O'Dwyer

with Martin Breheny

BLACKWATER PRESS

Editor
Adam Brophy

Design & Layout
Paula Byrne

Cover Design
Karen Hoey

ISBN 978-1-84741-168-6

Produced in Ireland by
Blackwater Press
c/o Folens Publishers
Hibernian Industrial Estate
Tallaght
Dublin 24

Contents

Martin Breheny's Acknowledgements

When John O'Connor of Blackwater Press and Mick O'Dwyer invited me to come aboard for this project my first reaction was to wonder where I would find the time.

But then, there's always time to do something you're interested in and since I have always regarded Mick O'Dwyer as one of the most fascinating, not to mention important, characters in GAA history, I was delighted to get the opportunity to work with him on this book.

My first memories of Gaelic football are of the Galway All-Ireland three-in-a-row team of 1964–66, one of the finest collection of players ever to assemble in any county. And since most of that great team were from my part of north Galway, they assumed true giant status in young eyes.

That they beat Kerry – Micko and all – in three successive championships made them all the more special. Revisiting that period for the book wasn't Micko's favourite part (although it was for me!) but he had so many remarkable years as a player and manager that he was more than compensated.

So then, thanks to Micko for inviting me to join him on this latest adventure and for being so accommodating in terms of time and travel which, more often than not, were designed to suit me rather than him. Thanks too to John O'Connor and his top rank Blackwater crew: Adam Brophy, Paula Byrne, Oisín Burke and Karen Hoey.

Ray McManus and his Sportsfile team provided most of the pictures to the style and standard we have all come to appreciate. Thanks too to Jason Clarke. As for my own family, Rosemary, Alan and Linda were, as always, wonderfully supportive and patient, drawing the line only when I occasionally broke into a Kerry accent after being exposed to Micko's Waterville lilt for so much of this year.

Martin Breheny
October 2007

Mick O'Dwyer's Acknowledgements

The trouble with acknowledgements is that you know that many people who deserve a word of thanks will be overlooked. So let me apologise in advance to those I don't mention – your support and friendship down through the years are very much appreciated.

As for the others, I'll start with those directly involved in bringing this book to fruition, from John O'Connor of Blackwater Press who first mooted the idea, to Martin Breheny who then picked up the ball and went on a year-long solo run which took him into every nook and cranny of my life and times. If ever there was a man suited for the job it was Martin, whom I have known for many years and who always brings great knowledge and skill to his writing.

Mind you, why I had Martin, who's from Galway, and John, from Offaly, producing my story is beyond me since both counties caused me awful grief as a player and manager.

Michael Fingleton, Managing Director of Irish Nationwide Building Society, is a great GAA enthusiast who always comes up with tickets for big games. He came up trumps again, this time as sponsor of this book for which I'm very grateful.

On the football front, I'll start with former Kerry Chairman Gerald McKenna, the man who decided it was worth taking a gamble on me as manager back in 1974. Did he know what he was letting loose? His successor, the late Frank King, was also a joy to work with even if I landed the poor man in trouble with the GAA authorities a few times.

The late Michael Osborne, one of the most dedicated football men I ever met, was largely responsible for bringing me to Kildare where I worked with so many outstanding people in what is a great football county. Declan O'Loughlin played a huge part in my move to Laois where County Chairman Dick Miller was also a joy to work with.

Then on to Wicklow where I was inveigled into service by Billy Timmins TD while the then County Chairman, Mick O'Hagan, was also very supportive as is his successor, Andy O'Brien. Great football people all. Of course, wherever I went my great friend Arthur French usually had something to do with it, using whatever it took to get his own way.

A word of thanks too to the hundreds of players I came across as a player and manager, men who light up the fields of Ireland in winter or summer.

Last, but by no means least, to my own family, my wife Mary Carmel and our four lads – John, Michael, Robert and Karl. Thanks for everything through the many years that I've lived this football-addicted life.

Mick O'Dwyer
October 2007

Preface

Give me a football, a field and a dream and I'm happy. I feel at home there. The world can load on its strains and stresses but I won't feel them, not while I'm involved in Gaelic football, a truly fantastic game that can compare more than favourably with any field sport in the world.

I'm on this earth since 1936 and, for as long as I can remember, football has been as much an inspiration as an interest and at this stage I doubt very much if it's going to change.

The game itself has moved from the relatively easygoing times of years ago to the professional approach that applies nowadays but, through it all, one basic principle has remained sound. It's still my parish against yours, my county against yours, as rivalries unfold from Kerry to Antrim, from Galway to Dublin and from Donegal to Wexford.

I have travelled through all 32 counties for more than fifty years in what I would regard as an on-going adventure. Apart from my native Kerry – the finest place on earth – I have had spells as manager in Kildare, Laois and now Wicklow, counties with a real passion for football and with the will and determination to indulge it.

The GAA has always been a wonderful influence on Irish life, not just as a sporting organisation but also as a national movement. Nothing unites people in this country like the common goal of achieving something together on the GAA fields, whether with club or county.

There is no better feeling for any county than when they win an All-Ireland football or hurling title. It makes their people feel so much better about themselves. But then it's not necessary to win the All-Ireland to create a sense of wellbeing. The joy on the faces of the people from Kildare and Laois when long spells without a Leinster title ended or the elation in Wicklow when the Tommy Murphy Cup was won in Croke Park this year (2007) will always remain fresh in my mind.

I see this book as a celebration of the great game that is Gaelic football. I have been lucky to win many trophies as a player and manager but ultimately the game is about all the participants and spectators. It is to them that I dedicate my story.

Message from
Michael Fingleton

It is a great honour and pleasure on behalf of the Irish Nationwide Building Society to be associated with this publication and, indeed, with Mick O'Dwyer who over the past fifty years has made such a unique contribution to the GAA both on and off the field.

He graced the field of play with distinction in the Kerry jersey and later as the manager of the great Kerry All-Ireland winning teams of the Seventies and Eighties.

He has successfully transferred his managerial talents to many other counties with equal distinction. He is a great ambassador for the game and his popularity throughout the length and breadth of the 32 counties is unprecedented.

May he add many more achievements to his long list well into the future. He is, and always was, his own man. I am personally delighted and privileged to have known him and to have him as a true friend.

Michael P Fingleton
Managing Director
Irish Nationwide Building Society
October 2007

In the Arms of an Obsession

I may as well come clean. I'm a double addict, an incurable case, totally beyond redemption. Football and driving took hold of me an awful long time ago and never let go. They shaped my life, my career and my very being to such a degree that I became a man possessed and obsessed. I have been blessed too, in many ways that I deeply appreciate.

The football and the car united as if by secret pact to send me in a direction that I could never have envisaged growing up as a kid in Waterville. Most peoples' lives evolve and change as they get older. Things that seemed so important at one stage take on a different perspective over the years. Interests usually broaden or narrow depending on circumstances and ambitions become fewer and more refined as life moves on.

Not for me, and certainly not in the area of football or driving. I have no idea why football took such a powerful hold on me all those years ago and kept tightening its grip as I got older. I have often said that football just wasn't in my blood – it is my blood. The fascination with the game became all-absorbing, all-consuming and it has never waned or diluted in the slightest.

I would dearly love to be still playing football. There have been many times, as I stood on the sideline watching a game, that I'd say to myself: 'God, what I'd give to be out there?' Having played in so many positions I know the particular requirements of each one in minute detail so I play every game through the mind's eye of individual players.

Having long experience both as a defender and an attacker was a huge help when I took up management. I was brought up in a Kerry scene where we played in zones and where the basic rules of engagement were that you tried to beat your man for possession and kick the ball to another zone where a colleague was supposed to beat his direct opponent. It was simple and straightforward and, because Kerry had a tradition of producing good players, it worked very well.

My experience all over the field widened my vision considerably. Playing in the half-backs gave me a real appreciation of how attacks could be launched from deep. I saw play coming at me like a wave but learned that if I could help stop the tide, half-back was a great place from which to ride back out when the worst had past. It also gave me practical experience of dealing with half-forwards, a busy lot with a deep bag of tricks. A few games against the likes of Seán O'Neill of Down would do more for a wing-back's football education than a thousand training sessions and a hundred hours of team talks.

When I moved to the forwards, I brought with me an understanding of how defenders thought. I knew what they liked and disliked, what they feared and how they ticked. I loved the freedom in attack, the constant mental battle with a defender who's trying to second guess you. He has to get it right all the time, every time, whereas a forward only needs to take a few chances to change a game.

Nothing compares to playing which is why I'd love to drop fifty years off the birth cert, buy a new pair of boots and be a young footballer starting out again. But then, my passion for the game is every bit as intense now as it was when my father bought that first football for me back in the early 1940s.

I can't explain it but I'm never as at home as when I'm on a football field. And it doesn't have to be Croke Park on a big day, although that's a thrilling experience. I love the whole scene surrounding football, the training, the planning, the tactics and even the bit of trickery. Every time I pass a pitch in any part of the country I think of the drama and excitement it has experienced over the years. If there's a game on, and I have a bit of time to spare, I'll screech to a halt and take a look in, even if it's only a junior challenge. Every game has its own particular fascination, whatever the grade, the county or the standard.

My wife, Mary Carmel, used to give me hell about stopping to look in on games when we'd be travelling somewhere but over the years she came to understand that she was married to a bloody lunatic who couldn't live without football and needed a regular fix from whatever source was available. And if that happened to be some unimportant club game on a windswept pitch, so be it.

Inevitably, I suppose, that obsession for the game was misconstrued by some people with small minds and begrudging attitudes. Long before I finished as Kerry manager, the word was out that O'Dwyer was making a fortune out of football although it wasn't until I went to Kildare that the rumour machine really cranked up. I was supposed to be travelling from Waterville to Newbridge by helicopter organised by the late Michael Osborne, a truly great football man who would do anything for his beloved Kildare.

Various sheikhs and other vastly wealthy racing people were reputedly shoving great wads of cash into my back pocket as I left St Conleth's Park after training. They had bought me a house, an apartment, a mansion or maybe even a castle, depending on the storyteller.

The rumours flew even higher when I went back to Kildare a second time. And so it went on and on. By the time I joined Laois at the end of 2002, I was reckoned to be earning more than the Taoiseach. And when I linked up with Wicklow last year, the deal was supposed to be so good that Sir Alex Ferguson became consumed by jealousy and stormed straight to his Manchester United bosses, demanding that he be put on the same pay as me.

You can just imagine Ferguson thundering into the Manchester United boardroom, and shouting: 'Bloody hell, boys, O'Dwyer's on more than me according to what I hear from Ireland. It's nay right – he's an amateur.'

Rumours of my vast earning power would have been all very comical if it didn't have such a nasty side. I was never one to give a toss what people thought of me but it's a different matter when groundless rumours begin to impact on your life. I didn't want ordinary GAA people thinking that I was a mercenary who was involved in management purely for money. For a start, it was untrue but apart from that it was irritating that an image of me was being created which was way off the mark.

There were so many snide references to my so-called deals in newspaper articles that I became infuriated enough to send a solicitor's letter to one particular columnist demanding that he either furnish evidence or shut up. In fairness, he apologised and the matter was left at that. However, the damage was done.

I have no doubt that some very senior people in the GAA hierarchy were stirring things up too. They disliked me a lot and distrusted me even more because they felt Kerry had outflanked them with commercial deals in the 1980s when, in fact, all we did was tap into the many opportunities that were staring us in the face. It suited the lazy, unimaginative GAA establishment (who had pushed their heads into the sand leaving their great big backsides to be kicked by other sports who were cashing in on sponsorship deals) to have a doubt hanging over me as some sort of money-grabbing rebel intent on wrecking old values.

It gave them a chance to prattle on incessantly about the threat to amateurism and how vital it was to keep an eye on managers' deals. I paid little attention to them but I am sure that all the rumours attracted the attention of the Revenue Commissioners.

It was understandable too because if they kept reading and hearing of this fella from Kerry who was reputedly earning a fortune out of managing teams, it was only a matter of time before they decided to check out if it were true. It came as no surprise then that after I left Kildare in 2002 I received a letter from Revenue informing me that I was to have a complete tax audit.

All aspects of my businesses and my personal affairs were to be investigated which they duly were. The tax people went through every cheque book, docket, file, ledger and invoice and they trawled through every bank account and every deal going back many years. I had no problem with that – they were merely doing their job and, with so many rumours flying around, they had every reason to believe I was up to all sorts of financial devilment. I had to present my case before a judge in Tralee but I was always confident that I would be able to show that everything was above board for the simple reason that it was.

I am meticulous when it comes to keeping receipts and mileage records which was just as well because I had to put it all before the tax inspectors. They waded through everything and were satisfied that all was in order and I have the tax clearance to prove it. I had no problem with the tax people, who were simply doing their jobs, but it annoyed me to think that the audit may well have been brought about by the malicious whispering campaign. For all I know, some powerful figure in the GAA may even have suggested to Revenue that they look into the affairs of that O'Dwyer bucko. I'm sure they would have been delighted if I had been outed as a tax defaulter as that would have helped in their spurious and unnecessary battle to protect amateurism. It would also have looked bad for me which would, no doubt, have pleased them greatly.

The truth is that my obsession with football has cost me money over the years. Granted, it was a help too, especially in the early years as it brought in business to the garage and the hotels. It's amazing the number of people I still come across who remind me that they got their cars fixed in my garage when something went wrong while they were on holiday in the area. Others will talk of staying in the hotels so there was no doubt that the football angle was an advantage in one sense. However, the more energy and effort I devoted to football, the less I gave to my businesses.

Mary Carmel would often say to me that if I devoted the same amount of time to business as I did to football, we would have had some empire. She was right. I passed up several business opportunities because of football. I wouldn't have had the time to concentrate on them so there was no point becoming involved in a half-hearted way.

I had a mad schedule in my days with Kerry. Leave Waterville at 6 pm to be in Killarney an hour later. It was boot to the floor all the way there and back. I'd try to be home in Waterville before midnight because we were running dances and discos in the hotels. I'd rarely be in bed before 4 am and I'd be out again early the following morning. I was never a big sleeper so I was able to keep that schedule up without feeling tired. In fact, I got a buzz out of being so busy.

I loved dealing with bands and band managers. The haggling, the wheeling and dealing and the odd argument added spice to it all at a time when the showband industry was going strongly in Ireland. They were all well able to look after themselves but I wasn't too bad either when it came to fighting my corner. I got very friendly with the late Tony Loughman who provided me with the best bands around at the time. Tony was a great character whose devotion to football – especially his beloved Monaghan – knew no bounds. It was always a pleasure dealing with him, even if we were always trying to outdo each other; it was part of the fun.

Joe Dolan, The Fureys, The Wolfe Tones, Brendan Grace, Christy Moore, Susan McCann, Margo and Royal Flush were all regulars while we also had a great relationship with a band from Limerick called Midnight. Then there were the Kay twins, who started their musical careers with the Artane Boys Band. They actually played in Croke Park for the 1969 final, the day I won my third All-Ireland medal. The bands who were playing the circuit at that time were damn fine musicians who never really got the credit they deserved in the media, although the public loved them. But then it wouldn't be the first or last time that the media were totally out of touch with the mood and personality of so much of the country.

I remember Margo asking me one time to book a new band that had come on the scene. She talked glowingly about them, especially the lead singer who turned out to be none other than her brother, a certain Daniel O'Donnell who went on to establish a massive reputation at home and abroad.

Between the hotels, the garage and the football, life was hectic. It got even busier when Mary Carmel's father died and we took over his undertaking business. There was scarcely a facet of business in Waterville in which we weren't involved and, on top of that, I was running the Kerry team. In fact, I was devoting more time to football than to business because, on top of the many trips to Killarney for training and all over the country for games, I was always thinking about football. So, while I might be physically present in the hotels or the garage, my mind would be wandering to such crucial matters as how best to get more ball into Sheehy and Egan. It was all-consuming from the moment I took the giant leap into the unknown at Gerald McKenna's invitation at the end of 1974.

That's why it's irritating to have accusations about being a football mercenary hanging over me. How dare people judge me when they haven't a clue as to my real motivation? What I got from the Kerry County Board in the 15 years I was in charge of the team wouldn't pay for my petrol but I didn't care. I wasn't in it for the money and that would later apply to Kildare, Laois and Wicklow too. Of course, there will still be cynics who won't believe me but frankly, I couldn't care less. If you worry about what others think, you'll never try anything. And if you worry about people of absolutely no consequence, it's a sign of a serious lack of self-confidence.

That doesn't mean that unfounded allegations shouldn't be of concern because if they go unchecked they have a nasty habit of taking on a sinister life of their own. For instance, the rumours over my arrangements with Kildare were plain crazy. People probably won't believe it – and I couldn't give a damn whether or not they do – but when I first met Michael Osborne and the other members of the Kildare Supporters' Club, money wasn't even mentioned.

They wanted me to come to Kildare and the only issues from my side were whether I was prepared to take on a big, new challenge and whether it would be feasible to commute between Kildare and Waterville. When I started making the journeys to Kildare, I received expenses as laid down by the GAA, which were paid to me by Michael at the end of every month. They were paid by cheque so there was a clear and permanent record of everything. It was the way both Michael, who was also a stickler for detail, and I wanted it because we both had a feeling that there might be questions asked later on.

The stories about flying up and down in helicopters were as untrue as the claims that I was earning a fortune with Kildare. Not once while I was with Kildare did I fly by helicopter to training. And there were no private planes either. In fact, when I started out, I was driving an old Mercedes that I had taken in below in the garage in Waterville.

The routine for the Kildare job was a lot more mundane than some would have you believe. I'd leave Waterville at around 2.30 in the afternoon and head for Newbridge. I'd have a quick meal after training and spin back down again, usually arriving home at around 2 am. Sometimes, I'd stay in Kildare for a few nights but in the early days I drove up and down an awful lot.

But then, unlike many others, I love driving. I have driven millions of miles over the years and enjoyed every one of them.

Where possible, I drive at night when the roads are quieter and I can motor along at a decent speed. Some of my travelling companions would have you believe that I'm a mad driver who puts the fear of God into passengers. They like to exaggerate, although I do admit that I wouldn't be one to dawdle along when I have a good car, an open road and a destination to head for.

Thank God, I have been very lucky on the roads, especially when you consider the amount of mileage I have put up. I had a tip one time back in the mid-Eighties near Ballincollig in Cork when a tractor pulled out in front of me. We collided but I was driving a sturdy Mercedes which withstood the impact and I escaped uninjured, even if the car took a battering. That has been the extent of my escapades on the road.

There was no way I could have taken over in Kildare, Laois or Wicklow if I didn't love driving as much as I do. I have always found it very relaxing to sit into a good car, turn on the tape (as it used to be) or the CD. Before the days of the bloody mobile phones, there was no way of reaching me in the car so I had peace and quiet to work things out. Most times, football matters would be swirling around in my head, mile-by-mile, hour-by-hour.

Before a match, I'd be working out how or where my teams might sneak an advantage and afterwards, I'd replay the game over and over again in my mind, going through every individual performance. If we lost, I'd try to rationalise exactly what went wrong and make a mental note to try something different the next time. If we won, it was a question of reliving the best bits while sorting out any problems that arose. There's nowhere better to do that than on your own in a car with the countryside flying by.

I love being on my own which might seem like a contradiction because I'm also very sociable and like being with people. I have attended thousands of functions over the years and still enjoy them but I have always been happy in my own company too. I was lucky that I never drank alcohol because it meant I could leave a function in the early hours of the morning and drive home and still be as fresh as a daisy the following morning. I have no doubt that being a non-drinker was a great help in keeping me fit and focused over the years. Anyway, I always felt that anybody who owns a bar shouldn't drink alcohol because it's all too easy to become your own best customer, a sad tale that has been told many times over in all parts of the country.

An alcohol-free life has certainly worked for me. I never had enough hours in the day to do everything I wanted so I would have regarded sitting in a pub for a few hours knocking back pints as a scandalous waste of time.

No, give me the mountains, the sea or the golf course any day. There's nothing nicer than driving through the countryside on a pleasant day. It's only in the last year that I got to know Wicklow in all its beautiful detail and, while nothing can ever compare to Kerry, I'd have to admit that the Garden County comes close.

Several times in the course of this year I would stop somewhere in the Wicklow mountains, take a brisk walk and soak in the magnificent scenery and serenity. I can do it because I love being on my own so much. I even like to play golf on my own at times. I did it quite a bit when I was managing Kildare. Sometimes, I'd stay in Kildare overnight and head out to the Curragh or the K-Club at around seven in the morning and play a round. Because I was on my own I could play two balls or concentrate on some particular aspect of my game such as chipping or putting which I found a great help in the ongoing battle to get the handicap down. I got it to seven at one stage but I never had enough time to really work on it. I would have loved to have been a scratch golfer and I'm convinced that I would have been if I had more time to play, but it just wasn't possible because of the demands from football.

Football kept me away from another great passion – motor rallying. If I hadn't become so consumed by football, I would have taken to rallying. In fact, I had prepared a car for the Rally of the Lakes one year but I couldn't compete because it clashed with a Kerry game and I never bothered much after that. I love speed – in fact, if truth be told, I would have given anything to have a go in a Formula One car. It's unlikely to happen now but you never know!

Cars have always held a fascination for me, not just for the thrill of driving but for the way they allow you to be alone with your thoughts while travelling from A to B. I'm one of those people who can quite happily be on my own among crowds too. One winter in the early Eighties I decided to undertake a world tour. Mary Carmel wasn't into all the long-distance travel but she insisted I go anyway because it was something I always wanted to do.

I travelled light with a carrier bag only, jumped on a plane in Shannon and headed for Singapore. From there it was on to Melbourne, Adelaide, Sydney, Fiji, Honolulu, San Francisco, Chicago and New York before jetting back home. It took 31 days to complete and really was a wonderful adventure. The fact that I was alone didn't bother me in the slightest. Many people have said to me that they couldn't go on a trip like that without company but I was quite happy taking in the sights, doing my own thing and relaxing in various cities right across the globe. I'm a country boy at heart but I also like to experience cities and towns. Once I know I can go back to the sea and the mountains, I'm happy. I love the roar of the crowd but the sound of silence can be blissful too.

I have always managed to keep a balance between the enjoyment of being part of a team situation and the need to have quiet times away from it all. Yes, I'm obsessed with football but I'm also blessed in many other ways. Blessed that I had a talent which was encouraged; blessed that I was from Kerry where I could indulge it at the highest level as a player; blessed that when I took over as Kerry manager the greatest collection of Gaelic footballers in the game's history were maturing; blessed that I got so much fun out of managing Kerry, Kildare, Laois and now Wicklow; blessed that I had the good health to pursue my dreams and ambitions.

Away from football, I have been blessed too, not least that I was born into a home which gave me values that would sustain me through life, not to mention encouraging my football ambitions which came to dominate my life while also impacting on those around me.

For a woman who has no interest whatsoever in football, Mary Carmel made one hell of a contribution to the GAA which, at times, she must have hated because it took up so much of my time. Our four lads, John, Robert, Karl and Michael, enriched our lives in a special way so, as I readily admit, my list of blessings makes rewarding reading. None of the lads were lucky enough to win an

All-Ireland senior medal but I won four so I have one each for them. I also won eight National League medals; they can have two each of those!

Actually I must root around the house sometime to see where the medals are. They're there somewhere but I never bother with them. Winning an All-Ireland is as much a state of mind as anything else. The medal is grand but the memory and the sense of achievement is what really counts.

Of all the blessings a person can have, health is the most important of all and I'm glad to say I have been very lucky in that regard. The ankles and the knees get a bit sore at times but that comes from old war wounds and is to be expected. Otherwise, I'm in grand condition, especially since I had a little heart procedure earlier this year.

I'm really disappointed with the attitude towards health and fitness in this country. It frustrates me that the Departments of Health, Education and Sport don't get together to work out a plan to make physical fitness an important part of people's lives from the minute they can walk.

I'm a member of the Irish Sports Council and I'm sure I drive the others mad by constantly going on about the need to make physical education a central part of the school programme. The habits that people form when they're very young tend to stick with them and that includes taking exercise. On the other hand, if kids don't get into the routine early, they are unlikely to start later.

Fitness for life, as opposed to fitness for sport, should be on the school curriculum right from the start but while everyone seems to think it's a good idea, nothing is being done to put it on a formal footing in our schools which is a travesty. The days when kids got exercise walking to and from school are gone so it has to be on the curriculum. Cost shouldn't be a consideration because, in the long run, the benefits from having a fitter, healthier society would be incalculable, not least in cutting down on medical costs in hospitals and elsewhere.

I often wonder what direction my life would have taken if I wasn't interested in football or if I had been born away from Kerry. I would certainly have loved to have tried my hand at golf or rally driving and, in terms of field games, I would have taken up rugby if the opportunity arose.

I regard it as a great game, perfectly suited to the Irish temperament. Playing rugby wasn't an option in south Kerry, so I'll never know if I would have been good enough to get on the Lions team!

Out-half or wing-forward would have been my favourite positions. I came close on one occasion to playing for Sunday's Well seconds in Cork, thanks to an invitation from my good friend, Jim Buckley, who played at wing-forward for Ireland a few times back in the early 1970s. Jim worked in insurance and used to call on me regularly. He told me one time that he could arrange for me to play for Sunday's Well if I was interested. I jumped at the chance. He was planning to play me at full-back but I had to pull out at the last minute because a football game was fixed for Waterville on the same day. I was fierce disappointed and, for one reason or another, I never did get a chance to play rugby afterwards which I greatly regretted.

But then finding time for anything outside of football was always one of my big problems. So much to do, so little time. That's what happens when your life is governed by a force over which you have no control. And if I'm honest, I have to admit that football controlled me rather than the other way around. And it won't change now, I reckon.

Jobs for the Big Boys

Of all the jobs in inter-county management, three stand out as the most desirable. Any manager or coach worthy of the name would have to be excited by the prospect of taking over in Kerry, Dublin or Galway, in that order.

Every county has its own appeal but that trio top the attraction list in terms of glamour and tradition. So much so, that any manager who didn't feel a tingle of excitement at the possibility of walking into those dressing-rooms should be checked for a pulse. I was lucky enough to manage Kerry for 15 seasons in what was a record-breaking period for the county and I could have returned many years later but I declined. I was offered the Dublin job in 2004 but turned it down for very specific reasons and I was linked to Galway in 2006 but nothing came of it because the timing was wrong, both for me and them.

There are good reasons why Kerry, Dublin and Galway would be the top three targets for any manager. Kerry is the spiritual home of football, a county so steeped in the culture and tradition of Gaelic football that it comes as second nature. It has had its valley periods but they never last as long or sink as deep as in other counties. Good Kerry teams are one of the enduring constants in the GAA and despite the challenge from other sports I don't see that changing in the foreseeable future.

Dublin haven't been as successful as Kerry – although they are a very comfortable second in the All-Ireland table – but they do possess a sense of glamour all of their own which comes from representing the capital city and a population of over one million people. Galway radiate their own special aura too and, from a manager's viewpoint, would always be attractive because they have a history for producing top class players. There's a natural flow to

Galway's approach which any coach would love, provided he believed in stylish, constructive play as I most certainly do.

I had so many great years as a player and manager with my beloved Kerry that when the chance came to return towards the end of 2006, people might have thought I would jump at it but that was never going to be the case. I was sounded out as to whether I was interested but there was always going to be only one answer. For a start, I had just taken over in Wicklow so it would have been dishonourable to walk away from them, but even if I had been available, I wouldn't have taken the Kerry job.

I had done my time in Kerry and could see no reason to go back. Coaching teams is all about testing your team and yourself and after managing Kerry to eight All-Ireland titles there would have been very little challenge for me in returning all those years later. That would have been spotted very quickly by the players so things probably wouldn't have worked out and the last thing I wanted was to be remembered for messing up a fine team.

Anyway, Kerry appointed a right good manager in Pat O'Shea who did an excellent job in 2007 in steering the team to become the first since 1990 to retain the All-Ireland title. With Séamus Moynihan and Michael McCarthy retired, he had to rearrange the defence and judged it just right by bringing in two fine young talents in Pádraig Reidy and Killian Young.

O'Shea showed his credentials with Dr Crokes and carried on with Kerry and I would be quite confident that he will enjoy a lot more success with this squad. They have won three of the last four All-Irelands, losing the other one by a single score. It is some record. There's a sound balance to the team and when you have a forward like Colm Cooper, anything is possible. The 'Gooch' would have got on any forward line on any team in any era, including the great Kerry side that I managed. So who would have lost out? I really don't know but I definitely would have the 'Gooch' in there. Maybe we would have played seven forwards! He has unbelievable skill and balance and, in terms of vision, he's the best I've seen since the 'Bomber' Liston. It's great to see a player like 'Gooch' in full flow. Everything about his game is totally natural which makes him the unbelievably talented player that he is.

Now if only Dublin could find somebody like the 'Gooch'. They have a lot going for them but lack the touch that Cooper brings to Kerry. Over the years, I often wondered what it would be like to manage Dublin. How would I gel with their approach to the game? How would they react to me? There was always a fascination about the Dublin scene and, having been involved in so many great battles with them as a player and manager, I reckoned it would have been exciting to be on the their side of the fence for a while.

Dublin have played a huge role in my football life, first during my playing days and even more so as a manager. Indeed, it was ironic that the day I featured on the Kerry squad for the last time in Croke Park coincided with the launch of the Dubs and the Heffo era.

It was back in May 1974 when Kerry and Roscommon replayed the National League final. I was among the substitutes (I retired a few weeks later) for a game which Kerry won quite easily. In these days when Croke Park is packed almost every time Dublin play, younger people will find it difficult to understand why a Dublin v Wexford first round Leinster championship game would be downgraded to curtain-raiser status on a double bill with a League final replay.

The answer is simple. Interest in Dublin football was very low at the start of the 1974 championship season as they had failed to win a Leinster title since 1965 and had fallen well down the pecking order. Less than 23,000 people turned out that day and it was estimated that at least half of them were there for the Kerry v Roscommon game. I have no recollection of watching any of the Dublin v Wexford clash before going into the dressing room to prepare for our game, but then it wouldn't have meant a whole lot because neither side were seen as serious championship contenders.

It changed pretty quickly as Dublin began their upward climb that day and ended up as All-Ireland champions four months later so maybe I should have kept an eye on them against Wexford after all. Some 16 months later, I was in charge of the Kerry team that beat Dublin to begin a decade of fiercely intense rivalry. It shows how quickly things can change because that looked an unlikely scenario on that May afternoon in 1974.

The possibility of me managing Dublin many years later might have seemed like heresy back in the days when I was leading Kerry in the near-annual battle for supremacy with Heffo's boys but it very nearly came to pass in 2004. It wasn't something that I actively pursued but my friend Arthur French, always a mover and shaker in football and business circles, discovered after Dublin were knocked out of the championship that they wanted me to replace Tommy Lyons. John Bailey was Dublin County Board Chairman and he had discussions with Arthur to find out whether or not I was interested. I was having some problems in Laois at the time over poor attendance at training and, while I was always one to honour my commitments, I wasn't going to be treated like a fool if others weren't prepared to put in as much effort as me.

While all this was going on in Laois, Arthur set up a meeting with Bailey and Michael Fingleton, the head man at Irish Nationwide. We met for lunch at the K Club so that if any GAA people spotted us, they would think we were out for a round of golf, rather than discussing the Dublin job. I have to say I was very tempted to have a go. Bailey was extremely anxious that I take over and told me that if I agreed, he would be able to sell the idea to the Dublin County Board. I told him I would think about it and we left that meeting on the basis that the job was mine if I wanted it. Certainly that was the impression Bailey gave me.

I went away to think about it and weighed up all the options very carefully. I had a suspicion that some people in Laois wanted to see the back of me and if that were the case, I wasn't going to stay where I wasn't wanted. It transpired afterwards that the extent of the opposition to me was exaggerated as the Laois squad and key County Board officers were keen for me to stay, but I wasn't too sure of the situation during some crazy days that October.

While I was still mulling over the Dublin situation, I was spotted chatting to Bailey at the All-Ireland ladies football final in Croke Park and suddenly a very lively cat sprung from the bag. We didn't even discuss the Dublin manager situation that day but shortly afterwards word broke that I was in the frame for the job.

The impact was immediate and the odds against me taking over in Dublin tumbled dramatically. It would have taken a considerable amount of money to trigger the change but obviously there were informed whispers in the long grass. The reaction was interesting. Some high-profile Dubs made it clear that they were horrified at the prospect of an outsider taking charge, let alone an outsider from Kerry who had been involved with a team that had brought them such heartache. It seems they felt it would be akin to Osama Bin Laden becoming US President.

Normally, I wouldn't give a hoot what anybody thought but this was different. The manner in which Dublin had treated its three previous managers (Tommy Lyons, Tommy Carr and Mickey Whelan) proved just how irrational the supporters – and in some cases the County Board – could be, and frankly it was worrying.

Whelan quit after taking dog's abuse following a League defeat in 1997; Carr was voted out despite having the backing of the players in 2001; and Lyons left after a disappointing 2004 campaign during which a despicable element of the Dublin support felt entitled to abuse him when Westmeath pulled off a shock win in the first round of the Leinster championship. Lyons is a good manager who did a damn fine job with Offaly and who changed Dublin's fortunes in 2002. It didn't work out for him from then on but the pictures of Dublin supporters screaming abuse at him as he headed for the dressing room after the defeat by Westmeath were seriously disturbing.

Was that what I could expect? The danger was that with so many former Dublin stars unimpressed by the prospect of me taking over, it would have been easy for them to whip up opposition. That, in turn, would have transferred very quickly to a section of the supporters so if Dublin lost a few League games, I would probably be booed out of Parnell Park. Now, I love football but life is too short for that!

The more I analysed it, the more I became convinced that it would be the wrong move to take the job. I had the full backing of everybody in Laois and Kildare when I joined them but I knew it wasn't going to be the same in Dublin. Much had been made over the years of the Heffo v Micko rivalry so if I were appointed in Dublin some of their supporters would have regarded my arrival as a betrayal of the county's heritage.

Heffernan used to say that beating Kerry in an All-Ireland was always like a double All-Ireland to him, but I'm not sure how he would have felt if a Dublin team managed by me beat Kerry. It might have been a little less sweet for him and many other Dubs too. Actually, I'm not sure how I would have felt either. Leading Kildare to an All-Ireland semi-final win over Kerry was uncomfortable enough, but it would have been twice as difficult to be involved with Dublin against Kerry.

As the possible implications sunk in, I realised that despite the obvious appeal of managing a Dublin team than can fill Croke Park for virtually every championship game, it wasn't a good idea. Besides, the Laois situation had righted itself so I decided to stay. Bailey was very disappointed when I told him but he understood my reasons. At least I think he did.

I had told him in the course of our discussions that if I took over, I had absolutely no doubt Dublin would win an All-Ireland in the next few seasons. I believed they would do it anyway and am very surprised that three years later, they still haven't managed to even reach the final.

I have never been one to criticise other managers and I'm not going to start on Paul Caffrey. He does things his way and good luck to him and in fairness, Dublin have won three successive Leinster titles but that's never enough in a such a proud footballing county where, like Kerry, success is measured in All-Ireland titles only. The rest is only window dressing.

Having come so close to taking over in Dublin, and also because they're so high-profile, I always keep a close watch on how they're progressing. To be honest, it has been painfully slow. So what would I have changed if I joined them? The first priority would be to set them up in such a way that they were able to counter the top teams on a consistent basis rather than the hit-and-miss scenario that continues to undermine them. I would start with the defence. One of Dublin's main problems is that they play too many attacking defenders. It seems to be an in-built thing with them. They all want to go forward at every opportunity which is a good trait in a defender, provided he knows that his primary duty is to prevent the opposition from scoring.

As a unit, the Dublin defence is poor at man-marking. They're so attack-minded that when they start to go forward, they seem to forget about their opponents. The amount of space available to opposition forwards against Dublin is amazing. Indeed, I would regard it as one of the main reasons that Dublin have continued to fall short on the really big days.

It's an area I certainly would have worked on, had I become involved. I'm not saying that backs should concentrate solely on defence but they must regard it as the first priority, not just when the opposition are coming at them but also when play is at the other end of the field. The Dublin defence has been poor on positioning and is far too easily wrong-footed, mentally and physically, by smart forwards.

Another aspect that has really intrigued me about Dublin is the make-up of the squad. Had I taken over, the first thing I would have done is gone out and trawled the junior and intermediate clubs for talent. I can't believe that in a county with so many clubs, so few junior and intermediate players make the senior team. It's something I would be very conscious of because it was the same in Kerry before I took over. The attitude up to then seemed to be that if a player wasn't with a senior club, he couldn't possibly be good enough for the county team. I never believed that and brought in lads from all clubs, big and small. It worked too as more than half of the great squad that won eight All-Ireland titles were from junior and intermediate clubs.

Something else I find difficult to understand about Dublin is why so many of their players are clones of each other. It's as if they're factory-produced, having had the individual flair knocked out of them somewhere along the way. They play a very rigid type of game which I can only assume comes from the restricted nature of the coaching they receive at club level in their formative years. But then you're going to get that in very big clubs where it's not possible to work with lads as individuals.

Country clubs must make do with what they have which means that every talent, however modest, is encouraged and nurtured whereas in the big Dublin clubs there's probably a tendency to concentrate on the best to the detriment to the rest. They can afford to do that because of the large numbers involved but they could be missing out on a young player who is slow to develop. Yet, with proper coaching, he could become a better county player than the young star who looks the part at the age of 12 or 13.

Facts don't lie so there has to be something wrong with Dublin's under-age system where, despite having by far the biggest pool of players, their last All-Ireland minor success was in 1984. Compare that with Laois, a county with a population of only 50,000 people, who have consistently turned out excellent minors. Really, Dublin should be asking themselves some hard questions as to why they're failing so dismally at minor level because it really is inexcusable.

Apart from nurturing talent from the lower levels and getting the defenders to do the basic marking job first before thinking they are as talented as Alan Brogan going forward, I would also work on raising confidence levels.

Insecurity is a terrible affliction for any sports person and there's no question that it seems to affect Dublin more than the other top teams. For instance, it's thirty years since they last beat Kerry in the championship which is a shocking indictment of a county that would see itself as our biggest threat. That has to be a confidence issue as much as anything else in different circumstances. I would love to have gone into that Dublin dressing room and worked at getting them playing with a real swagger which befits a team from the capital city. I'm not a professional in the psychology department but I know how to make lads believe in themselves, something that's clearly a problem in Dublin.

There's still hope for this Dublin squad if they acquire more self-belief, sort out the defence and if their forwards play less like robots and express their individual talents to a greater degree. All the better too if they find a few players from the lower grades who can freshen up the scene.

One of the interesting developments around the time I was contemplating taking the Dublin job was the manner in which it became a subject for large bets. Bookmakers claimed to have taken big money once the word went out that I might be in the frame. As for those who thought they were onto a coup, sorry folks, you jumped the gun.

How times have changed. Betting with bookmakers was largely unheard of in the GAA up to relatively recent times, yet here we had a situation where large sums were being placed on my next move. If people were prepared to bet on something as unpredictable as that, it makes you wonder what lengths some might be prepared to go in other areas of the GAA. I'm no expert on gambling but, with all sorts of spread-betting becoming increasingly popular, there's always a risk that somebody will try to either influence the outcome of a game or, at the very least, manipulate the winning margin. There have been various rumours about that type of nefarious carry-on from time to time and, while there's no proof that it's actually going on, it would be naive to believe that it couldn't happen.

If Kerry and Dublin are the two really big glamour counties, Galway is also a scene that would interest most ambitious managers. I was linked to Galway before taking over in Wicklow in 2006 but nothing came of it because they decided to retain Peter Ford for another year. I have to admit that I would have fancied Galway, had the opportunity arisen at the right time.

They play an attractive brand of open football which I like and which I would enjoy coaching. There's a natural rhythm to their style which has remained in place over the years. It was evident again with their minors this year. They beat Kerry and Derry with pure football which was a joy to watch. I was very impressed by their full-forward Michael Martyn and corner-forward Damien Reddington who was as cool as the 'Gooch' when his chance came to kick the winning goal in the All-Ireland final. I'd be very surprised if that pair don't make an impression at senior level. With the exception of Kerry, no county produces more eye-catching football than Galway when they're going well. Apart from the quality of football that they produce, I would have liked to manage Galway just to see them from the other side, rather than being on the receiving end as happened me with Kerry in the 1960s and Kildare in 1998 and 2000.

Offaly caused me quite a bit of grief as a player and manager too so it would have been ironic had I ended up there, a possibility which also emerged in late 2006. I was approached about the job and met a few County Board officials to discuss things. I was quite interested at the time becuse I always admired Offaly football but they took too long to get back to me. By the time they did, I had already agreed to join Wicklow. I don't know why it took Offaly so long because if they had come back earlier I would have given very serious consideration to taking over. Pound for pound, Offaly have been the highest achievers in the country since the early 1970s and deserve enormous credit for winning so many All-Irelands in football and hurling off such a small population. They're struggling of late to maintain the incredibly high standards they set for themselves, but Offaly have always been capable of re-emerging pretty quickly which is a great tribute not only to their capacity to produce good players but also to their self-belief.

I was approached by other counties over the years too, including Cavan and Carlow, but I didn't really fancy any of them at the particular times the chances came along. Whatever about managing, there's scarcely a county where I haven't conducted coaching sessions at some stage, ranging from Donegal where I was quite friendly with Tom Conaghan, all the way down to Wexford. But then, wherever I got the call, I felt I couldn't refuse which is still the case.

Having been on the circuit for so long, I suppose I've picked up some tricks along the way, but the basis of everything has always been well-executed simplicity. Fill a player's head full of theory and he'll under-perform because he's not working off instinct.

As a player, I always loved trying off-the-cuff things and, in fairness, we were allowed to do that in Kerry. It was a policy I took with me into management where it served me well too. After all, there wasn't much point trying to come over all technical with the likes of Pat Spillane who just wanted to have the ball all day.

But then I was like that myself. In fact, I would have had a bit of a reputation for being selfish but I was a good kicker so I always fancied my chances when I got within shooting range. I recall one All-Ireland final – I think it was 1969 against Offaly – when I was playing in the full-forward line with Mick Gleeson and the late Liam Higgins and obviously they thought I was taking too much on myself.

They would always be giving out to me for not passing the ball which became something of a joke between us. Anyway, on this particular day, Higgins shouted across to Griffin: 'Don't give the ball to O'Dwyer because you won't get it back.'

I yelled back: 'Grand, but who'll get the scores?'

Next thing, Higgins gets the ball, pops it out to me and I kick a point. 'Now lads, who's getting the scores?'

Quick as a flash, Higgins shouted back: 'Yeah but who's giving you the ball?' Griffin and Higgins would often remind me of that day afterwards. Griffin was a right character. I recall travelling to matches with himself, Mick O'Connell, Gerry Riordan, Johnny Culloty and our much-revered coach, Dr Eamonn O'Sullivan who would insist that we said the Rosary.

Griffin, a really mischievous devil, would quite often forget his lines, probably deliberately, and break into a fit of laughing which didn't go down too well with Dr Eamonn. 'Boys, boys, no laughing, the Rosary must be taken seriously'. Somehow, you can't see little episodes like that happening en route to games nowadays.

In those days team talks and motivational speeches were kept short and simple, which was no bad thing either. Being from Kerry, we operated on the confident basis that, most times, we were better than the opposition which was often the case so we just got on with the game. Times were changing when I took over as Kerry manager so I had to move things along but I still kept the team talks as short and simple as possible.

Never once in over thirty years in management have I planned a speech in advance. They were – and are – always off the cuff because they're more sincere and effective that way. I'd regard myself as a good motivator but then it depends on the players in front of you too. They have to have an inner sense of self-motivation if they're to be successful – otherwise you're wasting your time and all the sophisticated team talks in the world won't change anything.

As for superstition, I wouldn't be big into it although I have maintained a ritual with the match programme down the years. For some reason, I got into the habit of always carrying a rolled-up match programme in my left hand as we left the dressing-room. I've long since reached a stage where I'd think there was something missing if I didn't have it. It became such an extension of my hand that anytime I forget to bring it out, I send somebody back into the dressing room to get it. Maybe I want it as a baton to conduct things with but, whatever the reason, it's a practice I'm unlikely to shed now.

I'm a creature of habit in some ways although I'm still prepared to take up new challenges, even if that didn't extend to Dublin and all its sideshows. Kerry, Kildare, Laois and now Wicklow were different which is why I took them all on at various stages. And I'm still at it, doing my level best to help Wicklow's graph line maintain its upward turn.

A Walk down Wicklow Way

Maybe the gods who guard the Railway End goal in Croke Park felt guilty after all. They hadn't looked me straight in the eye for 25 years since cruelly disabling the Kerry defence to allow Seamus Darby crack home that famous Offaly goal near the end of the 1982 All-Ireland final. I had long since given up on them.

They had turned on me in my Kildare days too, jealously guarding Galway's interests in the 1998 All-Ireland final by denying Dermot Earley and Brian Murphy, both of whom had good goal chances in a late, desperate push for survival only for one to fly over the bar and the other to hit the post.

And, as if to prove that the Railway goal really had it in for me, the jinx hit again in the 2004 Leinster final replay when Kevin Fitzpatrick had a great opportunity to bring Laois level in the last minute against Westmeath but his shot spun wide. I tell you, that bloody goal was haunted when I came to Croke Park.

Or so I thought until the first Saturday in August 2007 when my luck finally changed. More importantly, Wicklow's luck altered in the most dramatic circumstances late in the dying seconds of the Tommy Murphy Cup final. If somebody had suggested twenty years ago that I would find myself dancing an excited jig on the Croke Park sideline after Wicklow scored a goal to win a competition for weaker counties called after Laois great, Tommy Murphy, I would have dismissed it as demented nonsense.

But then the great thing about life is that you never know where it's going to lead you next. And if you do, it's because you don't want to take chances or live anywhere near the edge. That's not for me which is how I came to find myself savouring Wicklow's win almost as much as anything else I had experienced over the years. No doubt, the 'Boy Wonder' himself, Tommy Murphy, enjoyed the occasion too. He was a proud Laois man but I'm sure he would like to have seen Wicklow do well too.

It was ironic that Tommy Gill should have scored the late, late goal that beat Antrim in the final because if you asked me a year earlier to name some Wicklow players, he would have been the only one to spring instantly to mind. Even then, that would have been partially down to the high profile he earned with Rathnew over the years.

So how then did I end up managing a county whose players I didn't know and who were trapped way down in football's basement? After all, when I took over in Kerry, the immediate target was an All-Ireland title while Leinster titles were the big priorities with Kildare and Laois. It was different in Wicklow where there is no tradition of success at any level.

And that was what really intrigued me about them. Not that I woke up one morning with a yearning ambition to manage Wicklow but, as so often happens in life, circumstances conspire to choose a direction you would never have anticipated for yourself. They most certainly did in the case of Wicklow and me.

I have known Arthur French for more years than either of us care to remember. He's from Claremorris, Co Mayo, originally and a great football man. His passion for the game is incredible and over the years I got to know him through golf outings, the odd bit of business and various other activities. He would drop into the Kerry dressing room from time to time after we won big games, even if it was breaking his heart that it wasn't his native Mayo that had Sam Maguire.

Arthur lives in Straffan now and, among his many business interests, has an auctioneering firm in Leixlip. His love of football meant we had an awful lot in common and over the years we became firm friends. He knew that irrespective of how it went, 2006 was going to be my last season with Laois and, while I hadn't thought beyond that, he started plotting.

I heard later that the first mention of the possibility of me going to Wicklow came a few days after Dublin had hammered Laois in the Leinster semi-final. Arthur met another friend of ours, Billy Timmins, Fine Gael TD for Wicklow, at a funeral and afterwards the chat turned to football.

Wicklow had a terrible season in 2006 and as an avid supporter, Billy, who won an All-Ireland club medal with Baltinglass in 1990, was bemoaning the county's bad fortunes. It seems that in the course of conversation, Arthur and Billy hatched a plan that they would sound me out for the Wicklow job when the Laois campaign was over.

Some time after Laois were beaten by Mayo in the All-Ireland quarter-final replay, Arthur casually mentioned to me that Wicklow were looking for a new manager and suggested it would be an interesting challenge to take on.

My response wasn't encouraging: 'Are you mad, Arthur?' I hadn't taken any time out of management since 1995–96 and, in the meantime, had spent ten seasons with Kildare and Laois. Still, he kept bringing up the subject of Wicklow.

'Sorry, Arthur, I'm taking a break. Anyway, where did you get such a daft notion from?'

He then proceeded to do what he always does when he wants to get his way. He dropped the subject for a while before casually slipping it back in. Would I meet Billy Timmins just to throw a few ideas his way? Oh all right then, anything for a quiet life.

I met Billy in the Ambassador Hotel in Kill on 11 September and we talked for around three hours. Just as I had done with Kildare and Laois, I outlined what I thought was required for Wicklow to put down a solid base. I had no intention of throwing off my coat and rolling up my shirt sleeves to help with the work but I had plenty of experience on the basics needed to get the show on the road and was happy to pass them on to Billy who would devise a plan to put to the County Board.

He wrote everything down and went away and I thought that was the end of the matter as far as I was concerned. However, he called back a few days later with a proposal. He had drawn up an extensive list of things Wicklow were prepared to put in place if I took the job. It was clear they were very serious so how could I refuse? I had been cornered again, just as happened in Kildare and Laois. I talked it over with Arthur and told him that, since it was his mooching away in the background that put me in this position, he would have to come aboard with me if I was going to take on another big challenge. He agreed and we decided that if the Wicklow County

Board wanted us, we would give it a year. Billy was liaising with the then Wicklow County Chairman, Mick O'Hagan, and the board who were full of enthusiasm for the idea. Before I knew it we were heading for the Westbury Hotel off Dublin's Grafton Street for a formal press launch, no less!

Seán Mulryan, head man in Ballymore Properties, had come in as county team sponsor which was also a huge boost. Like Arthur, he is a great football man and had put his money into his interest for many years by sponsoring his native Roscommon. It's great to see wealthy businessmen like Seán supporting the GAA although very often you get the impression from the authorities that they don't approve. Why? I don't know, but then it's one of many mysteries I have long since stopped trying to figure out. Seán certainly deserves great credit because he continued sponsoring Roscommon even after agreeing to take on Wicklow. Of course, his sons play for Hollywood so he knows the Wicklow scene and was keen to play his part in giving the county team a boost.

So many media people turned up for the press conference in the Westbury that you would think I had taken over as Irish soccer or rugby manager, admittedly two improbable scenarios although they are as likely as my prospects of ever being appointed Irish International Rules manager.

Having agreed to take the Wicklow job, I began to wonder what I had let myself in for. If you were to listen to some people's version of Wicklow football, you would think it was all about fights and feuds, rows and ructions and locking referees in car boots. I never believed all that stuff because no county has a monopoly on problems or solutions.

Still, it was clear that morale on the inter-county scene was at a low ebb in Wicklow. For whatever reason, 2006 had been a disaster. Wicklow had won just one League game against Waterford, had been hammered by Carlow in the first round of the Leinster championship after being hit for four goals, and were dumped out of the All-Ireland qualifiers by Monaghan.

Hugh Kenny, a damn fine player in his time and who came very close to leading Wicklow into Division One in his first season as manager in 2004, had resigned so it wasn't easy to find much optimism around the county. Having won just one game in all competitions in 2006, Wicklow's ranking was so low that according to an *Irish Independent* rating table, only London were below them. In pure results terms, it was impossible to argue with that assessment.

Dig a bit deeper and you find that in Wicklow's entire history they have little more than thirty senior championship wins to their credit. They have never won a Leinster title but I was even more surprised to learn that they had never won a senior championship game in Croke Park. They have never beaten Dublin in the championship, had just one win over Kildare and Meath and only two against Offaly and Westmeath.

So, if you were judging Wicklow solely on county results, they were a disaster. But once you examine it more closely, you find a totally different scene. This is a proud footballing county with lots of fine clubs whose facilities match anywhere in the country. In many cases they surpass them. The passion to improve at county level is huge too. One of the first tasks for Arthur and myself was to get people on board with us who not only knew the Wicklow scene, but were passionate about it too.

We didn't have to look far. Kevin O'Brien, Philip McGillycuddy and Gerry Farrell were the ideal men for the job. They had all given great service to Wicklow at club and county level and were determined to put in whatever effort it took to move things forward. Those lads not only know Wicklow football inside out, they also have an in-depth knowledge of the game itself. I couldn't have got three better men if I had the pick of the whole country. And when it came to sorting out things at a practical level, we were very fortunate to be able to call on Martin Coleman and Jimmy Whittle, two of the best organisers I ever came across in all my long travels.

I would have known O'Brien best of all from his great career with Wicklow, Leinster and indeed the Irish International Rules team. Indeed, there were times in my Kildare days when I looked across the border with a sense of envy and wondered if he might like to join up with us. There was talk at one stage that he was considering switching to Kildare but it never came to anything. He would have had to leave Baltinglass which would have been an awful wrench because he is a fantastic club man and, to be honest, he didn't want to quit Wicklow either. From a Kildare perspective it was a great pity as he would have made a huge difference to them.

Having agreed to take over in Wicklow, I was adamant that, as usual, I would do things my way. For years I had heard about how Wicklow was, in fact, two counties separated by mountains and how the west and the east didn't get on. I could never understand that. Mountains aren't exactly unknown in Kerry either but they don't divide us.

I knew that to have any chance of lifting spirits and generating some momentum, we would have to get all of Wicklow pulling in the same direction and that involved roping in as many clubs as possible. So we decided to vary training from club to club. That wouldn't be possible in lots of counties but I was amazed to discover how many clubs in Wicklow had first class floodlights.

Where I come from in south Kerry, there isn't one club that could compare to a dozen or more in Wicklow when it comes to lights and other facilities. The fine facilities were a great plus in getting the show on the road because they gave us a chance to move around the county and show the supporters that we meant business. To be honest, I had no idea what to expect from the players or the public so I was pleasantly surprised to see the surge in interest straight away. In fact, I was overwhelmed by the response.

We decided to start off with trials so that I could get some idea of what was available. I thought we'd get through it in a few sessions but 120 players turned up. It was unbelievable. Everybody wanted to play for Wicklow it seems, including lads who hadn't bothered before. It was most encouraging to see such a level of interest but we had to spend so long on the trials that it left us way behind other squads in terms of putting down the basic fitness foundation. With so many players to check out, I probably left some good lads behind me but they'll get their chance again.

It was nearly all about trials and trying to put a panel together before Christmas which left us behind schedule with the training. But there was so much interest and energy around that the public couldn't wait for the start of the O'Byrne Cup where we were drawn against Carlow. It was amazing the number of people who turned out on cold nights just to see us training. We would let it be known where the sessions were taking place and by moving around the county everybody felt involved, but of course what they really wanted to see was an actual game.

Never in the history of the O'Byrne Cup did a first round game involving Wicklow attract such interest. Even the TV cameras were there with Setanta deciding it was worth covering. Nearly 3,000 people turned out in Aughrim for what developed into a cracking contest in which we beat Carlow by three points. That, in turn, led to a further surge in hype for the next round against Wexford. More television, another win and suddenly people were beginning to get carried away.

I wasn't because it was clear just how much work we had to do, even if we had two wins behind us. Next up were Dublin and, while we put up a decent show, they ran out comfortable winners. To be honest, I was half-pleased because I wanted to get back to basics and prepare for the League away from the media glare. Still, it had been a good month for Wicklow who had three games covered on TV from Aughrim for the first time in their history.

Any League section is tough when a team is coming from where Wicklow were a year earlier and I knew damn well that, hype or no hype, we would need to get very lucky to finish in the top four in a group that also featured Meath, Sligo, Cavan, Wexford, Antrim, Waterford and Tipperary. We targeted Antrim, Waterford and Tipperary as games we could win which we duly did, but we needed to win one more to finish in the top four and clinch a place in Division Three for 2008.

We had our chances too. We lost to Wexford and Meath by a goal each in games we might have won (we led Meath by five points at one stage) and went down to Cavan by seven. That left us needing to draw or win against Sligo in the last game to take a top four spot. We lost by four points and I remarked afterwards that Sligo were the best team we had come across, better even than Meath.

Nobody could have known at that stage that Sligo would go on to win the Connacht title for the first time in 32 years while Meath would end up as All-Ireland semi-finalists. So, when you look at the level of opposition we were up against, it was a fair achievement to finish in fifth place, even if it wasn't good enough to nudge us into Division Three.

Thomas Walsh made his debut for us in the Sligo game but if we had him earlier on, he would have made all the difference. The reason we couldn't play him ranks as another petty example of how bureaucratic nonsense can be used whenever it suits. Let me make one thing abundantly clear – I had no hand, act or part in Thomas Walsh's decision to switch from Carlow to Wicklow. I neither met nor talked to him until everything had gone through. It was his decision to switch, something he was perfectly entitled to do.

Naturally, it suited the Carlow County Board to blame me for the loss of possibly their best talent but instead of throwing out wild allegations about how 'Micko's fingerprints were all over this' they might have been better looking for their own fingerprints on the mirror.

Now the irony is that I might have ended up managing Carlow if they had moved quicker. They approached me about the vacancy which arose after Liam Hayes left but nothing ever came of it. Maybe that's why they were so angry when Thomas decided to leave Carlow for Wicklow. It was a sad reflection on Carlow who can try to offload the blame all they like when, in reality, the reason he left had everything to do with them and damn all to do with me other than perhaps he was keen to come on board a team I was managing.

To be honest, I was surprised – but delighted – when I was told that he was interested in joining Wicklow. He's a fantastic talent who would slot into any side in the country. It was a perfectly legal move because he was living in Bray and was joining the Bray Emmets club. He wanted to play football but what went on to stall his transfer was nothing short of scandalous.

Every possible obstacle was put in place in an attempt to block it. There was even a ludicrous situation at a Leinster Council meeting where the application wasn't dealt with because it had been signed by Michael Murphy, who is the Wicklow administrator, as opposed to Tom Byrne, the County Secretary. Michael had been County Secretary before taking over as administrator. Now what difference it made whether he or Tom signed the form is beyond me but the Leinster Council made a big deal about it which delayed the transfer for a while longer. It was crazy stuff but it left us without Thomas for some crucial League games and also prevented him from getting used to his new colleagues and the new system as quickly as we would have liked.

Still, we would have him for the Leinster championship which was always the priority. We were drawn against Louth in the first round and I genuinely felt that we had a great chance of beating them. They were going very well under Eamonn McEneaney but Wicklow would have no fears of them, especially after running Meath so close in the League.

Returning to Croke Park with a fourth county was always going to be a special day for me and it damn near was a historic one too as Wicklow came so close to breaking their championship hoodoo. We led by four points at one stage in the second half but Louth got a goal late on and in the end we had to settle for a draw.

It was on to Parnell Park for the replay a week later and not even extra-time could separate the teams. Again, we were hit for a late goal but the lads fought back in a manner which made every Wicklow person (not to mention this Kerryman) very proud. The show went on for a third Sunday, this time heading back to Croke Park for the second replay where Louth's experience finally told. They had been operating at a higher level for a few seasons and were better able to cope with the demands of three hard games on successive Sundays. They ran out comfortable winners in the end but it was clear that Wicklow had made real progress.

We would have loved to head straight back into the All-Ireland qualifiers, an avenue that was open in all the previous years since 2001 but, for reasons best known to themselves, Congress delegates approved of a daft proposal in October 2006 to lock the 'back door' to the bottom four teams in Divisions 2A and 2B.

The whole basis for introducing the qualifiers was to ensure that every county got a second chance, yet the GAA had closed off that avenue to eight so-called 'weaker' counties, confining them instead to the Tommy Murphy Cup. For a start, the concept of linking eligibility for the championship to performances in the League was totally illogical. All the more so when it was done in a season where the actual formation of the four Divisions for 2008 was only being decided.

Wicklow's record in the 2007 League was more than adequate to entitle them to a place in the qualifiers but then I would argue that every county should have got a second chance irrespective of where they finished. We even had the ludicrous situation where Offaly, runners-up to Dublin in Leinster in 2006, were banned from the qualifiers because they finished in the bottom four in Division 2A.

I let my feelings be known on the nonsense of if all which didn't endear me to the GAA authorities. That may explain why they had a cheap shot at me later on over what they perceived as my new-found interest in the Tommy Murphy Cup. Let me tell them this – I have a fierce competitive streak in me so whatever the game or the competition, I want to win it.

Besides, it was very important for Wicklow to maintain momentum and, in fairness, the clubs bought into that and were most accommodating in releasing their players so that we could have a decent shot at the Tommy Murphy Cup. As it happened, I ran into a small problem myself around then when I had to have a stent fitted to a heart artery.

I felt a slight tightening in my chest on my way out of the Dublin v Meath replay in Croke Park in June but didn't think a whole lot about it. I got checked out in Portlaoise hospital the following day but nothing showed up. Still, when I went home to Waterville I called on my local doctor, Patricia Gibson. Ever the thorough professional, she made contact with Dr William Fennell, a well-known consultant cardiologist in Cork University Hospital, and shortly afterwards I got a call from him suggesting that I should take a stress test.

I headed for Cork without even telling the family because I reckoned there was no point in worrying them. Besides, I wasn't remotely worried myself so why bother them? Anyway, when I got on the treadmill something showed up and I was told that there was actually a tiny clot in one of the arteries. Dr Fennell assured me that it wasn't serious and that it could be treated by fitting a stent. I was awake throughout the whole procedure and, impatient devil that I am, I'd have discharged myself immediately afterwards if I could. However, Dr Fennell insisted that I stay in for a few days much to the relief of my family who feared that if I got out, I'd be off to Croke Park straight away for the next game. They were probably right too.

Thankfully, the whole procedure was a great success but I was told to take things easy for a few weeks, something I'm not particularly good at. The wonders of medical science really are something to behold. Some years ago, my condition might have caused serious problems but it was all dealt with so quickly and effectively that I had no time to even think about it. Not that I was in any way worried. Dr Fennell was reassuring about everything and I'm glad to say that I'm feeling better than ever now.

I would always be a good man to have medical check-ups but as I never had any problems with heart or blood pressure, I never had a stress test. Now, I'm not a medical man but it seems the stress test is vital to show up certain conditions which is something everybody should be aware of.

No question about it, I got a warning but I heeded it and I'm in great fettle now. I got some lectures about diet (I'm cursed with a very sweet tooth) which I have taken on board too. Life went on without me in the Tommy Murphy Cup where Wicklow were drawn to play Offaly in the first round. Arthur took over the manager's bib and marked the occasion by presiding over a famous win in Aughrim.

Offaly led by seven points at one stage but Wicklow turned it around to win by five. I wasn't at the game but kept in touch by phone which was an interesting, if most unusual not to mention frustrating, experience for me. Waterford were next up in the semi-final and nothing was going to keep me away from that game, but I had to heed medical advice so we came up with a compromise. I could attend the game but was told to keep away from the sideline. Instead, I looked on from the clubhouse behind the goal in Aughrim. Naturally, I slipped into the dressing room at half-time. Leighton Glynn's performance would have improved anybody's heartbeat as he scored 1-3 in a fairly easy win.

At long last, Wicklow had reached a senior final to be played in Croke Park. It would be easy to dismiss the significance that had for the psyche of the county. Despite the fact that the final against Antrim was due to start at an ungodly early hour on a Saturday, it was still a very big day for Wicklow football and indeed for Antrim too.

Wicklow jerseys being worn proudly around Croke Park in early August was something that had never been seen before and was a real inspiration for the players as they made their way to the ground. Antrim footballers aren't exactly regular visitors either so there certainly was an unusual, if welcome, atmosphere around the great stadium. The game certainly didn't disappoint. In fact, it was one of the most enjoyable and exciting of the year, made all the more dramatic by the need to go into extra-time when Antrim kicked a late equaliser.

When they went a point clear late in extra time, it looked as Wicklow would once again leave Croke Park empty handed but all changed when Glynn placed James Stafford who set up Gill for the winning goal. It was tough on Antrim, who needed a break just as much as Wicklow, but we would have felt that after being a luck-free zone twice against Louth earlier in the year, we were owed a break.

It was a huge boost to end the season on a high and to have some silverware to mark what unquestionably has been a year of progress. Of 16 O'Byrne Cup, National League, Leinster championship and Tommy Murphy Cup games played, Wicklow won eight, drew two and lost six. Of those we lost, two were against 2007 provincial champions (Dublin and Sligo), one was against an All-Ireland semi-finalist (Meath), another was against a team that won promotion (Cavan) while our Leinster championship conquerors (Louth) had been in Division One and later reached the last twelve in the All-Ireland race.

We put down a platform this season and raised the profile of the county team but it's no more than the beginning of a long process which Wicklow themselves must advance. That involves improving coaching systems, setting and working towards targets even when things go against you, getting the balance right between long- and short-term objectives and sticking with them no matter what happens.

The population of Wicklow is growing all the time and it's up to the County Board to get their structures right so that they can exploit the openings created by the growing numbers. I would be quite happy that will happen. I have found the Chairman, Andy O'Brien, who took over shortly after I came in, a top class operator and I have no doubt he will lead the board in the right direction. However, they must get help too from the Leinster and Central Councils, certainly when it comes to investment, because it can be difficult for any County Board to cater for towns where the population has increased considerably in a relatively short space of time.

There's enormous potential for the GAA in Wicklow to expand and improve but it will only happen with hard work and a sense of obsession to achieve something. In fairness, I have been impressed by the drive and determination I have experienced over the last year but it's only a starting point.

It would be wrong to assume that because progress was made this year, it will continue of its own accord. It won't. Players, clubs, the County Board and the general public all have their part to play, not just in isolation but on a united front, designed to reach a stage where Wicklow can seriously challenge for a Leinster title. It's a realistic target over the next few years if the attitude and the application are right. Winning the Tommy Murphy Cup won't change the face of Gaelic football in Wicklow but it gave a glimpse of what it's like to be winners in Croke Park. Now, imagine if Wicklow could press on and win a Leinster title. That has to be the aim and, however difficult it is to reach it, the prizes are out there if they really want to make it happen. Based on what I have seen so far, I'm convinced they do and I have no doubt Wicklow's graph will rise at a steady pace over the next few years. I'll be doing my best to see that it does.

Business and Pleasure

I grew up as a spoilt child. At least that's what I was told later! But then I was an only child which I suppose did bestow certain advantages on me that weren't readily available to others at a time when big families were very common in Ireland.

Both of my parents were from very large families themselves. My father, John, came from a family of 15 while my mother (Mary Galvin) was one of 16 children. My father, a devoted nationalist, believed passionately in the Republican side and was actively involved in the 1916 Rising and the Civil War.

Nobody knew the mountains, boreens and woods of Iveragh like he did which proved helpful when he and his colleagues were forced to go 'on the run'. For months they lived in caves as war raged all across south Kerry. And even when a degree of peace was finally brokered, there was so much animosity, bitterness and suspicion on all sides that lives were still at risk. My father decided it was time to sample a new world so he took the cattle boat to Canada.

His big sporting interest had always been beagle-hunting, a pursuit he again took up on his return home some years later. He married my mother who had been born on Scariff Island before the Galvin family moved to the mainland where five of her brothers, Seán, Paddy, Mike, Jim and Batt, would later play football with Derrynane. The Galvins were a great football family and from as early as I can recall, my mother was encouraging me to play the game.

I spent the summers in Derrynane fishing with my uncles and grand-uncles but football was also an abiding passion. My father was more into fishing and shooting than football but when he spotted my great interest in the game, he too encouraged me. The problem was that footballs were in scarce supply at the time so I came up with a cunning plan to procure one. My mother worked in the Butler Arms Hotel and, from time to time, surplus tomatoes fell into the hands of her scheming son who sold them on to his friends at a penny each.

Delighted with my industry, I watched my piggy bank grow until I had what I estimated was enough to buy a football. I'm not quite sure I actually had the full amount but I handed it over to my father who completed the transaction on his next visit to Tralee.

He had set up a taxi service on his return from Canada and the US, where he had spent a number of years, so we were in the lucky position of having transport at a time when few others in the area had. It also meant that he travelled to Tralee fairly regularly so I could keep nagging him about buying a football. Anyway, he returned one evening with what I thought was the most beautiful creation in the entire world.

I looked at it as if it were a precious gift from God, rolled it around in my hands, smelled the shiny new leather and was so proud of my new possession that I hardly wanted to take a kick in case I lost it. I quickly learned that being the sole owner of a football had several advantages. Not only could I play away to my heart's content any time I wanted to, I also became something of a local celebrity as all the young lads in the area were keen to share in the opportunities that the new arrival presented.

So, I came up with a business deal. In what was probably the first sign that I had a nose for an opening, I devised a system whereby lads became part of an O'Dwyer co-op, involving the football. It was simplicity itself. Any lad who wanted to join in our games had to become a member of the exclusive club, which had an entry fee of six pence. It worked and very soon I had established a thriving business.

Naturally, as the owner of the football, I retained control of it. I brought it down to the Millerick Gardens every evening, checked that all the would-be participants were fully paid-up members and then it was match time. I was in a doubly lucky position: enjoying playing the game I loved while also making a tidy profit. In fact, as the numbers increased I saw room for expansion and, having accumulated a nice little pot of money from my first venture, I bought a second football which I rented to another group.

We wouldn't miss a single evening and it was in those loosely organised, unrefereed games that lads honed their skills. We went without shoes in the summer, kicking the ball with bare insteps which wasn't too painful in dry weather but a different proposition in rainy times when the leather soaked up water and became so heavy that every kick brought agony. Still, it didn't stop us playing our games and dreaming our dreams.

You don't see kids going barefoot anymore and thank God for that. You won't see a group of lads out in a field either, playing football among themselves, which is a great pity. Everything has to be organised and, while they'll turn up on given nights for training (well most of the time anyway), how many will take a ball and head down to a field to practise their shooting? Very few it seems and the results are there for all to see. You will find senior inter-county players who have great difficulty kicking the ball over the bar from thirty yards range which is unbelievable. But they have grown up in a culture where practising the basic skills doesn't matter nearly as much as it used to.

Nowadays, it's all about game plans, psychology and other mumbo-jumbo. It makes me laugh at times when I read some of the nonsense that's spouted about preparing and motivating teams. I often get the impression that some coaches and analysts believe they are impressing the rest of us uneducated eejits with their in-depth knowledge of how to plan properly. They like to show off how much they know – or think they know – even if, in many cases, it's all second-hand wisdom. Make it sound good, therefore it is good, that seems to be the motto. And if you throw in some reference to an American football or baseball coach, all the better.

Let them have their manuals, their charts, their clipboards, their videos and their buzzwords – it doesn't alter the fact that Gaelic football is a simple game. For example, the forward who can kick the ball over the bar on a fairly consistent basis from thirty or forty yards is a priceless asset. And the only way to become accomplished in that art is to practise, practise, practise. All you need is a ball and a set of posts. In fact, two jackets thrown seven yards apart will do for a target, yet how many modern-day players work on such a basic skill on their own?

It happened years ago because kicking a football was a regular pastime. Okay, they were simpler times with less pressures and distractions but there's still no reason why players can't do more on their own. Times were certainly simpler in the Waterville where I grew up. Lads played football, went fishing or shooting, worked if there was anything going and emigrated when it dried up, which was quite often.

I was born in 1936 so some of my earliest memories coincide with the World War Two years when rationing was common. I remember Harry Mansfield, the local shopkeeper, handing me an orange one day and, believe it or not, I had absolutely no idea what it was. Oranges were scarce items around our area at the time and, since I hadn't seen one before, I didn't know what to do with it. Still, since it was round, I reckoned that it must be a ball of some sort and proceeded to boot it down the little hill outside the shop. Harry saw what I'd done and, thinking I was an ungrateful little brat, proceeded to lecture me on the error of my ways. His annoyance at seeing this young lad kicking a delicious orange down the road was understandable and I'm not sure he believed me when I explained that I hadn't a clue what it was.

Waterville fared better than many other small villages in Ireland during the war years because of tourism and fishing but nonetheless very few families remained untouched by emigration.

For those young men who remained in the area, football was the great social outlet, one which hooked me from the moment I became aware of the pleasures attached to the games, the contests and the personal challenges. The addiction bug had bitten and was never shaken off.

Donal Kennedy, a teacher in the local primary school, was a great football man and when he left the area he was replaced by John McCarthy who would exert an even bigger influence on my career. He had an endless devotion to football, often transporting far more of us than was legal, safe or comfortable to games in his Morris Minor. Where would the GAA have been without people like him? All over the country, people like John McCarthy ferried youngsters around, which was mighty important in those days when cars were so scarce.

Equally importantly, from my viewpoint, John was a delegate to the Kerry County Board and kept bringing my name into conversations with fellow delegates from around the county who didn't have a whole lot of interest in what happened out Waterville way.

He was a great man but there was a period when I was less than impressed by his views on the direction my life should take. Together with my father and mother, he wanted me to head for St Brendan's College, Killarney, as a boarder when I finished primary school. St Brendan's was one of the finest Gaelic football nurseries in the country but the thought of leaving home and boarding in Killarney filled me with an unspeakable dread. I regarded the prospect of being locked up in a college instead of being able to wander free as the equivalent of prison. No doubt, it was an exaggerated view of life in St Brendan's but I was so convinced it was true that I just couldn't put it out of my mind.

I found myself in a tricky situation, lining up against such a formidable and persuasive trio as my parents and my teacher, all of whom were doggedly determined to extend my education in St Brendan's. I felt cornered but, stubborn little devil that I was, I had no intention of giving in without a battle so I bolted over to my grandmother (Nora Galvin) in Derrynane and told her of what I felt was the most serious plight in world affairs at the time.

To my great delight, not to mention relief, she backed me and my parents eventually relented. The St Brendan's idea was scrapped and instead I was sent to the local technical school in Waterville. I had a few good years there, even if I wasn't all that enamoured by the academic side of life. Of course, football continued to fascinate me and I picked up my first 'major' title when Waterville won a Kerry technical schools' competition. Our win was made all the sweeter by the fact that we beat the 'townies' from Tralee in the final. Good! A small but important victory for the underdog.

There weren't many openings around Waterville for young school leavers back then but, home bird that I was, I wanted to stay in the area and was lucky enough to get a job as an apprentice mechanic in Austin Lucey's garage. My starting wage was a princely £2 a week. With my father being a taxi man, I was always tinkering with cars and quickly settled into my new life, even if football occupied far more of my thoughts and ambitions than the workings of the internal combustion engine.

In those days, virtually all car parts had to be repaired. They were only replaced if there was no possibility of getting a few more miles out of them. It made for great mechanics, people who had to improvise and figure things out. Nowadays, everything is done by computer which is much handier but doesn't demand the same sense of craftsmanship or ingenuity from those involved.

I had a natural aptitude for mechanics. It was also a good job for a footballer as all the work with engines, gear boxes, back axles and so on, strengthened the hands and fingers. I have no doubt it was a big help to me, just as I believe Jack O'Shea's ball handling was improved by his work as a plumber many years later.

Things went well for me in Lucey's and when Austin decided it was time for him to leave the business, he proposed that I buy it. I had some money saved but still had to find £1,350. That may look like spending money to people these days but it was a hell of a lot of cash back in 1956.

Borrowing was the only option and, flushed with the optimism and fearlessness of youth, I had no qualms about going into debt for what I was certain would be a sure winner. My father took a different view. Neither a lender nor a borrower be – that was very much his motto. As for going guarantor for me with the bank, he wouldn't hear tell of it. In fairness, that was in keeping with the mood of the time. People feared debt and with good reason, but I reckoned I couldn't lose because I knew the car business and the people in the area. I applied to the Munster & Leinster bank and quickly discovered that they didn't quite share my enthusiasm for the venture. Well, not at first anyway, but after listening to the rough outline of what passed for a business plan, which was based on the simple premise that if they lent me the money I would work every hour of the day in order to repay it, they relented. I was on my way.

It was tough work but I enjoyed it. Being involved in football was a big help to the business, especially when I started to make an impression with Kerry. That's the thing about the GAA family – we tend to stick together, not just in our own areas but throughout the country. Over the years, I developed contacts everywhere around the country which were very useful. More than that, they became friends, people I'd call into if I was in their area while they would drop in on me anytime they were down Waterville way.

One such man was Reg Armstrong, who had the franchise for Opel cars in Ireland. Reg had been a top motor cyclist but also loved fishing and was a regular visitor to Waterville. He would arrive down in his big Opel Admiral car which was a mighty impressive machine and when it came to promoting the virtues of the brand, he was in a league of his own. I got to know him very well and after I had settled into owning and running my own garage and began to think of expanding, he suggested that I become the Opel dealer for the area. I knew there wasn't much of a market for the Admiral around our parts but Opel had plenty of smaller models, including the very popular Kadett, so I said I'd give it a go. Within days he had delivered seven cars and a long and fruitful business relationship had started.

There were none of the big car transporters in those days so when I needed to have cars delivered, I would bring a few lads up to the Opel depot in Ringsend to drive the new cars back down to Waterville. We would leave at six o'clock in the morning and be back that evening, but we thought nothing of it. That's probably where I developed such a love of driving. I had got a taste of it earlier on when I worked with the Luceys who were involved in a number of businesses, including fish exporting.

I would drive to Shannon Airport quite regularly but there were times when we went much further afield, as far away as Kilmore Quay in Wexford and Belmullet in Mayo. The hours were long and exhausting but I was young and thought nothing of it. Besides, the extra cash came in handy.

Once I started selling Opel cars, business expanded quite rapidly and among the ventures I became involved with was a self-drive company. I'd take in cars, do them up and let them out for self-drive. Cars were a lot less reliable then than they are now but because I was able to do the repairs myself, the self-drive business made good sense.

The combination of building a business and a football career occupied my every waking moment but there were many of those because I was never one to sleep very much. I have one of those metabolisms that doesn't need much sleep which is just as well, given some of the crazy commitments I have undertaken over the years. Suffice to say that if I slept eight hours a night, I wouldn't have got through half the workload.

I was so busy in my sporting and business life early on that I don't know where I found time for anything else, not least relationships. But, despite the hectic schedules, I had the good sense to spot a young lady by the name of Mary Carmel O'Sullivan at a dance in Fogarty's Hall. She was a receptionist in the Southern Lake Hotel and it really was a case of opposite attracts because she had no interest whatsoever in football. Neither of us could possibly have known back in the early 1960s that football would play such a massive role in our lives. I was still well short of my playing prime but, since most players tend to drift out of the county scene in their early thirties, it would have been fair for her to assume back then that my career would be over by the late 1960s.

It wasn't. I squeezed every last ounce from my playing time, taking it all the way to 1974 before heading down the management road, one which I'm still travelling to this very day.

I married Mary Carmel in February 1962, a year Kerry went on to win an All-Ireland but that success did nothing to change her mind about football. The only game she every attended in Croke Park was the 1964 All-Ireland final against Galway and, when Kerry were losing at half-time, she decided she had enough but she couldn't get out because the gates were locked. The second half didn't get any better for Kerry or Mary Carmel who felt trapped inside the place. She made up her mind on the spot that it was the last time she would ever visit Croke Park, a promise she kept.

In fact, she never attended another game in which I or any of our sons were involved. Her total lack of interest in football was in direct proportion to my damn obsession for the game. We could never have managed if we didn't accept and understand our different interests.

We were so busy in those early years that there weren't enough hours in the day. Shortly after we got married, we built a house onto the garage. My uncle, Jim Galvin, came down from Dublin to build it and, if memory serves correctly, it cost around £2,500. Some time later, a good friend of mine, Billy Huggert, put his house up for sale and we bought it for £2,000.

At the time, you could get a bar licence for a hotel if there were 12 rooms on the premises so we extended the house. However, in order to get one license another had to be quenched somewhere so a solicitor friend of mine, John Molan, acquired a licence through his contacts and transferred it to us. We now had our own hotel, the Villa Maria.

Mary Carmel ran the hotel. She had an exceptional talent for it which was just as well because I was so wrapped up in the garage and the football that I hardly ever had a minute to spare during the day. I had also become the local undertaker, having taken over when Mary Carmel's father died. My main involvement with the hotel was late at night when we ran dances and discos. I'd be up until nearly dawn but it never bothered me.

Having got the Villa Maria up and running, we joined up with Pat Foley, Des Nangle and Dr Alan O'Sullivan and bought the Sea Lodge Hotel (which would later become the Strand Hotel) off Austin Lucey. A few years on, we bought out the other three so we now had two hotels, a garage and an undertaking business. The O'Dwyer empire was expanding.

There was so much going on in my business life that, in ordinary circumstances, football should have drifted down the priority list but I just couldn't let that happen. It left Mary Carmel carrying a massive load but, for a woman who had no interest in football, she was mighty understanding when it came to allowing me to indulge my obsession. But she accepted from early on that she had married a man and his football and that nothing could separate them.

As for our sons, I'm afraid the O'Dwyer name meant that they were never going to be judged solely on their merits. It's always a drawback for a son when his father has had a good playing career because the young lad is watched like a hawk from the day he first ties a boot lace. My involvement as a player and manager for so long made it even harder on our lads.

Maybe that was why our son Michael had no great interest in football in his earlier years, preferring the beagle-hunting, although he did become involved with the club later on.

John, who was Kerry-U-21 manager for the past two years, played a few League games in my later years with Kerry but it wasn't easy for him or me. I was being accused of pushing my own son, while he knew that he was being scrutinised much more than any other young fella who was trying to make the breakthrough. If I hadn't been managing the team, he would have done better but then I wouldn't be the last manager to discover how difficult it is to have sons challenging for places.

Some Tyrone supporters made life very hard for Mickey Harte when he played his son Mark on the team a few years ago, and I wonder to what extent Joe Kernan's decision to step down as Armagh manager was influenced by his sons' playing careers. There will be four Kernan lads challenging for places on the Armagh team in the coming years and, if Joe were manager, it would be next to impossible to call it correctly on all fronts. Maybe he felt it was better left to others. If so, he was probably right.

Our twins, Karl and Rob, were on the Kerry minor squad together in 1987 but – like the seniors – they ended up losing a Munster final replay to Cork. Three years later, Karl was on the Kerry squad that won the All-Ireland U-21 title.

I'll be in trouble for saying this but Rob would probably have been the best player of them all but he was unlucky with back injuries. However, he did manage to win an All-Ireland junior medal in 1991.

I will deal elsewhere with the unfair manner in which Karl was treated by Kerry after the 1992 Munster final defeat by Clare, but his subsequent contribution to Kildare proved many people in Kerry wrong.

I often wonder how the lads would have fared if I had been like their mother and had no interest in football. In terms of their playing careers, it could possibly have been better for them. They wouldn't have faced the same scrutiny which would have given them a chance to develop without people comparing them to their father. Also, they would have got a fairer chance in Kerry. Still, we can't change who or what we are and the lads had to live with being sons of the maddest football man in the country. They didn't seem to mind, thank God.

Ghost Train to Heaven

We queued up to pay the one shilling admission, growing increasingly impatient as we came close to the Hill 16 gates. We wanted to get inside as quickly as possible to join a whole new magical world, the shape of which had been formed in our minds by a combination of Micheál O'Hehir's vivid descriptions, other people's stories and our own schoolboy images.

I had just turned 17 years of age and, together with my good friend Eric Murphy, I was about to step through the gates of Croke Park for the very first time. The great adventure had long been in the planning. However, it all depended on whether Kerry reached the All-Ireland final. It was 1953 and a time when Kerry were beginning to re-emerge from what was, by their standards, a lean period during which they hadn't won an All-Ireland title since 1946 and hadn't been in a final since 1947. That final against Cavan had been played in the Polo Grounds in New York so, as Eric and myself raced up the steps and onto Hill 16 on 27 September 1953, it was the first time in seven years that Kerry colours were waving in Croke Park on All-Ireland final day.

Naturally, we had charted Kerry's progress throughout the summer with great interest. Clare had been easily beaten in the Munster semi-final setting up another Munster final with Cork who had beaten Kerry by no less than nine points the previous year. Kerry were better prepared this time, winning by four points and booking an All-Ireland semi-final clash with Louth who were going very well at the time. However, Kerry hit them with three goals to win by five points, much to the relief of Eric and myself whose plan was about to come to fruition. At long last, we were heading for Croke Park.

Eight years earlier, I had attended my first Munster football final. Some local men had hired my father's taxi to take them over to

Killarney for the game against Cork. My father slipped the little nine-year-old in with them and off we headed. Cork were strong at the time and beat Kerry by five points en route to winning the All-Ireland but the main memory I can recall from the game is being awestruck by how big the players appeared. They looked ten feet tall and built to match but then heroic figures always look massive to nine-year-old eyes.

I was especially taken by the Cork centre-back and captain, Tadhg Crowley, an imposing figure who seemed to hold the Kerry forward line virtually on his own. Losing to Cork was fierce disappointing, even for a young lad watching his first Munster final, but the day, the occasion and the atmosphere made a huge impression on me. I told myself I needed more of that.

It was something I also felt after my first visit to Croke Park eight years later. The whole experience is still fresh in my memory, probably because it was such an exciting voyage of discovery for a young lad who had never been further from home than Tralee and Killarney. Now we were headed for the capital and All-Ireland final day. We travelled on the 'Ghost Train', the special excursion that travelled overnight bringing Kerry supporters to Dublin for big games.

Eric and myself set off from Waterville in good time on Saturday evening. It was a ten-mile cycle to Caherciveen but it was no more than a hop to two fit young lads for whom the prospects of attending an All-Ireland final in Croke Park was so inspiring that we would have galloped through fields of nettles and walked over six-inch nails to get on that train. It left Caherciveen at around 9.30 pm, heading out on the long journey through the night.

The 'Ghost Train' was a Kerry ritual, taking excited hordes to Dublin for what was regarded as the greatest show on earth – the All-Ireland football final. Eric and myself brought sandwiches and tea aboard to nourish us on the long journey; others took something a little more fortifying and, as it began to take effect, there were regular outbreaks of raucous singing which added to the sense of occasion if not exactly to musical enlightenment. The thrill of being on that train was something special and, as I stared out into the dark autumn night wondering where exactly we were, little could I have known how Croke Park and All-Ireland finals would become such a large part of my life. The journey was long but such was the level of excitement and anticipation of the great day which lay ahead that nobody slept. Besides, passenger comfort wasn't top of the priority list when the 'Ghost Train' was being designed.

It was nearly 7 am when we arrived in Kingsbridge (now Heuston) station on a grey Sunday morning. So this is Dublin, the capital city. We wandered slowly along the quays staring into the Liffey and taking in the endless lines of buildings and criss-crossing streets. How do people live in a city, I wondered? How do they know where to go, since every street seemed the same as the next? Do they not miss the open country, the fields, the rivers, the mountains, the peace, the freedom? That was my world and I had no understanding of anything different and very definitely not of city life. Having said that, I still don't know how anybody lives in large cities. I love visiting Dublin but don't ask me to live there – I'd grow sad in a week and mad in a fortnight.

All-Ireland final morning or not, religious obligations called so we found a church and stood at the back for a quick Mass before turning onto O'Connell Street where we had breakfast in a café. As the morning moved on and the All-Ireland atmosphere began to grow, we were reminded for the first time of Kerry's opponents. O'Connell Street was awash with saffron as Armagh supporters made their presence felt with a degree of exuberance normally associated with counties who aren't used to being involved on All-Ireland final day. It was, in fact, Armagh's first appearance in the final and nobody in Kerry knew very much about them other than that they had beaten Roscommon by a point in the semi-final.

In our confidence and our innocence, we couldn't possibly envisage Kerry being beaten even if it had been seven years since their last All-Ireland win. My heroes on the Kerry team were John Cronin, Ned Roche and, of course, Tadhgie Lyne, the big star of the time. It wouldn't have been regarded as one of the great Kerry teams but they were under such pressure to end the drought that they dared not return home without the Sam Maguire. Kerry people wouldn't really have rated Armagh as serious opponents at that stage which was a risky business, especially if over-confidence was allowed into the dressing-room. Obviously, it wasn't.

The first thing that struck me about Croke Park was the sheer size of the place. We arrived early, took what we thought was the best vantage point on Hill 16 and began to soak up the occasion and the atmosphere. Before very long, it became clear that this was no ordinary All-Ireland final. As the crowds swelled way beyond expectations, it grew from over-crowded to uncomfortable to chaotic to dangerous. The official attendance was given at 86,155, the highest up to then but it was later estimated that at least another 8,000 got in for free after gates at the Hill 16 end were knocked down. This was long before all-ticket games so there was no way of coping if an exceptionally large crowd turned up. The terraces were packed way beyond capacity and, while stand tickets were available on the day of the game, the fact that they cost five shillings meant that many Kerry fans, in particular, opted for the terraces. Armagh had so many supporters that they dominated everywhere on both stand and terrace.

It was estimated afterwards that Armagh supporters outnumbered Kerry by five to one and that there were more than 100,000 who wanted to attend the game. Over 5,000 people never got into the ground and were forced to listen to Raidio Éireann's commentary outside. Now that had to be the ultimate definition of hell, standing outside Croke Park on All-Ireland football final day unable to get in because the capacity ceiling had been smashed.

I was glad that we had arrived early enough to get a place on Hill 16 but it quickly turned into such a seething mass of humanity that there were times when it was impossible to remain in one place. It was dangerously over-crowded but safety issues didn't feature very high on the agenda back then. Amazingly, nobody got killed or seriously injured. As wiry young lads, Eric and me were able to literally go with the flow which was just as well in the circumstances.

Micheál O'Hehir's colourful descriptions of Croke Park had created an image of the place in my mind which lived up to all expectations. I marvelled at how green and lush the grass looked and how so many people could come together at the one time. The sheer joy and excitement of being present for such a marvellous occasion provided an abiding memory which has never left me. Of course, there was no way I could have known that day that in just six years I would be playing there in my first All-Ireland final.

The 1953 final may not have gone down in history as one of the best but it certainly was exciting. Big Mal McEvoy was in inspired form at midfield for Armagh and it turned into a dogged battle of wills between two evenly-matched teams. Kerry were leading by two points with six or seven minutes remaining when Armagh were awarded a penalty. We couldn't believe it. Were Kerry going to throw it all away? And we after travelling so far to be here!

The awarding of the penalty proved controversial. Meath's Peter McDermott was the referee and he adjudged that Kerry goalkeeper Johnny Foley had touched the ball on the ground. Back then, goalkeepers were treated the same as outfield players when it came to picking up the ball. Anyway, Foley was penalised and Armagh full-forward, Bill McCorry, a man with a big reputation as a penalty taker, lined up the kick.

There can be no more dramatic incident than a penalty kick late on in a closely contested All-Ireland final. The massive Armagh crowd were willing McCorry's kick into the net but he got his angles wrong and blazed the ball wide. The match was decided. Kerry went on to win by 0-13 to 1-6, picking up another All-Ireland title and breaking Armagh hearts. Amazingly, it would be another 49 years before they would finally win an All-Ireland title.

The journey back home was long and tiring but that didn't matter. I had seen Kerry win an All-Ireland final; also I had been to Croke Park, the theatre of dreams for every young Kerry lad. It was after 3 am on Monday morning by the time we reached Caherciveen station and 5 am by the time we got home to Waterville. For weeks afterwards, I would regale anybody who was prepared to listen about the wonder of it all and, since Kerry football was the subject, I was never short of an audience.

The funny thing was that neither Eric nor me ever contemplated a Kerry defeat because, like every kid in Kerry, we grew up thinking of the county as winners. That's still the case which is why football has come to play such a central role in Kerry history. It's the ultimate expression of the county's identity, passed on from generation to generation in a seamless way. Naturally, there have been times when Kerry struggled – I was part of it myself as a player in the Sixties and early Seventies – but we always see it as a temporary blip that will correct itself at some stage. And right through the history of the championship that has proved to be the case.

I have no doubt that Kerry's reputation has helped enormously in psyching out opposition. That's why Kerry have always been good at winning All-Irelands with moderate teams. If it's a modest year, Kerry nearly always win because they know how to and they have the self-belief to see it through.

Playing in Croke Park has always helped Kerry too. It's the place where Kerry players prove themselves to their peers. It's as if the green-and-gold was made for Croke Park and right to this day Kerry see it as a home from home, a place where our teams can showcase their skills both individually and collectively. Everything in Kerry has always been geared to reaching Croke Park, an objective which, in fairness, is made easier by the fact that Cork were (and are) the only county who consistently challenge Kerry in Munster.

That's a big help to Kerry and was certainly very important in the glory years between 1975 and 1986 because ourselves and Cork were so far ahead of the rest that we knew we would march into Munster finals virtually unchallenged. It meant we could time our training to perfection so that we peaked when we needed to, starting with the Munster final in mid-July.

It suited Kerry perfectly and we made full use of it. Cork were in the same boat but they couldn't match us in most of those years which left them seething in understandable frustration. They would have won an awful lot more over the years had they been in any other province.

Of all counties, Cork must have welcomed the opening of the 'back door' as it gave them a chance to live a second life away from Kerry, unlike pre-2001 when, so often, their season ended in Munster.

Kerry's dominance in Munster has impacted on the development of football in Clare, Limerick, Tipperary and Waterford too. Lads in those counties were more inclined to concentrate on hurling because it offered them a better chance of success than football which was perfectly understandable. That's still the case today.

Being the leading light in what has always been essentially a two-county football province when it comes to sharing out the big honours suits Kerry and nobody gained more from it than myself, both as player and manager.

I'll probably be accused of treason against Kerry by suggesting that the system should change but I have long favoured the 'open draw' All-Ireland championship. The 'back door' has its attractions but nothing could ever quite compare with the thrill of the straight knock-out championship. It was hard and unforgiving but it was incredibly exciting.

The trouble was that it took too long to run off, stretching as it did from mid-May to late September. My idea would be to have a real League competition in the early part of the year, let clubs take over for a month or two and then run off the straight knock-out championship fairly quickly.

Under the current provincial system, some counties go into action more than a month ahead of others, whereas if you had 32 teams all starting at the same time, the championship could, barring draws, be run off in five rounds and take a maximum of ten to 12 weeks as opposed to nearly twenty at present.

In order to make sure that the GAA maintained a high level of exposure, the hurling and football championships could be staggered, rather than running simultaneously as happens at present. I'd love to see something different tried, rather than slavishly adhering to provincial systems which feed into the All-Ireland. That would be fine if there was no club activity but the current formats are playing hell with the club scene.

An 'open draw' football championship would generate massive interest. Imagine Kerry going up to Markievicz Park to play Sligo, or Tyrone coming down to play Wexford in Wexford Park. The argument will be made that a straight knock-out championship would reduce revenue but why is making money such a big ambition in the GAA? It's certainly not to filter any of it back to the players.

If, as seems likely, the 'back door' is to be retained, consideration will have to be made for provincial champions who lose All-Ireland quarter-finals getting a second chance. Why should the rest get a reprieve while provincial champions are eliminated if they lose a quarter-final? I'd suggest that the four provincial winners play off among each other with the two winners qualifying for the All-Ireland semi-finals, while the two losers play two surviving qualifiers to complete the semi-final line-up. That would be much more equitable than the present system.

It's only right that we should be constantly looking for a system that's fair for everybody. It's difficult to find one and there will always be anomalies since some counties are weaker than others, whether due to population or concentration on football or hurling to the detriment of the other tradition. That doesn't mean the GAA shouldn't keep looking because it owes it to the players and the supporters to get a fairer format.

It's great being from a county like Kerry where football has always been a religion (we would continue to do well whatever championship system were in use), but what about all the counties who know at the start of the year that the best they can hope for is to pull off one surprise win somewhere along the line? And then there's tradition, the silent manipulator that seems to dominate the psyche in many counties. That's fine if it's a winning tradition, but what if it's not? Look at how long it took Donegal, Derry, Armagh and Tyrone to make the All-Ireland breakthrough. In fairness, they all did in the end but it shouldn't have taken until well in to the GAA's second century. It makes you wonder to what degree a losing tradition delayed their progress.

Kerry, on the other hand, have benefited from the power of a winning tradition. It never dawned on me as I set out for my first visit to Croke Park in 1953 that Kerry might lose. They had won 16 All-Ireland titles up to then – more than three times Ulster's entire total at the time – so my young mind would have seen northern teams as somewhat inferior. I suspect that 17-year-olds from Armagh might have had a reverse feeling and would have preferred to see anybody but Kerry in that final.

Who knows, maybe that even transferred itself onto the Armagh players too as they missed some great chances that day? Losing the 1953 final had a serious impact on Armagh who wouldn't win their next Ulster title for all of 24 years. As for me, the subsequent years became more and more exciting as I began the transformation from boy to man and headed into a new phase of my football life. Still, the memory of climbing up the steps at the back of Hill 16 and getting my first look at Croke Park in all its splendid glory has never left me. Nor will it.

Anyone See My Munster Medal?

If a good start is half the battle, then I was well short of halfway 18 months into my senior career with Kerry. In fact, I had already played in two games which have been rightly classed among the worst performances ever produced by Kerry teams. Just as well I was only a young fella. The more senior lads had to shoulder the blame, thank God.

Waterford and Kildare had beaten us in championship and League games in the space of nine months, leaving Kerry feeling like a once-proud empire tumbling wildly towards oblivion. Waterford's sensational win in the 1957 Munster championship is still talked of as one of the biggest upsets in GAA history, although given the chaotic nature of the Kerry set-up that day, it shouldn't have come as such a great shock.

Obviously, lessons weren't learned either because in early February 1958, we lost a League game to Kildare by 3-10 to 1-0 in Naas. Tadhgie Lyne got our only score against a Kildare side that looked like supermen by comparison with us. Once more, we were heading for ridicule among Kerry fans who had ground work laid for them by a report in *The Kerryman* which opened with a quote from Cormac, a one-time High King of Ireland: 'Bury me at Nás na Ríogh and face me towards the rising sun.'

Kerry supporters would have been happy to bury us anywhere as they regarded us as having brought disgrace to our county and embarrassment on ourselves. I was just learning the trade but it was still difficult to come to terms with a championship defeat by Waterford and a League trouncing by Kildare.

This wasn't what I anticipated playing for Kerry would be like as I grew up in Waterville with the dream of becoming a county player swirling around in my head. Not that I thought it would ever come to anything because players from south Kerry, and especially Waterville, didn't feature in the county's plans. It was something people in the area came to except, even if they greatly resented it. If it weren't for Seán McCarthy, a local teacher who was delegate to the County Board, I would never have got a look in with the Kerry minors in 1954.

He sang my praises to anybody who was prepared to listen and eventually managed to get me a trial which I thought went fairly well. Not well enough to get on the team, it seems. I was among the substitutes for the first Munster championship game against Waterford which ended in a draw. I wasn't picked for the replay either but one of the cars ferrying some of the players to Kenmare broke down and I was called in at corner-forward. I scored 1-6 in a landslide win and felt that would secure my position for the final against Cork. It didn't. I must be in a very small minority of players to have scored 1-6 in a championship game and still be dropped!

I was down to number 18 for the final, further back still for the All-Ireland semi-final and was outside the 21 altogether for the final against Dublin which Kerry lost by a point. Nobody ever explained to me why I slipped down the pecking order, although I had my own suspicions that it was because I came from south of the Laune river, an area deemed superfluous to requirements by the main power brokers in Kerry football at the time.

I felt hard done by but I was young and enthusiastic and even being close to the team excited me. I knew I was better than some of those who got in but there was nothing I could do about it. Having played against Waterford, I should have got a Munster medal but it never materialised. I can only assume it was handed to somebody with a more fashionable football address.

Two years later, I won my first Munster medal at midfield alongside Ned Fitzgerald (Maurice's father) on the Kerry junior team. Well, at least the first Munster medal I actually got. My eagerness to pick up tips on how to improve my fitness nearly wrecked me that summer. Ronnie Delaney came down to Waterville as part of his training for the Olympic Games in Melbourne so I decided I'd keep an eye on what he was doing. Day after day, he pounded the sand dunes and, as an eager 20 year-old, I decided that if it was good enough for an Olympic athlete of Delaney's stature, it was good enough for me. So off I'd go through the sand dunes, clocking up the miles and thinking of the advantages it would give me on the football field.

The difference was that the Olympics were some months away whereas I was in the middle of the football season. Anyway, I wasn't ready for such heavy work and it nearly crocked me. We played Waterford in the Munster junior final and I was as stiff as a board. It was as if stones were tied to my ankles but, luckily, Waterford didn't offer much opposition so my sluggishness was overlooked by the selectors. I played well against Monaghan in the All-Ireland semi-final which ended level but, with the heavy training still taking its toll, I was poor in the replay and was replaced. Still, I had learned a valuable lesson about training which would prove helpful in later years. What Ronnie was doing was right for him at that stage of his preparations and would have been right for me at another time of year, but not then. Unfortunately, there was nobody around to tell me that at the time. Like many other important tips, I picked it up by myself.

Under-performing for the juniors wasn't exactly what I had in mind as part of the grand plan to get into the senior side, an ambition which looked to have stalled after the disappointing effort against Monaghan. However, my form held good for Waterville and south Kerry and I got the senior call-up with Kerry for the start of the League in October. It was a huge honour, even if I expected to be among the substitutes, initially at least. But I got into the team for the first game when four of the selected side withdrew for various reasons, mostly I suspect because they couldn't care less about the League and had closed down for the winter.

I was astonished that any player would turn down a chance to wear the green-and-gold but their lack of interest was my big chance. Carlow were the opposition in Tralee and I was chosen at right half-back. The weather was bad, the crowd was small but I still felt ten foot tall as I ran onto the pitch as the first Waterville man ever to play for Kerry. I was beginning to live the dream and, full of the confidence of youth, had no doubt whatsoever that I was plenty good enough to be on the Kerry team.

Usually, Carlow wouldn't have been seen as a major threat to Kerry, certainly not in Tralee, but they had some excellent players around then, one of whom it was my bad luck to come up against that day. Brendan Hayden was a talented forward and didn't take long to show the rookie from Waterville that there was more to county football than he thought.

Hayden gave me a right roasting, kicking three points from play and two more from frees. I struggled with the quicker pace of the game, wasn't comfortable on the ball and left the pitch wondering if this would be my first and last game as a Kerry senior. We won by three points but that did little to raise my spirits because I knew that the verdict from the Kerry public would be damning. I was left off for the next game and didn't get a look in again until the following May when I played in a challenge game against Cork which went well enough to convince the selectors to retain me for the start of the championship against Waterford.

In these more sophisticated days when everything is planned down to the last detail, it's difficult to believe that even in a county like Kerry it was all very haphazard fifty years ago. We even had a row over who should be team captain for the year. It was one of those stupid, inter-club disputes but, with the County Board failing to take charge, it spun out of control and ended up as a seriously divisive issue which, among other things, resulted in our regular goalkeeper, Donie (Marcus) O'Neill, not travelling to Waterford for the championship game.

The system of linking the captaincy to the county champions or the champions in a division is fraught with problems, not just in Kerry but anywhere it's used. The captain should be chosen by those in charge of the team so that the best leader gets the job rather than a player who's nominated on the basis of his club's success.

Many of the more successful counties, including Kerry, still apply the old system, arguing that there's no need to change a winning formula. Trouble is, it's not a successful formula and has no basis whatsoever in logic or fairness. It's a throwback to a different age and definitely has no part in the modern game. For example, I was allowed to choose my own captain in Kildare and opted for Glenn Ryan who turned out to be a superb leader. That's the sort of man you need as captain, someone who is guaranteed to be on the team, has strong leadership skills and commands respect on and off the field.

At one stage in 1957, I was in line to be Kerry captain in my first season because of Waterville's success but it would have been utter madness to ask a 20-year-old who was struggling to break into the team to inspire a group that contained proven players with leadership qualities. The whole sorry business over the captaincy cost us dearly that year, leading as it did to a change of goalkeeper for the Waterford game. O'Neill later wrote a letter to the County Board, rightly complaining about the way the whole affair had been handled and was handed a six-month ban for his efforts. Back then, you dared not take on the system.

Apart from O'Neill, some other star names, including Seán Murphy and Tom Moriarty, were absent for the Waterford game for various reasons, leaving us with just 16 players on the day of the match. Given all the other chaos surrounding the team, it was surprising that we had travelled to Waterford the night before the game, a decision which may not have been the wisest either as I'm not sure everybody saw fit to get as much rest as they should.

We headed for the pitch with Denis O'Shea as our only substitute so John Barrett, a reporter with *The Kerryman* and a handy club player, togged out too in case of an emergency. Despite the utter shambles of the preparations we would have been expected to beat Waterford fairly easily. They hadn't beaten Kerry in the championship for nearly half a century and, despite our problems, we still had some brilliant players who would have been expected to steer us through. Galway, the reigning All-Ireland champions, had beaten Kerry by five points in the League final a fortnight earlier but only after a strong finish so why should there be any reason for us to fear Waterford? I wasn't selected for the Galway game and was one of six changes for the Waterford tie.

Everything went okay for about forty minutes. We weren't exactly giving a dazzling display but still managed to lead by six points with twenty minutes to go. However, to their great credit, Waterford never lost hope and struck for two goals. The unthinkable was unfolding in front of us and our nightmare became a reality when Waterford centre-back Tom Cunningham booted over the winning point in the last minute. Waterford 2-5 Kerry 0-10.

No sooner were we back in the dressing room than the implications of what had just happened began to sink in. What would be the reaction back in Kerry? Would it be safe to go home? Would any of us ever play for Kerry again? Kerry people couldn't believe the awful news when word began to filter through back home. Gerald McKenna, who was based in Dublin at the time, was so stunned that when he heard the result read out on Raidió Éireann he phoned the sports desk and asked if they had made a mistake. They hadn't, but we had.

That game has gone down in both Kerry and Waterford folklore, albeit for different reasons. So much so that it's only right, in the 50th anniversary year of a remarkable encounter, to recall the identities of the players involved. It remains painful for the Kerrymen but I'm sure Waterford still feel a surge of pride every time that day is mentioned.

Waterford: Gerry McCarthy; Mick Prendergast, Mattie Lonergan, Con Crowley; Mickey O'Connor, Tom Cunningham, Jimineen Power; Séamus Power, Seán Forde; Georgie White, Noel Power, Billy Kirwan; Jim Timmons, Jimmy Whyte, Tommy Power.

Substitutes: Bill Daniels, Seán Roche, Seán Ormonde, Jimmy Maher, Patsy Donnolly, Larry Guinan, Ed McCarthy.

Kerry: Tom Barrett; Jerome O'Shea, Ned Roche, Tim Lyons; Mick O'Dwyer, John Dowling, Micheál Kearins; Tom Long, Mick O'Connell; Paudie Sheehy, Ned Fitzgerald, Tadhgie Lyne; PP Fitzgerald, Tom Collins, Dan McAuliffe.

Substitutes: Denis O'Shea, John Barrett.

The long journey home to Kerry involved a stop-off in Youghal where sorrows were drowned by those who saw a few pints as an escape from the horrors of the day. We must have looked a sorry bunch, some boozing, others moping, but everybody feeling empty and useless. Never having touched alcohol, I wasn't involved with the drinking faction of the party. I have always felt that, having survived that night without a pint, there was never any question of me taking up drinking. Instead, I just sat there, trapped between despair and bewilderment. All my life, I had dreamed of playing for Kerry and when the big chance arrived I was part of a team that had blown it spectacularly against Waterford.

I had a mixed day against Billy Kirwan, a very good wing-forward, who would have been very much at home on stronger teams. Still, Waterford were good enough to exploit Kerry's chaos and the fear for all of us as we headed home that night was that we would be written off as collective failures, deemed unworthy to ever play for the county again. Thankfully, time is a great healer and there would be other chances for most of us. In fact, two years later, eight of the team that lost to Waterford were on the Kerry team that beat Galway in the All-Ireland final. What a transformation.

There was more pain to come after the Waterford defeat when Kildare embarrassed us in that famous League game in Naas in early 1958. These really were worrying times for Kerry football. The All-Ireland win of 1955 seemed a long way off and, in the interim, we hadn't even won a Munster title, a situation that seemed unlikely to change as we traipsed out of Naas with our reputations again in tatters. There was a further scare to come when Tipperary nearly beat us in the first round of the Munster championship in Thurles. I got a late goal which helped us to a two-point win on a day when nobody could have seen much hope for Kerry. But, as has so often happened right through Kerry history, the sight of the Cork jersey can awaken us to something new and exciting in the most unlikely circumstances. They were raging hot favourites to win a third successive Munster final but we overwhelmed them in the Athletic Grounds and won by ten points.

It brought me my first Munster senior medal but more importantly it gave Kerry a huge lift at a time of great uncertainty. One win never makes a season but in a county like Kerry, there's always a belief that something can kickstart a surge which will take on a life of its own. We sensed that something was stirring after the 1958 Munster final win because we were due to play Derry in the All-Ireland semi-final. Derry had won the Ulster title for the very first time so obviously there were doubts as to how they would cope with Croke Park and the new challenge. We knew very little about them, other than they had brilliant players in captain Jim McKeever, who would go on to win the Footballer of the Year award, and Seán O'Connell, who would be my direct opponent.

Nowadays, every detail of every team is available, but back then you relied on whatever scraps of information you could pick up, which usually weren't very many. Even those that were procured couldn't be relied on so you just had to improvise on the day. It was my first semi-final so I was as apprehensive as the Derry players. They reacted very positively to the new surrounds, bringing their impressive Ulster form to Croke Park and spreading the ball around as if they knew every blade of grass in the place. Still, I was doing okay on O'Connell but was switched off him when Tom Moriarty had to retire with a broken leg.

O'Connell scored a goal late on as Derry went on to win by a point. I was especially disappointed that it was O'Connell who struck for the crucial goal as I have always felt that if I had still been marking him, he wouldn't have got the chance. That's not cockiness or arrogance – it's just that I had done well on him prior to being moved. Of the three semi-finals which I lost as a player, this was the one I felt we really should have won because we hit no less than 17 wides over the hour.

We gained some measure of revenge on Derry in the following season's League final which we won by a goal on a day when I had another great battle with O'Connell. Astonishingly, it was Kerry's first League title win since 1932. Four months later, I would be the proud holder of my first All-Ireland senior medal after we beat Tipperary, Cork, Dublin and Galway on the way to the title.

Dublin pushed us the hardest, eating into our big lead late on but we held on for a two-point win on a day when Mick O'Connell gave a fantastic performance. It was altogether easier in the final where Galway never got into the game. They had a very impressive looking line-up, including the 'Terrible Twins', Seán Purcell and Frank Stockwell at centre-forward and full-forward respectively, Mattie McDonagh and Frank Evers at midfield, but we beat them surprisingly easily, 3-7 to 1-4. That scoreline suggests we took them apart but we didn't get on top of them until the final quarter on a day when Seán Murphy gave a brilliant display at right half-back. Things went well for me on the other wing too – indeed, the whole defence impressed as is clear from Galway's low return.

Who would have thought that just over two years after losing to Waterford and 18 months after being humiliated by Kildare, Kerry would be back as All-Ireland champions? It was an exciting time for me because I had now firmly established myself on the team and was growing in confidence all the time. I was still only 23, had won all the major honours available and was looking forward to much more success.

What I, or indeed anybody else in Kerry, didn't realise was that the face of Gaelic football was about to change and that we wouldn't be part of it. New forces were massing in the north and the west that would leave us behind for quite some time. We'd pick up an All-Ireland in between the two revolutions and another one afterwards but we'd also have to admit that the Swinging Sixties belonged not to Kerry but to Down and Galway.

Down Days and a Lost Kingdom

So which was better – the Down team that brought the Sam Maguire Cup across the border for the first time in 1960 and enjoyed the experience so much that they held on to it again in 1961, or the Galway team that won three All-Irelands in a row between 1964 and 1966?

It's a great debate for people who like to compare teams and, since there's no way of ever knowing the definitive answer, everybody can make a convincing argument to support their particular viewpoint. For what it's worth – and I played against both on several occasions – I believe that if the teams were pitted against each other in their prime, Down would win.

That's not to say they had better individual players than Galway but I reckon that Down's style of play would have caused more problems for Galway than vice versa. Frankly, I believe Down would have out-muscled Galway and not always fairly either.

Down were tough, physical and aggressive and could be quite cynical too when it came to fouling, especially outside the scoring range. If they felt play needed to be stopped, they did it and worried about the free later. That made them very hard to play against and, since they had brought fitness to a new level for that era, they gave themselves a decided advantage in terms of out-lasting opponents.

Galway had a few lads who weren't exactly shy in imposing their physical presence either but it wasn't done in the same systematic way as Down. Galway were more of a pure footballing side than Down which is why I suspect that if the sides clashed, Down would have ground out a victory. I'm not accusing Down of being ruthless hit men who thumped their way to glory but there's no doubt that they were tough and hard. They had a lot of skill woven through the side too but they brought a cynical edge to their play which was difficult to counteract. Throw that into the mix with so many excellent individual players, including a superb half-forward line of Seán O'Neill, James McCartan and Paddy Doherty, and you had the ingredients for a hugely effective side.

That trio played a big role in the great Down story of the early Sixties but there was a lot more to it than just a collection of good players coming together at the same time. Down's development was part of a patient plan that had been devised some years earlier. It wouldn't have come to anything of course if they didn't have high-quality players but, equally, those lads might never have won an All-Ireland if new organisational structures and targets hadn't been put in place.

Maurice Hayes, who was County Secretary at the time, is generally credited with being the man with the vision and ambition to plot a new way forward to change the course of Down football. Players were made to feel important, training schedules and methods were changed and, over a period of time, Down discovered that they were on to something special.

They were more progressive than the rest of the country at that time. They were definitely well ahead of Kerry in terms of how players were treated which was probably understandable. Down believed that they had to do something different to win their first All-Ireland, whereas Kerry assumed they would continue winning All-Irelands by carrying on as usual. If it was good enough in the past, it's good enough now – that was the Kerry motto.

Down took the scene by storm in 1960 and Kerry weren't ready for them. Galway had beaten Down easily in the 1959 All-Ireland semi-final and we had beaten Galway even more convincingly in the final. So, when Down retained the Ulster title in 1960 and edged out Offaly in an All-Ireland semi-final replay, we didn't see any serious threat from them.

We should have been warned after losing the 1958 All-Ireland semi-final to Derry but, having won the All-Ireland a year later, we felt we were a cut above Ulster teams, including Down even if they had beaten us by two points in the 1960 League semi-final.

None of the sides from the six counties had ever won an All-Ireland title up to then and Cavan were the only Ulster team to have made any real impact so northern teams weren't rated by the big powers like Kerry, Dublin and Galway.

However, Down's new approach was to yield rich dividends. They trained harder and became fitter; they looked after their players; they worked on tactics; they were aggressive and mobile; they studied the opposition; they inter-changed players; in short, they were ahead of their time. On the minus side, they also introduced a degree of negativity which must have been pre-planned. They had no qualms whatsoever about fouling a player well out the field.

The free had to be taken from the ground back then giving them time to regroup which they did most effectively. I would be the first to pay tribute to Down for the many positive and creative aspects they used such as off-the-ball running, support play, accurate passing and ball retention, but there's no doubt they also exploited as much negativity as they thought they could get away with. There were no 'ticks' or yellow cards which meant that, provided a challenge wasn't of the seriously 'dirty' variety, a player could foul as much as he liked without any consequences other than giving away a free.

Down used that to good effect so it was very difficult to build up any momentum against them. They would have been in trouble in the modern game where a loud sneeze can draw a yellow card and a follow-up cough leaves a player heading for the dressing-room. Down would have had to adapt to that and they were probably good enough to do so. At that time, they didn't need to; they could foul all day but as long as it was done far enough away from goal it didn't damage them.

I know they have always denied that deliberate fouling was part of their plan but I played against them often enough to suspect that it most definitely was. After all, it was hardly a coincidence that they did it so systematically.

The advantage they gained through those tactics would have been useless if they didn't have good players which they most assuredly did. Apart from their deadly half-forwards, they also had a well-organised, tenacious defence, led by captain Kevin Mussen,

Leo Murphy and Dan McCartan, while Joe Lennon and Jarlath Carey were solid and reliable at midfield.

Still, when Down qualified for the 1960 All-Ireland final, Kerry weren't all that concerned by the prospect of taking them on. All things being roughly equal, we felt that Kerry would always beat Down on the big days. The trouble from our viewpoint was that things weren't equal. Down were better prepared and made it count.

I was at left half-back that day and found myself marking Seán O'Neill, a wonderful player who could slot in anywhere in the attack, including full-forward where he built a huge reputation. He was a handful, yet even though I did okay on him and he didn't do much damage, Down still won by eight points.

We were devastated. It didn't take disgusted Kerry fans long to let us know that it was the county's biggest ever defeat in an All-Ireland final up to then. We could have no complaints about losing the game but the margin of victory flattered Down. We were behind at half-time but came back to draw level before they got a lucky goal, followed by a penalty from which Doherty added their second goal. There was no way back for us and Down closed out the game, something they were very good at doing.

It was a lesson for Kerry in how times were changing but it wasn't heeded. Once again, there was a sense that everything would come right for us, just as it always seemed to. It was the wrong approach. Down may not have been eight points better but they definitely deserved to win. They were fitter than us so that was one area we should have addressed immediately but we didn't. The following August they beat us again, this time in the All-Ireland semi-final where their greater stamina was just as crucial as in 1960. Physically, they were much stronger too and we reckoned afterwards that they must have done some weight training which would have been unheard of in other parts of the country.

It was all square at half-time in the 1961 semi-final but we scored just one point in the second half and Down ran out comfortable six-point winners. The margin didn't flatter them that day – they really were that much better than us. It was obvious that we needed to adapt to what was happening around us but we still seemed to think that being from Kerry would be enough to turn things around. And very often it was.

The following season supported that theory. We were looking forward to another All-Ireland final clash with Down but they were thrashed by Cavan in the Ulster final, handing the initiative right back to us. We swept past Cork by 16 points in the Munster final before dismissing Dublin easily in the All-Ireland semi-final to set up a final clash with Roscommon which would turn out to be possibly the worst of all time. I say that as somebody who was involved in it which is unusual because players tend to don rose-tinted glasses when looking back at big games they won.

Frankly, this was a terrible affair, just indeed as the Kerry v Roscommon final of 1980 was too. The 1962 success had a special significance for Kerry in that it brought the county's 20th All-Ireland and it also banished the bad taste of the Down defeats over the previous two seasons. But whenever or wherever you find Kerry people reminiscing about the past, they'll pass over the 1962 final as it was no more than a statistic in the record books.

Cavan were expected to build on their win over Down but they seized up against Roscommon and lost by two points. We didn't rate Roscommon at all and, as events transpired, we didn't have to, even if there was a lot of hype surrounding them. The famous incident in the Connacht final against Galway that year when the crossbar broke while the Roscommon goalkeeper, Aidan Brady, was swinging off it as the ball sailed over the bar, had got lots of publicity. Galway were leading comfortably at the time but, after a long delay to repair the crossbar, Roscommon were a different side and went on to win by a point. Galway were a better side but got caught out which was good news for us as they would have been much harder to beat in the All-Ireland final.

All neutral GAA people wanted Roscommon to beat us in the final, if only for the sake of Gerry O'Malley who had given such wonderful service to the county over many years. It was a nice sentiment, even if quite naturally it didn't register with us. It didn't seem to have much impact on Roscommon either, as they were exceptionally poor that day and we didn't have to do anything remotely special to beat them.

We badly wanted another chance to tackle Down in an All-Ireland final and were sure it would come in 1963 but it never did. Instead, we had to make do with a National League 'Home' final clash and this time we beat them by a point in a most unusual game. It was played in mid-May when you would expect good conditions but a gale force wind swept through Croke Park. It was behind us in the first half and we built up a six-point lead (0-9 to 1-0) at half-time in what was a tough, rugged game. We had realised by then that in order to have any chance of beating Down we had to stand up to them physically, which we certainly did. They had bullied us in 1960 and 1961 and we weren't taking it any more. We didn't get a single score in the second half but defended doggedly, restricting Down to just five points. They would later claim that the absence of the suspended James McCartan, who had been sent off in the semi-final against Galway, cost them the game but then we had serious injury worries going into the 1960 All-Ireland final so these things tended to balance out over a period of years.

I don't know how I actually managed to play in the League final because on the Wednesday before the game, a concrete manhole clattered down on my toe back in the garage. The toe was badly crushed but I was so determined to play that I asked Dr Tom Prenderville to concoct some sort of treatment. He prepared a poultice which I applied but the pain was still crucifying and, to make matters worse, I couldn't possibly get the heavily bandaged toe into a football boot.

Still, I refused to accept that I couldn't play so I cut the top of the boot to let the toe out. I got an injection to numb the entire area just before the game and went out to play against no less a man than Dan McCartan. I had been switched from left half-back to centre-forward that year and was relishing my new role. I had played all my football with Waterville as an attacker and was delighted when I got the chance to move up front with Kerry.

The switch meant that I now had experience in defence and attack, something that was very good for me as a player and would later stand to me as a manager. I never had any problems with switching lads from defence to attack, or vice versa, provided they had the necessary versatility as the likes of Ger Power, Ogie Moran, Tommy Doyle, Seánie Walsh and Tom Spillane did.

I never knew what was in the injection I got for the League final although I suspect it would have knocked out a horse. It got me through the game but the pain was unbelievable afterwards. I was probably stupid to play but it didn't matter what anybody told me – I wanted to line out against Down and nothing, least of all a bloody lump of concrete, was going to stop me. I was damn lucky I didn't lose the toe. The pain was ferocious on the night of the game so Dr Jim Brosnan gave me another injection. I should have rested up after that but a few days later myself, Mick O'Connell and Tom Long were off to New York as guests of John Kerry O'Donnell to play in some fundraising games. I was told to give the toe a chance to heal but had no intention of listening. As far as I was concerned, I was invited to New York and had to play.

But then I was never the most sensible when it came to minding myself. In 1979, I got a fierce bad facial injury in a club game. At the time I was 43 years old, an age when most sane people would have packed in their playing careers but I was still getting such enjoyment out of it that I couldn't let go. I was in my fifth season as Kerry manager and enjoying that too but nothing could ever compare with playing which was why I continued until I was 48 years old. Even then I didn't want to pack it in.

In 1979 I got a kick in the face in the south Kerry final and had to be rushed to hospital in Cork for treatment. My good friend Peter Huggert drove me across and he had to stop at least three times because I kept passing out. I was damn lucky I didn't lose the sight of an eye. There were real concerns for a few days but, thankfully, I have good healing powers so everything was okay. It didn't take long for me to get restless so I signed myself out of hospital against doctors' advice and a week later I was back training the Kerry team again. Six months later I was playing club football and continued for another five years. The madness of it all, yet I wouldn't change a single thing. I have always believed that players should play for as long as they possibly can because nothing will ever match the special feeling of being out there doing what you love best at whatever level.

Injuries are a hazard of any field game but you can't let them take control of your attitude. Back in 1962, I had my nose burst in a League game against Cork but was due to play for Ireland against the Combined Universities a week later and wouldn't entertain the thought of missing it. So I had this cage thing made to protect my nose and went up to Croke Park to play for Ireland on the day after St Patrick's Day. We had a good team but still lost by two points. It was risky for me to line out that day but I ignored the dangers. I took quite a few knocks to the nose over the years and am paying the price now with my sinuses which give me a bit of trouble.

If Mary Carmel didn't know for sure before we got married the lengths to which I would go to play a football game, it dawned on her very quickly after our wedding in February 1962 because it was only a month later I headed for Croke Park looking like an alien with that special cage to protect my nose. I think she knew then that she had married a madman!

But when you're young, you feel indestructible. I always tried to see injuries as no more than nuisances which definitely shouldn't be allowed to interfere with the important business of playing football. One time, I broke my thumb but was so desperate to line out in a club game with Waterville that I had it strapped to a finger and played on anyway. It wasn't easy but I did okay. It was my nature to play through any pain barrier which is probably why I have never had any time for players who exaggerate injuries. If a broken nose and a crushed toe were the worst I experienced up to 1963, I quickly realised the following year that there were injuries which simply couldn't be ignored. What's more, they came at a time when Kerry were heading into a serious slump.

Winning the 1962 All-Ireland final and the League title eight months later left us feeling really good about ourselves. Down seemed to be in decline and Cork were no great threat, leaving Dublin as the most likely side to cause us problems. At least, that's what we thought.

So much so that at the start of the 1963 championship, we felt that Kerry were bang in line to win their first two-in-a-row since the early Forties. Cork did nothing to disabuse us of that notion in the Munster final and we beat them fairly easily. I played well and was very happy with my form but little did I know that I was about to head into the most depressing period of my playing career.

Between August 1963 and May 1965, Galway met Kerry in two All-Ireland finals, one semi-final and a National League 'Home' final. They won all four. We didn't even manage to score a single goal in any of the games. It was a miserable period for Kerry and even more so for me personally as a series of injuries robbed me of what should have been my prime years.

Other than winning an All-Ireland minor title in 1960, there was no real sign of a Galway surge in the early 1960s, certainly not to the degree that it developed. Seán Purcell's great career had run its course and, while Galway were always likely to be competitive, we didn't worry too much when we saw them emerge from Connacht as our semi-final opponents in 1963. I recall the late Jack Mahon telling me many years later that Galway were incensed when they read that some Kerry player had talked openly in an interview about how we wanted to play Dublin in the final.

That may have motivated Galway but it made little difference throughout the first half or early in the second half of the semi-final when we moved five points clear and seemed to be playing well within ourselves. One more point might have seen Galway off but they got a lifeline when Pateen Donnellan snatched an opportunist goal. He was down injured near our goal but, when a high lob dropped in, he made a miraculous recovery, grabbed the ball and punched it to the net. Pure cuteness! And it wouldn't be the last time that Pateen's quick thinking turned games during that period, or indeed the last time that the Donnellans would be a thorn in my side as Michael did more than his share to thwart Kildare in 1998 and 2000.

Galway went on to win the 1963 semi-final by two points, leaving us in a state of total shock. My personal nightmare was about to begin. In early January 1964, I broke my ankle playing for South Kerry against UCC but, typical of my impatience, I came back too soon and broke my fibula in a seven-a-side tournament in Sneem on St Patrick's Day.

It was a different world for injured players back then. County Boards forgot about you when you weren't able to play. You had to look after your own rehabilitation and, if there were costs involved, you footed the bill yourself. When the plaster came off, my leg was wasted away and only for Patie Dennehy, an ex-army man from Ballinskelligs, my recovery would have been much slower. He worked wonders but, after having two bad injuries in the space of a few months, my fitness was way behind everybody else.

I was back for the All-Ireland semi-final against Cavan and was picked at centre-forward. It was a crazy decision. I could only run in straight lines, couldn't twist or turn properly, couldn't sprint, was slow off the mark and found it hard to get off the ground when I tried to jump for the ball. All in all, it wasn't how you'd like your centre-forward to be for an All-Ireland semi-final! I got away with it against Cavan, who were quite poor that year but still somehow managed to beat Down in the Ulster final. We hammered them by 12 points but I suspected it was a false dawn. And so it was. Galway had learned a lot from their 1963 final defeat by Dublin and were a whole lot more potent a year later.

I was in a bad mood going into the 1964 final. It's the worst feeling in the world heading into a big game knowing that you're not fully fit and that you're up against an opponent who is at the peak of his game as Galway centre-back Seán Meade was. Meade was in the classic mould of doggedly defensive centre-backs who tried to keep opponents within arm's length all the time. He'd nudge and he'd pull all day so pace was the obvious way to trouble him but I didn't have the legs to put him to the test which was very frustrating.

I did no better against John Donnellan, another tough customer. But then I wasn't the only Kerry forward who didn't perform that day. Enda Colleran, Noel Tierney and Bosco McDermott had our inside forwards tied up while Martin Newell was a stylish wing-back alongside Meade and Donnellan. Behind them, Johnny Geraghty was an outstanding goalkeeper. A mixture of wonderful athleticism, lightning reflexes and endless courage for such a small man, he was a special talent as Jo Jo Barrett discovered when he let fly with a thundering shot early in the second half which Geraghty turned out for a fifty. That save inspired Galway and deflated us to such a degree that we were well beaten long before the end.

Galway were full value for their five-point win, a margin we cut to three when we met them in the 1965 final. Once again though, they were very much the better team. If 1964 was frustrating for me, the 1965 final was a total disaster, In fact, it was my worst ever performance for Kerry in a major game. Once again, I shouldn't have even been playing. I had been suffering from an injured ankle but came on as a substitute against Dublin in the semi-final and scored 2-1. I don't know how I managed it because I could only run in straight lines but, having scored so much in a short time, everyone (except me) thought I'd be okay in the final.

I wasn't. I started at full-forward against Noel Tierney, a massive presence at full-back who was then at the top of his game. Taking on a man like that was no job for a fella with a bad ankle. I never got into the game and should have been taken off but we didn't have a whole lot of talent on the bench so I had to carry on, knowing full well that I was going to make absolutely no impact. After all, this was a Galway defence that conceded just one goal in three All-Ireland finals and semi-finals in three seasons so you needed to be in the whole of your health to find a gap.

Having said that, I would have loved to have taken on Meade and Tierney when I was at full fitness but I never got the chance because our paths didn't cross again in the championship during my playing days. Galway had also beaten Kerry in the 1965 'Home' League final when a last minute goal by Sáamus Leydon ruined us. We would always contend that big Mattie McDonagh didn't just lift the ball directly off the ground but shovelled it along for six inches before picking it up and passing to Leydon, but the referee allowed the goal and we were beaten.

That goal was a source of great debate right up to the time that Mattie died. We became good friends over the years and had many a passionate discussion on that goal. I'd accuse Mattie of cheating and he'd just laugh and say: 'Micko, you need to get your eyesight tested, sure the ball was six inches off the ground.' On one occasion we were playing golf in some outing when I saw Mattie strolling down the adjoining fairway towards his ball and I yelled across at him: 'Don't pick it up Mattie, you won't get away with it this time.' He loved the crack over that goal.

He was a mighty man, a great player and a lovely person. He did for that Galway team what James McCartan did for Down. Both were real warhorses who had the power to take on defences but they had skill and smartness too. Mattie was, of course, the only Connacht man to win four All-Ireland senior medals, a record that's unlikely to be beaten in the foreseeable future, if indeed ever. If any man deserved that honour, it was Mattie. I'd go so far as to say that Galway probably wouldn't have won any of the three titles in the Sixties without him. One of my great regrets was that I was away in Spain when he died so I missed his funeral but, judging from the number of people from all over the country who travelled to Ballygar to pay their respects, it was clear that he was held in the highest esteem everywhere which was a fitting tribute to a great man.

The only Galway v Down championship clash of that era was in the 1965 semi-final which Galway won by three points. It couldn't be classed as a definitive test to decide which was the better team of the Sixties because Galway were in their prime whereas Down had slipped quite a bit from the heady heights of 1960 and 1961. Galway people would argue that their side had more pure footballers than Down and also that Down won two relatively handy All-Irelands.

Against that, Down had a tougher route in Ulster than Galway had in Connacht. In fact, there was one year when Galway were given a bye directly to the Connacht final. Also, I have no doubt that the Kerry teams that lost to Galway in 1964 and 1965 weren't as good as the teams that lost to Down a few years earlier. That view is supported by the fact that, whereas we recovered from the Down defeats to win the All-Ireland in 1962, we fell away after the Galway experiences and didn't even win Munster in 1966 or 1967.

By the end of 1965, I was a very unhappy camper. The injury blight left me frustrated and, although I was still only 29 years old, I was beginning to think that maybe the body was flashing out warning lights. They turned into blazing headlights in February 1966 when my ankle went again in a League game against Cavan which, to make matters worse, we lost.

I had to go off after just three minutes and I decided enough was enough. My pace was gone, I had become an easy target for moderate defenders and all the signs were that my inter-county number was up. So, I quit as a player. I didn't have to of course. I could have patched up the ankle, hobbled on and, seeing that I had topped the poll for the election of selectors at the January convention, I could always propose myself for a place on the team!

I wasn't interested in playing purely for its own sake. If I wasn't fully fit and able to contribute then I had no business playing. I continued as a selector, again topping the poll in 1967 in what was another grim year for Kerry. It's always a bad season when we lose to Cork but this was a second successive defeat and, as if to underline how far back we had gone, Cork didn't win either All-Ireland. As we sank lower, Wicklow nearly beat us in a League game towards the end of the year and, a week later, Louth did. And in Tralee too where a bewildered crowd let the Kerry players know in no uncertain terms what they thought of their efforts.

This was as low as it got for a very long time. Kerry people would usually be upbeat about the future but that definitely wasn't the case at the end of 1967 which marked the end of a fifth successive season when our championship attempt had been a shambles. I wasn't getting any satisfaction out of being a selector and still had a great desire to play, one that had been reborn with the club.

The injury problems had cleared up, I was feeling good about myself and decided: 'To hell with this retirement business, I'm going to give it another shot.' A few of us got together and came up with the idea of playing a Kerry Past v Present challenge game in Tralee in February 1968. It was a 'no-win' situation for the Present team who were always going to be judged harshly because things had been going so badly, but that didn't matter. Something needed to be done to lift morale in the county.

The Past team included many great names, including Mick O'Connell and Séamus Murphy who had also drifted out of the scene but who would re-emerge as key figures.

I scored 1-8 and was back in business. Seven months later Kerry were in an All-Ireland final.

It was quite a transformation in a short space of time but then Kerry have always been capable of doing that and so often Cork are the catalysts. They certainly were in 1968. They led us by seven points after eight minutes in the Munster final at which stage we're looking at each other and wondering if we're headed for an absolute disaster. Bad enough to lose two successive Munster finals to Cork, but a third? I don't think it had ever happened up to then so we knew what lay in store for us if we had to face the Kerry public after another black day. I don't know if that frightening prospect lay at the heart of our revival but, whatever the origin, we launched a revival which saw us finish on no less a tally than 1-21 to Cork's 3-8.

We could well have lost the All-Ireland semi-final to a fine Longford team that had won the county's first and only Leinster title but Culloty came to our rescue late on with a great save and we edged home by two points. We were back in an All-Ireland final where, almost inevitably, Galway or Down were waiting. It turned out to be Down who beat Galway in the semi-final.

Naturally, all the talk in Kerry was of revenge for 1960 and 1961 but it didn't turn out that way. Down got two early goals and, while we battled back, it was always a losing cause. They won by two points but were full value for a bigger win as our goal – from a Brendan Lynch free – only came in the final minute. The awful run had continued as we had now lost three All-Ireland finals in five years.

Despite that, I was quite happy with my own game and felt that my decision to return had been fully vindicated. And it got better over the next two years when we won an All-Ireland double and I picked up a Texaco Footballer of the Year award in 1969.

If 1960 was my best year as a defender, 1969 was definitely my best as a forward. I ended up as the country's top scorer but, even more importantly, Kerry won the All-Ireland beating Offaly (0-10 to 0-7) in a fairly nondescript final. Ten points should never be enough to win an All-Ireland final (it hadn't been since Cavan's win over Meath in the 1952 replay and hasn't been ever since) but it was that day so we have to give credit to the defence.

I had scored freely throughout the year, accumulating a total of 8-96 in 22 games which probably accounted for my winning the Texaco award – a great honour as only two Kerrymen, Seán Murphy and Mick O'Connell, had won it previously. It was all the more special for me because it arrived at the age of 33 after I had come out of retirement.

A year later, Kerry were again All-Ireland champions, I was top scorer and this time the Texaco went to wing-back Tom Prendergast for his fine contribution to our wins over Cork, Derry and Meath. The 1970 championship was historic as the first to feature eighty minute games. It was quite a change for players to go from thirty to forty minute halves and, while it led to much higher scoring, it also meant that one-sided games simply dragged on for far longer than they should.

That's the thing about the GAA. It can be fierce conservative for years and then produce something as radical as increasing the duration of a game by twenty minutes.

I don't recall any change in our training schedule for the increased demands of the eighty minute game but obviously nobody else did anything about it either as we encountered no stamina problems en route to another title. Eighty minute games were too long, not from a stamina viewpoint but because the nature of football or hurling isn't suited to it. That emerged as the general view and a sensible compromise was reached for the 1975 championship when the duration of games was cut to seventy minutes.

One of the great memories from the 1970 final was the cracking goal scored near the end by midfielder Din Joe Crowley. He cut through and blasted the ball to the net for as fine an individual goal as you will ever see in a final. If he was there for a hundred years, he probably wouldn't have scored another goal like that but he made it sound afterwards as if it was something he'd been practising all along. Still, he was entitled to boast about it because it was one hell of a goal.

After what Galway had done to us in the mid-Sixties, we were determined to match their three-in-a-row in 1971 but were walloped out the gate by Cork in the Munster final. We returned the compliment – admittedly not by as much – a year later. However, a new force had emerged from the midlands in the form of an Offaly team that emulated Down from a decade earlier by winning a first ever All-Ireland and retaining it a year later.

I got my first taste of management in 1972 when I took over as Kerry player-manager for the closing stages of the National League which we won with a comfortable victory over Mayo in the final. Johnny Culloty took over as trainer for the championship where we fancied ourselves big time, especially when we hammered Roscommon in the semi-final. However, just as Down had done in the early Sixties, Offaly had assembled a talented, well-organised team and, having made the breakthrough in 1971, were oozing with confidence a year later.

My pace was going, which at the age of 36 was understandable, and I didn't really enjoy either the drawn final or the replay. The drawn game was a dull affair where my only happy memory was of punching the equalising point. Kerry would always fancy themselves in a replay but tradition didn't count much this time. With Willie Bryan catching everything around midfield, Offaly blitzed us in the second half, eventually winning by 1-19 to 0-13, a margin which, I'm sorry to say, is a record defeat for Kerry in All-Ireland finals.

It was my last All-Ireland final but we got a small measure of revenge on Offaly in 1973 when we beat them in the League final. That was my last big outing in Croke Park as a player and I scored five points which was a nice way to sign off. We didn't realise it at the time but Kerry had now become League specialists who shone in spring and withered in summer. It would take a few years and a frank admission that we had allowed ourselves to fall behind the times before we could start turning things around.

Apprentice Boys March On

Kerry football was in a troubled state at the end of 1974. Now that may sound ridiculous to counties who have had little success but Kerry always judge themselves by the highest standards and when they dip below those, the soul-searching begins, as it did in the autumn of 1974.

It may have been only four years since we had won an All-Ireland title and the National League crown had been collected for a fourth successive season in 1974 but the underlying trend was worrying.

League titles have always been regarded as no more than tasty little extras in Kerry. It's grand to win them but during my playing and managing days we never worried too much about them, and the same applies today. As a player, I won eight League medals which are nice mementos of good spring campaigns but all eight together wouldn't come remotely close to matching one All-Ireland medal.

I won the last four League medals consecutively between 1971 and 1974, the first three on the pitch and the last as a substitute when Kerry beat Roscommon in a replay. My Kerry career ended in May 1974 when I decided that, since I was heading for my 38th birthday the following month, I should heed the body clock and leave the inter-county stage to younger men.

It was the right call because I would have hated the 1974 Munster championship. There's nothing more frustrating for any sports person than having the brain prompting you to do the right thing only for the body to declare: 'Not anymore, my friend, I've had enough of this.' It eats into you because you know it's never going to get any better. In fact, it's certain to get progressively worse. Still, I could have had no complaints. Not many players are still on the inter-county scene at 37 but it would have been tempting fate for me to celebrate my 38th birthday by training for the Munster championship.

Cork were reigning All-Ireland champions in 1974 and had a fine team that walloped all before them in 1973. There were years, later on, when Kerry sailed through the championship without having to answer any hard questions but Cork were every bit as comprehensive in the 1973 campaign, beating Clare by 17 points, Kerry by seven, Tyrone by 15 and Galway by seven, to win their first All-Ireland since 1945.

I played in my last Munster final in 1973 which turned out to be a miserable experience for Kerry. I pointed six frees and we scored 1-15 which would have been enough to win most games but our defence was ripped apart, conceding 5-15 which was an utter embarrassment. Bad enough to lose to Cork but to be hit for five goals! We couldn't wait to get back home and hide.

Of course, that was a seriously good Cork team, although not good enough to put 5-15 past Kerry if we were mentally tuned for the challenge which we obviously weren't. Maybe it was the big defeat against Offaly in the 1972 All-Ireland final replay that knocked the heart out of the squad but, for whatever reason, we were shamefully inept against Cork nine months later.

That Cork team should have won more All-Ireland titles. They had a lovely balance all over the field but they fell into the oldest trap of all in 1974. Their easy win over Kerry seemed to convince them that retaining the All-Ireland title was a formality. They didn't rate a re-emerging Dublin side as a real threat and were hopelessly ill-equipped to respond when the pressure came on in the semi-final. A year later, they were eaten alive by young Kerry lions, ending Cork's good days for a long time. Who would have thought that when they beat Kerry by seven points in the 1974 Munster final it would be their last provincial win for nine years? And who could possibly have envisaged that Kerry would transform so quickly from the shocking mess that was 1974 to an All-Ireland winning side a year later?

Coming after the disastrous Munster final of the previous year, the 1974 final was a total nightmare, one of the most depressing days Kerry had endured for a very long time. It was a wet, miserable Sunday in Killarney and the Kerry performance matched the awful weather. Kerry stayed with Cork for fifty minutes but were swamped for the remaining thirty (games were eighty minutes long then). Cork ran out the easiest of winners in what was Mick O'Connell's last game for Kerry. He came on as a substitute but couldn't do anything to halt Cork's powerful march to their third Munster title in four years. To put it bluntly, Kerry were a shambles.

And therein lay the worrying part. It was the first time since 1909 that Cork had won three of four Munster titles so we could be forgiven in Kerry for not being over-excited about having the League trophy as our guest for four successive years. After all, there's nothing worse for a Kerryman than being ranked behind Cork, not least because they love to keep reminding us about it.

Things weren't going well for Kerry at under-age level either. We hadn't won an All-Ireland minor title since 1963 which was a sacrilegious omission in a county like Kerry. Cork had won nine of the previous 11 Munster minor titles which suggested that their under-age systems were far superior to ours. It also gave them a steady stream of fine young talent which many thought would go on to dominate for years at senior level.

Johnny Culloty had been training the Kerry senior team but decided to step down after the 1974 Munster final. There wasn't exactly a wild rush to replace him amid the general air of despondency which prevailed in Kerry but when County Chairman Ger McKenna asked me if I was interested in taking the job, I didn't hesitate for a second. My playing days with Kerry were over and this was the next best thing. Ever since I was a kid in Waterville, I had been fascinated with teams and tactics. I had served for several years as a player and selector with Kerry and got a chance at management in 1974 when I took charge of the U-21 team.

We lost the Munster final by a point to Cork in Cahirciveen in a game we definitely should have won. Páidí Ó Sé blasted a penalty over the bar at one stage and a tidy Cork team, captained by Jimmy Barry-Murphy, held on to win by a point. It was fierce disappointing for me in my first year as a county manager but there were upsides. We had some brilliant young talent on that team while quite a few others had been on the 1973 team that won the All-Ireland U-21 final.

We're talking here about lads like Paudie O'Mahony, Jimmy Deenihan, Ger O'Keeffe, John Long, Paudie Lynch, Mickey Ned O'Sullivan, Tim Kennelly, Ogie Moran, Seánie Walsh, Páidí Ó Sé, John Egan, Barry Walsh, Ger O'Driscoll and Mikey Sheehy. It's a mighty impressive list, most of whom would go on to become legendary figures, although no one could possibly have predicted it at the time.

McKenna was obviously impressed with what I had achieved in Waterville prior to taking over the county U-21s and felt that with a new manager and a new squad, Kerry could become a serious senior side again. His eagerness to achieve that was no doubt multiplied by Dublin's return to the top spot. The sight of Dublin lording it on All-Ireland final day is always enough to leave Kerrymen muttering darkly in the night and waking in the morning with a fresh resolve to do something about it.

It would have hit McKenna more than most and the awful pain was doubled by Cork's dominance in Munster. Hell, Kerry's heritage was under threat. I told McKenna that if I was to take the manager's job I would have to be allowed to do things my way. There was no need to mention it because by asking me on board he had shown full confidence in my ability to kickstart what had become a slow-moving scene. He let it be known from the start that I would have his total backing and that I wouldn't have to be looking over my shoulder all the time. That level of sincere support would become even more important a few years later when an attempt was made to oust me.

Having got the manager's job, I made two immediate decisions. I would go with the bulk of the U-21 teams from 1973 and 1974 and I would concentrate totally on the championship and let the League look after itself. Backing youth meant leaving out some very senior players which was tough and I'm not sure they ever forgave me, but it had to be done because Kerry needed a new sense of direction.

The previous one had taken us a certain distance but times were changing in Gaelic football and we would have to be part of that. Actually, we would have to be ahead of it, as befits Kerry's status in the game.

It was just as well that McKenna knew I wasn't putting much emphasis on the League because we got a right lesson against Meath in the 1975 quarter-final. Expectations had been raised with a good pre-Christmas campaign where we drew with Dublin, beat Cork and lost to Offaly by a point. But it all came unstuck against Meath.

They beat us by five points but, in real terms, they were even more superior than the scoreline suggests. I have to admit I had serious misgivings about the future as we left Croke Park that March evening. Mind you, Kerry supporters had a lot more doubts, I'm sure. As for the players, well they were young and enthusiastic and would try anything I suggested so I decided to go for broke. I would train the life out of them, just as I had done with Waterville over the years.

We were always drawing from a small panel in Waterville so I reckoned we had to create an advantage for ourselves to take on the bigger clubs. We might not be able to match them in certain ways but, by God, we would be fitter than them. And it worked.

I decided to try the same thing with Kerry. In the run-up to the 1975 Munster championship, we trained like no team had done before. It was crazy stuff but they were young enough to take it and anyway, I believed it was the right way to go. Had I kept all older lads on the panel, they wouldn't have been able for the training and even if they were, they would probably have revolted. They had become set in their ways and wouldn't have taken too kindly to someone who had played with them laying down the law about a new and punishing routine. It was different with all those eager young lads who knew no different, so it made my job easier. Besides, it was the right thing to do because Dublin had raised the fitness bar and I knew that if we were to match them, we would have to be better prepared than them.

It was fascinating to watch how the squad changed. Mikey Sheehy had come in as a nice solid little lad with buckets of skill but he was carrying too much weight. He was also a bit lazy on the training field but we soon got rid of that and, as the pounds fell off, his skills blossomed into something really special. He would never have achieved that unless he was fully fit.

I had played with Sheehy in a League game in late 1973 and could see first hand just how much potential he had. He was a typical Tralee lad, a cocky little devil with a conjuror's instinct. He came on as a substitute against Cork in a League game and had obviously been told to kick any frees that came our way because I had missed a few. Now, however good he was, I was damned if I going to let a kid from the town throw me off the free-taking role. When we got a straightforward kick from 21 yards, he was all set to line it up but I shouted across at him: 'Hey, give me that ball.'

He looked a bit surprised but he threw it over to me and trotted off smiling. And yes, I did point it, but then it was impossible to miss.

It was to be the start of a great relationship between us and, boy, how his free-taking brilliance served Kerry over the years. And then there was Pat Spillane. When he first joined the panel, he wasn't a great kicker but he worked so hard on it that he became one of the best I ever saw. He could turn and twist and bang the ball over the bar without looking. It was all down to practice. He was helped too by his natural enthusiasm for everything he did. He hadn't a single doubt about his own ability and the more opponents tried to wallop him, the more he rose to the challenge.

By the time we set out for the 1975 Munster campaign, I knew we had a team that certainly wouldn't be short of fitness. I was disappointed that the GAA had decided to end the five-year experiment of playing championship games over 80 minutes. Instead, they cut it back to 70 minutes which was a pity from our viewpoint because the team was so fit that they would have had no problem with 80- or even 100-minute games.

I was really excited heading into the 1975 championship. We had taken a reality check against Meath in the League quarter-final, but a few months later everything looked much more positive. I could see the potential levels rising all the time and the only question was whether that could be transferred into a real force on the big occasions.

We beat Tipperary in the Munster semi-final after getting a fright in the first half. They matched us all the way to half-time but we overpowered them in the second half. I still wasn't happy with the fitness levels and decided to increase the training programme dramatically for the final.

There was a five-week gap between the semi-final and final which we turned into one of the most concentrated training periods ever seen. We trained for 27 consecutive nights which was unheard of then. It probably still is but I was a new manager with my own ideas and I had a young squad who were well able for everything that was thrown at them. The plan was to blitz Cork with pace and endurance on Munster final day.

It worked too. We led by seven points at half-time and also enjoyed the huge psychological plus of a brilliant penalty save by Paudie O'Mahony from Jimmy Barry-Murphy. From there on, it was a mere formality and we ended Cork's dominance and launched a run that would see us win eight All-Ireland and 11 Munster titles between then and 1986. Cork didn't really rate us in 1975. They had so many players with big reputations, an All-Ireland senior medal and All-Star awards that they felt vastly superior to us, while their younger lads had mostly happy memories of playing Kerry at minor and U-21 level.

Our 1-14 to 0-7 win was quite remarkable, given the extent of Cork's dominance a year earlier. In real terms, we weren't that much a better side but the combination of our fitness and enthusiasm, not to mention lots of developing skill, combined with Cork's belief that they were a notch above us, set them up for a crashing fall.

Elsewhere, things were going our way too. Our opponents in the All-Ireland semi-final were to be the Connacht champions which, for the first time since 1928, turned out to be Sligo. Winning Connacht after such a long, barren spell was a major achievement for Sligo. In fact, it was probably the peak of their ambition as they were reputed to have enjoyed themselves immensely in the period between the Connacht final and playing us. That was understandable, but combining celebrations in a success-starved county while preparing for an All-Ireland semi-final against a hungry Kerry team was never going to work. And it didn't. They were beaten before the start, much as Monaghan were in similar circumstances four years later.

Mickey Kearins, by far Sligo's best-known player and a man who had done so much for the county over many years, was past his prime in 1975 and we reckoned that if we held him in check we wouldn't have any trouble with the rest of the attack.

It could have been much different if Mayo or Galway had won Connacht. Galway had lost three of the previous four All-Ireland finals which was a shattering blow to their confidence, but they were a mighty experienced side who would have presented us with a completely different challenge, while Mayo would probably have done better than Sligo too.

Sligo put up a decent fight for a period but, as we suspected, lacked forward power and we skated to an easy victory, 3-13 to 0-8. Three games played and we still hadn't conceded a goal, thanks in no small way to our goalkeeper, Paudie O'Mahony, who saved penalties against Cork and Sligo.

So then, less than a year after taking over at a time of great pessimism in Kerry, I found myself preparing a team for an All-Ireland final. Ominously, and almost inevitably, Dublin were our opponents. What's more, they were chasing the two-in-a-row and were so well fancied that, publicly at least, we rowed along with the notion that we were wide-eyed innocents taking our chances against the slick city masters. We played on that as only Kerrymen could! We talked up Dublin from every angle on and off the field and were delighted that, in the main, the media bought into the idea that we were no more than hopeful youngsters who had got lucky against Cork and were even luckier that Sligo had come out of Connacht.

Deep inside the Kerry camp, the view was completely different. For a start, we reckoned Dublin had won a poor enough championship in 1974. Their return from the wilderness, complete with songs about Heffo's Army, Hill 16 and so forth, had been hyped to the heavens by a Dublin-based media. In fairness though, Dublin had given Gaelic football a fresh impetus when it was badly needed. However, it didn't alter the reality that Cork's arrogance had undermined them in the 1974 semi-final, while Galway, who were edgy anyway after losing finals in 1971 and 1973, completely lost their nerve in the final.

Also, we had noticed that the Dublin defence had leaked a surprisingly high number of goals in the 1975 championship.

Wexford had hit them for three; Louth had got four; while Derry had scored three in the All-Ireland semi-final. Now, we didn't mention it to anybody at the time but we reckoned they had serious problems which were being camouflaged by thick layers of hype. In fairness, Dublin had also scored a lot of goals but I had no doubt that our young, quick and mobile defence, built around John O'Keeffe at full-back and Tim Kennelly at centre-back, was far better than anything they had met previously. Corner-backs Ger O'Keeffe and Jimmy Deenihan were wiry customers, while wing-backs Páidí Ó Sé and Ger Power brought great balance to the line. Tipperary, Cork and Sligo had all failed to score a goal against us and we had only conceded an average of eight points per game.

My only fear going into the final was that we were short of experience. John O'Keeffe and Brendan Lynch had played in All-Ireland finals before but the rest were young and were coming up against a battle-hardened, physically strong Dublin team. If we were to win, it would have to be achieved through pace and constant movement so that we left Dublin thinking about us all the time, rather than settling into their own rhythm, getting Hill 16 behind them and making life very difficult.

The belief that our defence was well up to the challenge was proved correct on final day. Dublin scored no goals while we got two, the first from John Egan (that man poached so many crucial goals for us over the years) very early on and the second from substitute Ger O'Driscoll in the second half. In between, we were fairly comfortable too.

O'Driscoll had come on as a replacement for Mickey Ned who ended up in hospital after being hit a thunderous wallop by Seán Doherty as he flew through the heart of the Dublin defence midway through the first half. It was one of those shuddering clashes that you know will end up badly. And it did. Mickey Ned was knocked out, rushed to the Richmond Hospital and didn't fully come around until nine o'clock that night at which stage he was informed by a nurse that Kerry had won the All-Ireland.

He should have been on the steps of the Hogan Stand four hours earlier making his captain's speech after receiving the Sam Maguire Cup but instead that honour went to Pat Spillane who, even at the age of 19 years, wasn't short of a few words. That hasn't changed over the years either!

Doherty has since explained that, with everything happening at high speed, it could have been himself or Mickey Ned who ended up on a stretcher. Actually, there was no need for either of them to be damaged. Mickey Ned was jet-propelled that day and had so much confidence that he wanted to take on every Dublin defender. Laughably, there are those who would say he had it coming to him because he didn't get rid of the ball sooner. Since when is a player obliged to pass the ball to avoid ending up in hospital? It was an unsavoury incident which not only wrecked Mickey Ned's All-Ireland but also had a profound impact on his career as he was never quite the same player again.

But his injury galvanised the rest of the Kerry team who were well prepared anyway for anything Dublin might throw at them. We won by seven points which, in the context of where we started from 11 months earlier, was unbelievable.

The mighty Dubs had been beaten by a team of young fellas from Kerry with an average age of just over 22 years. I remarked in the dressing room afterwards that this was the best Kerry team of all time which might have been a slight exaggeration as they were still in their formative years. What I really meant was that they were going to be the best Kerry team of all time which they most assuredly were.

The sense of satisfaction at beating the Dubs was incredible. They had set the standard but we had raised it. We had taken them on with pace and they couldn't cope. They may have been a bit like Cork a year earlier, believing all their own hype and not paying enough attention to what the lads from Kerry were up to.

That final was to be the start of an unbelievable rivalry with Dublin which lasted right through my days as Kerry manager and extended into my periods in Kildare and Laois. Whether League, championship or challenge, every game against Dublin had a special edge. I'd have to say that the Kerry–Dublin rivalry of the 1975–85 period did an awful lot to raise the profile of Gaelic football at a time when it badly needed all the exposure and promotion it could get.

Who else, for instance, would draw a crowd of almost 26,000 for a routine League game in Croke Park as Dublin and Kerry did in November 1975? Dublin were really fired up for the game and won by four points which didn't bother us a whole lot as that League campaign was never going to be a serious target. However, the level of determination that Dublin showed that day should have been a warning as to their intent for 1976 but it didn't register with a young, footloose and fancy-free Kerry squad who were enjoying their new and exciting lives as All-Ireland winners.

The transformation in Kerry football in 1975 was as profound as anything that ever happened in the history of the game in the county. Our style had changed from catch-and-kick to a new, inclusive game where every player's individual skills were fitted into the pattern rather than the other way around. Catch-and-kick had served Kerry well but the game was moving on and if we didn't adapt we would have been left behind, just as we had been between 1971 and 1974.

There were complaints in later years about how we sacrificed basic Kerry principles in favour of a different style, but I couldn't have cared less. My job was to restore Kerry to what we regarded as its rightful place at the top of the pecking order and we achieved that in 1975.

Still, there were clouds gathering on the horizon. My description of the team as the best Kerry had produced was taken a bit too literally by some of the squad. By the time they realised that, the landscape had changed dramatically again. What's more, we would have been put through the ringer, me more than most, as sharp, critical arrows were fired in my direction. They came mighty close to hitting the target too.

Capital Punishment

If there are five pieces of advice I would dispense after my long years in management they are these: be your own person; always trust your instincts; take calculated chances; give your players confidence; and never select a player who is carrying an injury, irrespective of how good he is.

It's not a problem if the injury is only a little niggle, but if it disrupts training to any degree it should be regarded as serious enough to keep a player off the team. I speak from the bitter experience of having got it wrong, not once, but twice. And on both occasions it probably cost All-Ireland finals.

In 1976, Jimmy Deenihan and Ger O'Keeffe went into the All-Ireland final against Dublin carrying ankle injuries which restricted their training properly for the final. I played them, they struggled, Kerry lost – it was a bad mistake. They weren't the only ones who didn't come anywhere near reaching the peaks of a year earlier but that doesn't excuse playing them. It was my call and I got it wrong. I made the same mistake with Kildare in 1998. Niall Buckley couldn't train fully in the weeks before the final but I played him against my better judgement and it didn't work. It wasn't his fault – it was mine for selecting him, although I must say that my fellow selectors were very keen on starting him. That's where being your own man comes in. I should have said no, stuck by it and taken the consequences. As it was, I went with the flow and Kildare paid the price.

I should also have left O'Keeffe and Deenihan on the bench in 1976 rather than picking them as usual and hoping that everything would be okay on the day. It wasn't. In O'Keeffe's case, I was probably influenced by the fact that he was a devil for thinking he had pains and aches. He'd think there was something wrong with him if he wasn't complaining of a twinge. Tolerance of players who always seemed to be carrying some knock or other was never my strong point because I believed (and still do) that a lot of it was in their heads.

Clearly, that wasn't the case with O'Keeffe in 1976. In fairness, he was genuinely injured. It's easy to be wise afterwards but the reason we went with himself and Deenihan was that we didn't want to disrupt the defence too much. Besides, we had beaten Derry by 16 points in the semi-final and had convinced ourselves that everything would be fine in the final. That's the trouble with easy wins in semi-finals – they create a false impression. We knew that the Dublin full-forward line of Bobby Doyle, Jimmy Keaveney and John McCarthy would be a lot better than Derry's but we still felt we'd have their measure.

There's a natural defence mechanism that kicks in at times like that. You go with what you trust and hope it will work again. Hence the decision to stick with O'Keeffe and Deenihan, even if they weren't quite right. I knew right well that a whole lot had changed since that great day a year earlier when we stunned a Dublin team that had taken us for granted. Still, I thought (naively as it happens) that our natural flair and the big occasion would disguise the debilitating factors which were lurking very close to the surface.

They began the slow, unseen process of undermining the squad within weeks of the 1975 triumph. Just as you never see rust in a car until it breaks through to the surface, it was difficult to spot the gradual erosion of the collective will and determination of the team. It was inevitable, I suppose, that it would happen. Here you had a group of young fellas, most of whom hadn't yet reached their mid-twenties, enjoying the celebrity life of All-Ireland winners.

They were regarded as extra special, not just because it was evident that they had an unbelievable amount of talent but because they had lifted the spirit of the county at a time when Kerry supporters were convinced that the bad days would continue indefinitely. There are always opportunities for players who want to enter into the spirit of any occasion and some of the Kerry lads certainly embraced the social whirl more enthusiastically than was good for them. That's putting it mildly. Whatever the festival, fun or frolic, they were there, living it up in the most convivial atmospheres. There are plenty of hangers-on who want to befriend successful players and who create an environment where it seems like the fun never ends. And when it does, sure there's more to be found tomorrow night. I was well aware of what was going on in the winter and spring of 1976, but what was I to do about it as there's no ear more closed than a first time All-Ireland winner who doesn't want to be told?

The contrast between 1975 and 1976 could hardly have been greater. The team was the same but the mood or the focus weren't. Contenders had grown into champions and couldn't spot the grey clouds that were drifting in. In fact, we should never have survived the 1976 Munster final. We drew with Cork in the newly-opened Páirc Uí Chaoímh and, since they had come to Killarney twice in the previous two years, they had home venue again for the replay.

Cork's failure to beat us that day haunted them for a long time as they were definitely the better side but lacked the finishing touch to put us away. They led by seven points at one stage in the second half and were still four clear with five minutes to go. I stood there on the sideline, trying to figure out the move or the switch that might make the difference while deep inside I was very angry with the team, and myself too. Angry that they hadn't coped better with success, angry that I hadn't been harder on them, angry that a combination of both had left us in a precarious position.

And then, just when it looked as if the gods would complete their punishment, they began to turn a benign eye. Cork's Brian Murphy, a tenacious corner-back right throughout his great dual career, was adjudged to have crossed his own goal line when stopping a thundering drive from Seánie Walsh, and shortly afterwards Declan Barron had a goal disallowed at the other end. That was a six-point turnover in the space of a few minutes. The gods were with us all right! So was the momentum and when Spillane fisted the equaliser, you could sense the spirit draining out of Cork.

We outscored them in extra-time by 0-7 to 0-3 to win by 3-20 to 2-19. We were certainly the better team in extra-time but Cork should never have let us get that far. It was to be a defining game for Cork who wouldn't beat us again in the championship until 1983. In fact, they would suffer some humiliating defeats in the interim. Had Cork won Munster in 1976, they might have gone on to win the All-Ireland and the whole balance of power between us and them might have been a lot different over the following years.

Beating Cork in such dramatic circumstances looked to have ignited our season, a view reinforced when we thrashed Derry by 5-14 to 1-10 in the semi-final on a day when Sheehy scored 3-3. It was vintage Sheehy, the instinctive predator with the sniper's finish. That was to be the start of a series of easy semi-final wins over Ulster champions but, in hindsight, we would have been better off had Derry put us under a whole lot more pressure. At least that way we would have been able to identify the problems and set about solving them.

Lads knew that they hadn't minded themselves as well as they should have over the previous 11 months but the fightback against Cork, followed by the demolition of a good Derry team that had achieved the fairly rare distinction of winning successive Ulster finals, left them with a dangerously false impression.

It was only at that stage that we began to look towards Dublin who were back in the final for a third successive year. Some of our fellas seemed to think that it would be a repeat of 1975 but of course two important things had changed. One, we hadn't the same hunger or zeal and two, Dublin had undertaken a complete overhaul of their half-back line.

Heffernan had obviously identified the half-back area as being in need of serious repair and had brought in Tommy Drumm, Kevin Moran and Pat O'Neill. It worked exceptionally well. By the end of the campaign, Dublin had conceded just 1-45 in five championship games, compared with 12-45 in 1975. That's some difference, much of which was down to the tightened security brought by the new half-back line.

Dublin didn't have to do anything special to retain the Leinster title before beating Galway by a goal in a poor All-Ireland semi-final. So they turned up for the All-Ireland final without having given any indication that they were ready to raise their game considerably. It was the ideal situation for them.

We got an early sign of their intent in the final when Moran scooted through the heart of our defence in the opening minutes and whizzed a shot just wide. It was such a memorable burst that, to this day, you will find people who think he actually scored a goal. In fact, he might as well have, because that run set the tempo. It convinced Dublin that we were more fragile than a year earlier and left us facing up to the reality that they were right.

Moran was a special talent. Strong, quick, athletic, fearless and intelligent; it was no surprise that Heffernan and his co-selectors, Donal Colfer and Lorcan Redmond, ignored his soccer leaning and persuaded him to join the set-up.

His early surge in the 1976 final set the agenda for what turned into a horrible day for us. Paudie O'Mahony had to retire after twenty minutes with an Achilles tendon injury and we struggled all over the field, yet remarkably Dublin were only two points clear at the three-quarter stage. It wasn't a fair reflection of their superiority but their seven point winning margin most certainly was.

To add to the disappointment of surrendering the All-Ireland title, we had to live with the fact that it was Dublin's first championship win over Kerry for 42 years. In between there had been seven championship games between us, of which Kerry won six, while the 1941 All-Ireland semi-final had been drawn. To add to our misery in 1976, Dublin's win had been achieved with exactly the same winning margin as we had enjoyed a year earlier.

The message was clear. Dublin had learned their lesson in 1975, gone away, made the necessary corrections and cleaned us out. We had sat back and admired ourselves, ignoring the unquestionable reality that nothing remains static.

It was a painful lesson to take back home to Kerry to face a public who believed they had been badly let down, perhaps even betrayed. They rightly felt that there was an awful lot of talent in our dressing-room, yet Dublin had won by seven points so the blame game started.

Naturally, I was the main target which was fair enough. I had been given credit a year earlier, now I would take the hits. Nobody felt the 1976 defeat more than me but my motto in life has always been to look forward. We couldn't change 1976 but we could damn well change our approach for 1977. I badly wanted Dublin to remain at the top in Leinster because if we won the Munster title, we would meet them in the All-Ireland semi-final in a game that would almost certainly decide the destination of the title.

The big chance came on August 21 when Kerry and Dublin lined up for a contest that has gone down in history as one of the most memorable ever played. The defeat in 1976 had burned so deep into every Kerry soul that our 1977 season was based almost solely on the prospect of another clash with Dublin. Meanwhile, they saw it as the year to really stamp their authority by winning a third All-Ireland title in four seasons. A phoney war of sorts was fought out between us in the League final which we won by two points.

It didn't mean a whole lot to us while Dublin weren't unduly perturbed by losing it as they had been without Brian Mullins. In fact, they probably regarded it as a victory of sorts, believing that Mullins would be worth far more than two points which was probably the case. We took the League trophy, left it in a dark corner somewhere and looked ahead to the championship with nothing on our minds only beating Cork again and getting another crack at Dublin.

Cork gave us a real fright early on in the Munster final, leading by six points at one stage and by four at half-time. But with the strong wind behind us, we wiped them out in the second half as Spillane, Barry and Seanie Walsh, Sheehy and Egan cut loose. We won by 15 points. It was our biggest Munster final win over them in my spell in charge and, to be honest, they were a complete shambles once the game started to run away from them. I have no doubt that their spirit had been broken by the defeat in 1976. What else could explain the craven manner in which they capitulated over the final twenty minutes?

We had made some adjustments to the set-up from the previous year with a young Jack O'Shea slotting in at midfield where he was partnered by Páidí Ó Sé who switched from right half-back. We opted for that pairing because even then it was clear that Jacko was a special talent. Raw and inexperienced but special nonetheless. We put Páidí alongside him because of his strength, determination and courage. Páidí was never going to be a long-term option at midfield but, for that year, we felt he was the right man with Jacko. Ogie Moran moved from wing-forward to wing-back and Seánie Walsh had come into the attack. We were criticised afterwards for not playing Pat McCarthy at midfield but he hadn't been going well all year so why should we assume that it would all come right in the semi-final? We had made that mistake with Ger O'Keeffe and Deenihan a year earlier and weren't going to repeat it. Maybe we should have brought McCarthy in earlier against Dublin but then we were leading for most of the way so it wasn't as if we were in serious trouble all through. Far from it.

Dublin had exactly the same team as in the previous year but Heffernan had left the scene, having quit a month after the 1976 All-Ireland. Dublin's response was simple, yet clever. Rather than bring in a new manager who might disrupt the continuity that was running through the squad, they promoted from within, making Tony Hanahoe the manager as well as the captain.

It might have looked like a gamble at the time but Hanahoe had always been a hugely influential figure in the camp. Besides, he was surrounded by several strong, mature personalities who knew exactly what they wanted and how to achieve it.

Still, I was quite confident heading into the semi-final. The mood was right, training had gone well and our sense of determination had moved well into obsession territory. Everything was set up for a classic and it didn't disappoint. Dublin people would have you believe it was the best game of all time, which is understandable, but we have always found it interesting in Kerry that the truly great games always seems to be those that we lose.

No doubt though, it was a cracking game which wasn't decided until the closing minutes and which might easily have gone either way. The cold, harsh statistic – Dublin 3-12 Kerry 1-13 – may suggest otherwise but the truth is that we led by two points with six minutes remaining.

Now, if you were to believe people afterwards, you would think that myself and the Kerry selectors, Murt Kelly, Paud O'Donoghue, Pat O'Shea and Donie Sheahan, made a complete mess of everything from start to finish. Yet, Kerry led in the 64th minute and only for a defensive mix-up between John O'Keeffe and Ogie, Dublin would never have got in for the goal that changed the game. Ogie seemed to have the ball collected but Johnno knocked it in the direction of Hanahoe. He passed to David Hickey who kicked a precious goal. Worse was to follow for us as Bernard Brogan got in for another goal which definitely sealed our fate.

Everything happened so quickly that an eerie sense of numbness descended on our dressing room afterwards. Most categorically, Dublin were not five points better than us but that's what the scoreboard said and we had to live with it. The reality was that the game could quite easily have gone our way. I still recall an incident towards the end of the third quarter when Seánie Walsh carried the ball into the Dublin square before flicking it over Paddy Cullen's head from a tight angle. It looped across the goal where Moran collected and cleared. Had we got a goal at that stage, we would have won.

We might also have won had we been able to switch Walsh from full-forward to midfield. He was only twenty years old but was a marvellous talent who would have made all the difference when Dublin started to get on top around midfield late in the second half. Unfortunately, he had injured an ankle three weeks earlier and only had the plaster taken off on the Tuesday before the game. It was still bothering him and he felt he didn't have the mobility to make an impact at midfield. On such tiny margins are big things often decided.

It's easy to forget how times have changed since that momentous day more than thirty years ago. Dublin v Kerry would attract a full-house 82,000 crowd these days but the attendance for the 1977 semi-final was just under 55,000. It was an all-ticket game which was unusual – if, indeed, not a first – for a semi-final.

Dublin went on to win the final easily, beating Armagh by 5-12 to 3-6 which added to our misery as it proved beyond doubt that the semi-final was, in fact, the real final. The Dublin v Kerry game of 1977 is still shown regularly on TV as part of classic games series but I don't watch it anymore. It was painful then and I'm sure it would be now too.

Times have changed, Gaelic football has moved on and, to be honest, I doubt if the quality of that game ever quite matched what it was made out to be. I'm sure my views are influenced by being on the losing side, just as Dublin's rose-tinted version owes everything to the fact that they won.

That's fair enough because they had every reason to feel very satisfied at the end of a fourth season in which they had won three All-Irelands and reached another final. Kerry, on the other hand, were beginning a period of introspection during which they searched for clues as to why the whole new world that appeared to have opened up in 1975 had darkened so dismally. The public wanted a guilty party and it didn't take long for the detectives to look towards Waterville and me.

'Go Out and Win More All-Irelands'

There isn't a manager in any sport who hasn't felt paranoid at some stage. And for good reason too, because however well life may be bouncing along, you can be assured there's always someone out to get you. It's the nature of the business.

I didn't have to wait long after the 1977 All-Ireland semi-final defeat by Dublin to hear the rumbles of discontent echoing through the Kerry mountains. There was very little said publicly but privately a lot of influential people in the county had very definite plans for me, all of which involved a large door marked 'EXIT'.

My crime? Kerry had lost to Dublin in successive years, leaving the 1975 success as eaten bread so long forgotten than few could quite remember what it tasted like. I could and I had every intention of sampling a whole lot more, assuming of course that I was allowed to remain in the kitchen, a prospect which was doubtful for a time. There was a growing sense of impatience over what had happened in 1976 and 1977. Never mind that Kerry had been beaten by probably the best team ever produced by Dublin, or that, despite the five point margin in 1977, nothing other than luck, in terms of getting the breaks at the right times, separated the sides.

There was a deeper antipathy towards me than anything generated by those two defeats. It centred on two issues really. The view among my critics was that the 1975 success was a flash in the pan. I had gambled with a young team and got lucky. We had fooled Dublin once but it wouldn't happen again. There was also a wide strand of opposition against the style of play employed by Kerry. The catch-and-kick days were over but there was a resentment towards accepting that in Kerry.

Why that should be the case was beyond me. Yes, it had served us well in other eras but no game stands still and if Kerry wanted any reminding of how much they were being left behind, it came in the 1971–74 era. We won the League titles that nobody else seemed to care about but lost the championships to teams who were moving ahead of us.

Joe Keohane, the marvellous Kerry full-back from the 1930s and 1940s, would have been much to the fore in the battle to retain what he regarded as traditional Kerry values that should never be compromised. I always had great regard for Joe, who served as a Kerry selector with me for years, but our views on how Gaelic football was evolving could never be reconciled.

There were plenty of others too who believed that I was ruining Kerry football. Besides, the new style wasn't winning All-Irelands anymore so, towards the end of 1977, the campaign to get me out cranked up considerably. Gerald McKenna would be the key to my survival. But first he had to survive his own battle to remain as County Chairman. He was opposed at the 1978 convention by James Linnane, a highly respected priest from St Brendan's College, Killarney, who had a good coaching record with the college and had also trained the Kerry minors. He had several high-profile backers, influential men like Dr Jim Brosnan, Tadhg Crowley, Séamus Fitzgerald, Séamus Murphy, Tom Long and Donie O'Sullivan.

It was strange to have so many former team mates in the opposite camp but they were obviously convinced that I was taking Kerry football in the wrong direction. Donie O'Sullivan, who had played right up to 1974, was mooted as a successor if I was to be replaced. He has always insisted that he wasn't interested but at the time I believed he was. To be honest, I still hold that view.

If McKenna had been beaten in the election for chairman, I would not have been reappointed as manager. Or if I was, my control would have been diluted to such a degree that I couldn't possibly continue. McKenna was an excellent chairman but his loyalty to me wasn't helping his cause. Now, that might weaken the resolve of a lesser man but not McKenna. He believed in what I was doing and wasn't going to sacrifice his principles to help his election cause. He stood his ground and was re-elected.

I again topped the poll in the election for selectors and was joined by Keohane, Liam Higgins, Bernie O'Callaghan and Pat O'Shea.

The immediate heat was off as far as I was concerned but it returned in another form as McKenna's instruction on being re-elected was simple, yet immensely challenging: 'Go out there and win more All-Irelands.' Despite being reappointed, I knew that many people in Kerry were deeply sceptical. If Dublin had beaten Kerry over the previous two years, why should it change in 1978?

It was a question I repeatedly asked myself during the long winter nights and the more I looked at it, the more I came to the conclusion that, while there were areas and aspects to be sorted out, we had a lot more positives than negatives. Jack O'Shea would be a more significant presence in 1978; so would Seánie Walsh; Mick Spillane had come aboard and, most important of all, we found the man who changed everything – 'The Bomber'.

First though, a statement had to be made. Pat Spillane was dropped for the opening League game because we felt that he had been playing for himself, not the team, in 1977. Surprise, surprise, he didn't take the demotion very well. Rumours abounded that he was considering quitting the panel. Right. He was still some weeks short of his 22nd birthday, stone mad about football, had talent to burn and possessed enough self-confidence for an entire squad. Most of all, he was a Kerryman. Put it all together and ask yourself this – was he ever going to walk away from all that?

Maybe he wanted the selectors to believe that he would, but nobody gave it a second's thought. Spillane was Spillane. He'll come right. Besides, we weren't daft enough to contemplate leaving him out of the side for too long. Still, he had to be taught the lesson that, just because he had the energy of a steeplechaser, the determination of a ferret and the evasive skills of a swallow, it didn't mean that he could keep soloing the bloody ball all day. He didn't spend long in purgatory and it didn't do him any harm either!

We also decided that it was time to switch Ger Power out of defence. Anton O'Toole had run though him a few times in the 1977 semi-final and even before that it was becoming increasingly clear that Power wasn't happy at left half-back. He had unbelievable pace, loved being on the ball but wasn't really interested in man-marking an opponent. It was time to try him in the half-forwards. Besides, we were well off for defenders. The switch to attack was a marvellous success and Power would go on to have a great career up front.

There's no doubt, however, that the biggest single ingredient in turning things around in 1978 was the arrival of Eoin Liston. I used to hold trial games fairly regularly to have a look at new talent and to satisfy myself that we weren't missing out on anybody. I asked Ogie Moran one night if there were any young fella up there in north Kerry who might have something to offer. Ogie said that there was but he doubted if he would come in because he wouldn't fancy the hard training.

Anyway, Ogie arrives in with this giant of a man one night. He wasn't in the best of condition but you could see straight away that he had something special. He had great hands and was well able to fetch the ball. He was deceptively nimble on his feet, had immense strength and a good sense of positioning. Definitely one to work with.

We had some incredible talents in our forward line but we lacked a real ball winner, someone to target with high lobs if the occasion demanded. 'Bomber' had played basketball so his hands were lightning quick which, in the hand pass era as it existed back then, would prove very helpful. Ogie warned that if we pushed the newcomer too hard, he might baulk at the hard training. I took it on board but reckoned that it was something we could work on. And we did!

Boy, did we make Liston suffer over the years. By a lucky coincidence (for me and Kerry), he got a teaching job in Waterville which meant he was right on my doorstep and I could work on him and with him. Some of my happiest times were spent working with 'Bomber' because I was convinced that, with proper coaching, he could become an amazing player which he eventually did.

Most evenings after school, he would head down to the pitch and I'd join him for one-on-one sessions. Donal Brosnan would be inside in the goal, kicking the ball out between us and, competitive devil that I was, I'd try anything to beat 'The Bomber'. I was well into my forties at that stage but was still playing good club football so I used every ounce of cuteness against him. When he'd win the

ball, I'd be tackling, harassing, blocking. It must have made a rare
sight as this giant figure, who was still way short of his prime, tussled
with a man who had played senior football for Kerry before he was
even born.

If we weren't on the football field we'd be playing golf,
basketball, badminton or just about any other sport we could find.

I did my level best to persuade him to leave Beale and join
Waterville but he was too dedicated to the home club to do that. I
admired his loyalty but often cursed him for it because he would
have made a great difference to the Waterville team. He most
certainly had a massive impact on the Kerry team because he quite
literally gave our midfielders and half-forwards something to aim
at. It was a new weapon in our armoury, one that would help sink
Dublin in the most dramatic fashion.

With 'Bomber' serving his apprenticeship as our new full-
forward and Seánie Walsh settling with Jacko at midfield, there was
fresh impetus to the scene heading into the 1978 championship.
The League hadn't gone well but that didn't matter in the general
scheme of things. We wanted to arrive at the championship starting
gate with a team that was capable of setting the agenda, rather than
reacting to it as we had done against Dublin in 1976 and 1977.

A rather tempestuous clash – actually that's a polite description
of what was a nasty game – against Dublin in Gaelic Park, New York,
in May 1978 showed just how intense the rivalry had become. Heavy
rain made conditions awful and led to all kinds of frustrations
which eventually spun out of control. It was claimed afterwards that
Kerry deliberately got stuck into Dublin to show that they wouldn't
be intimidated, but it certainly wasn't pre-planned in such detail. I
was never one to show my hand in a meaningless challenge game,
much less one played in New York a month before the start of the
championship. However, there was no way we were going to be
pushed around either. At that stage, Dublin were double All-Ireland
champions and would have felt that bit superior to us. We couldn't
stand for that.

Familiarity had, I suppose, bred a certain level of contempt
among both sets of players and, once the rancour set in, the game
took on a disturbing life of its own as fists and mud flew, lads were
sent off and recriminations began. It got plenty of publicity back

home and certainly whetted the appetite for a likely All-Ireland final clash later on. It also left Kerry feeling that little bit better about ourselves, not just because we had won the game but because it had put down a marker with Dublin.

Both sides returned home, utterly convinced that they would meet again in the All-Ireland final four moths later. The truth was that Dublin and Kerry were miles ahead of the rest. Cork were chaotic and unable to offer us a decent challenge in Munster while the rest didn't count. Connacht and Ulster were in poor shape and while Offaly were beginning to emerge in Leinster, they were still some way behind Dublin, even if they did run them to three points in the 1978 Leinster semi-final.

It was the only real test Dublin got en route to the All-Ireland final as Carlow, Kildare and Down were blown away. We had it even easier, walloping Waterford, Cork and Roscommon. It was as if the gods had booked their seats for a Kerry v Dublin final on 24 September and weren't going to have it spoiled under any circumstances.

Dublin love to recall the 1977 semi-final clash as the highpoint of their rivalry with Kerry in that era but we much prefer to dwell on the 1978 final which, by any standards, was quite remarkable. Our winning score of 5-11 – and I love reminding the Dubs of this – was by far the largest ever scored against them in an All-Ireland final. It was also the biggest winning margin in an All-Ireland final since Mayo beat Laois by 18 points in 1936.

Those two noteworthy feats were achieved in circumstances which looked totally improbable for the first twenty minutes when Dublin compressed us so tightly into our own half that we could scarcely breathe. It was seriously worrying and not at all what I had envisaged. Our forwards had been flying in training, so much so that I was convinced they would clean out the Dublin full-back line of Gay O'Driscoll, Seán Doherty and Robbie Kelleher.

Dublin had brought Kevin Moran back from Manchester United to play at centre-back and, great and all as he was, I felt that Ogie, who was our captain that year, could make progress on him. It's not easy to switch in and out of codes, even if you are a professional. It was claimed later that Kevin had pulled a hamstring in training on the Tuesday before the game and that this seriously impaired him in the final. It didn't seem to bother him in the first twenty minutes as Dublin swarmed all over us. Jimmy Keaveney clocked up the points and Dublin galloped into a five point lead.

Bloody hell, what's happening here? I'm trying to figure it out when 'Bomber' trots over and tells me that he has a pain in his knee and another down his neck.

'I can't move, I'll have to go off,' he declared.

'Not a bloody chance,' I yell at him. 'Get back in there and run it off. You'll be all right. For God's sake, this is an All-Ireland final, man.'

It wasn't the most scientific analysis of his predicament but that could wait until the medics examined him at half-time. Besides, I had enough worries without a man on whom I was pinning so much hope complaining about pains. By the end of the game, he would have ensured himself of a place in All-Ireland folklore after scoring 3-2. Curiously, we heard no more about pains in the neck!

Notorious sceptic that I am about players contracting mystery ailments, I asked him later how come the aches had gone.

'Don't know. But they got a bit better when I made a decent catch and once Egan got the goal, I didn't feel a thing,' he replied. Ah, the magic of positive thinking, not to mention a change in fortunes.

Egan's goal changed the entire complexion of the game. Dublin were so comfortably in command at that stage that they started to showboat. Their backs wanted to be forwards while forwards became self-indulgent and, in between, Jacko and Seánie were gradually asserting themselves against Mullins and Brogan.

Still, we badly needed a break. We had scored just one point in the first twenty minutes which was a shocking bad return and the fear was that if Dublin tagged on a few more points and the game lurched towards half-time with us facing a seven- or eight-point deficit, confidence would begin to drain away.

In boxing parlance, we were on the ropes, clinging on for survival. However, Dublin misjudged the extent of their superiority, became sloppy and were hit with a powerful counter punch in the form of Egan's goal which was born of over-carrying by Bobby Doyle. Mick Spillane reacted smartly, thumping the free as quickly as possible in the direction of 'Bomber' who fed Jacko. Then it was on to Pat Spillane who passed to Egan and his flick just cleared Paddy Cullen's fingers for one of the sweetest goals I have ever seen.

The sense of relief was unreal. We had played rubbish, yet we were back in the game. Mikey Sheehy's bizarre second goal is the most discussed and documented in GAA history. Well, apart maybe from Séamus Darby's goal in the 1982 final.

Dublin remain adamant that Cullen was harshly penalised by referee Séamus Aldridge after he had clashed with Ger Power and, to be fair, they could call on some reliable witnesses to support their case, starting with the Kerry forwards who were in the vicinity.

Being a smart boyo from Tralee, Mikey wasn't going to reject Robbie Kelleher's generosity in handing him the ball and, before Cullen could shout, 'Hey ref!' it was nestling in the Dublin net for what was probably the cheekiest goal ever scored. Sheehy has often told since how I kept staring in his direction at half-time as if trying to figure out how he had been so brazen as to attempt that chip at a crucial stage of an All-Ireland final when just about every other free taker in history would have tapped the ball over the bar. And yes, he is right. I would have given him a right earfull had he missed.

Because of its sheer wizardry and audacity, Sheehy's goal came to be regarded as the match winner but I don't think that's the case. Egan's goal, for a start, was more important in that it brought us back into the game at a time when Dublin looked to be steaming to victory. But the goal that really killed off Dublin came two minutes into the second half when Jacko shot for a point but the ball flew straight into the arms of the 'Bomber', who dispatched it to the net. That put us five points clear and, having scored three goals in less than 15 minutes, there was a feeling that more were available. And so there were. 'Bomber' added another two as Dublin's challenge melted in miserable blue streaks which left their supporters stunned as we raced to a 17-point win, 5-11 to 0-9.

The sense of satisfaction afterwards was overwhelming. It was vindication for the team, for me and for Gerald McKenna who had stood by me. Those who had claimed that we were contaminating Kerry football with our hand passing were quite happy to share in the glory, conveniently ignoring the fact that most of our goals had been scored with the hand.

I don't think anybody was in any doubt as they left Croke Park that evening that they had seen the end of one era and the beginning of another. Our team was still quite young and had taken on a new dynamic which would stand the test of time, albeit with a few adjustments. Dublin needed to rebuild, certainly in defence, and even then it was going to be difficult to recover from such a terrible defeat.

To their great credit, they reeled off their sixth successive Leinster final win in 1979 after completing a courageous comeback against Offaly. However, they had Jimmy Keaveney sent off and, while they managed to beat Roscommon without him, we were confident as we lined up against them for a fifth successive year.

We weren't asked one hard question en route to the final. In fact, we were criticised for running in 9-21 against Clare in the Munster semi-final, something which I always felt was unfair on us and patronising towards Clare. We hadn't reached such lofty heights without having a strong panel, so the pressure for places remained intense. Once the championship came it was 'game on' and there could be no holding back because if one player slackened off there were others on the bench more than anxious to replace him. Nobody takes any pleasure in beating weaker opponents by 36 points but it would have been far more insulting to Clare if we had eased up against them.

Anyway, that was probably our peak year so it would have been impossible to rein the team in. They dismissed Cork by ten points in the Munster final and put 5-14 on Monaghan who had won the Ulster title for the first time in 41 years. It was their bad luck that the All-Ireland semi-final paired them with us rather than Roscommon or indeed Dublin.

Playing in Croke Park for the first time is always daunting but all the more so when an entire squad is experiencing it for the first time. We had heard reports about how Monaghan had devised various plans to knock us off our stride but they never materialised and we won by 22 points.

The great rivalry that has always existed between Kerry and Dublin ensured massive interest in the All-Ireland final but it was a bit phoney really because both sides knew the truth. The gap between us had widened substantially in a year and, although Ger Power was out injured, Tommy Doyle was a more than adequate replacement and we won by 3-13 to 1-8 despite having Páidí Ó Sé sent off.

With Dublin in decline, our lead at the head of affairs looked certain to widen. Offaly were improving but would take a few years to mature and there wasn't much else happening in Leinster. Ulster continued to produce the most competitive provincial championship but their champions came up short in Croke Park for several years, while Galway and Mayo had been relegated to second and third place by Roscommon in Connacht.

It was there that our next big challenge would emerge, one that should have succeeded in 1980, a year in which it was decided that, because we had inflicted such a heavy defeat on Clare in 1979, we should get a bye into the Munster final. I could see the logic – as we were so far ahead of everybody except Cork, there didn't seem much point in subjecting teams to routine humiliations.

Cork were always our barometer in Munster and they probably thought they had narrowed the gap to manageable proportions when they beat us by a point in the 1980 League final. It was our policy at that stage not to train collectively for the League so it was surprising we even got that far. We would probably have won too if Sheehy were fit to play but the defeat didn't exactly leave us wrapped in dejection as we headed out of Páirc Uí Chaoimh.

We would be back for the Munster final a few months later and, with our training schedule on target, Cork were facing a completely different outfit. It was all very depressing for them at that stage. We were a class above them and both they and we knew that if the script ran any way close to plan, the result was inevitable. Once again, that proved to be the case.

Another July Sunday in Cork, another easy win (by nine points this time), another vintage display by the forwards who racked up 3-13 and another All-Ireland semi-final date ahead. It was becoming routine by now, even if there was a novelty value to the semi-final as Offaly had finally wrestled power from Dublin in Leinster, winning their first provincial title for six years. Because they were new to the semi-final scene, we probably underestimated them. We knew all about the marvellous skills of Matt Connor but reckoned he couldn't beat us on his own. He didn't either but he made a damn good try, scoring 2-9. The only other Offaly player to score was Gerry Carroll but his contribution of 2-1 took the Offaly total to 4-10, an alarmingly high concession rate for a team that believed it was setting new standards.

We scored 4-15 so there was never any doubt that we would win, especially since we led by 12 points early in the last quarter. Still, there was cause for concern. Connor and Carroll had scored 4-4 from play between them, leaving our defence and indeed our goalkeeper, Charlie Nelligan, helping us with inquiries. We played down Offaly's late recovery as best we could, citing complacency once we had opened a big lead, but we were still sufficiently concerned to change our two corner-backs for the final against Roscommon.

Out went Ger O'Keeffe and Mick Spillane to be replaced by Jimmy Deenihan and Paudie Lynch. That tightened the defensive bolts considerably but problems had erupted at the other end as 'Bomber' was ruled out with appendicitis. And to compound matters, Ger Power, who was captain, had a hamstring injury. Suddenly, our odds-on rating was beginning to look precarious.

It was amazing how we seemed to lose a key player for nearly every final. It was Power in 1979, Liston in 1980, Pat Spillane in 1981 (although he came on as a substitute and stood on one leg for the last few minutes), Sheehy in 1984 and of course we were without Deenihan for all of the 1982 campaign.

Going into the 1980 final without 'Bomber' really worried me. We had beaten Roscommon easily in the 1978 semi-final but they had improved immeasurably in the interim. They had also gained what they thought was a sizeable psychological boost late in 1978 when they completed a senior and U-21 double over Kerry in Dr Hyde Park.

The senior game didn't matter a damn as it was only a tournament outing to raise funds for the building of a staff HQ in Croke Park, but the U-21 was an All-Ireland final. Now, why Kerry agreed to play an All-Ireland final in Roscommon's home ground is beyond me but they did and it proved costly. Roscommon won by a point which, when coupled with the senior success, pumped plenty of confidence under their wings for when we next met.

There's no point sugar coating anything about the 1980 All-Ireland final. It was a rough, untidy, fractious affair for which Roscommon were solely and totally to blame. Our game was based on quick movement on and off the ball and Roscommon had clearly spent lots of time on the training ground devising ways of stopping us. Our style was an open book, one we had employed over several seasons, so why would we want to become embroiled in a dour war of attrition?

It made no sense at all for us but Roscommon had obviously calculated that it offered them their best chance of success. Ironically, circumstances changed dramatically when they raced into a 1-2 to 0-0 lead after 12 minutes. Clearly, they hadn't legislated for such a positive situation and, instead of pressing on, they became defensive and negative. It was a terrible mistake because we weren't playing well and there would have been more scores available to Roscommon in the first half had they remained more progressive going forward.

I know my view that Roscommon over-indulged in deliberately negative play has upset many people in the county, including the great Dermot Earley, as honest a player as ever laced a boot. All I can say is – look at the video. And even that doesn't show everything that went on. The free count supports my claim as it was two to one in our favour. Presumably referee Séamus Murray from Monaghan wasn't happy with the Roscommon approach either.

We scraped through by three points in the end on a day when Sheehy, who shipped some very heavy punishment, scored 1-6 of our 1-9 total. I have always said that, while I believe we were unlucky to lose the 1982 final, we should have been beaten in 1980. Roscommon played the wrong game in what was their biggest chance of winning an All-Ireland since the 1940s and paid a heavy penalty. It was a great pity for a team that would probably have won a title in another era. They had won four successive Connacht titles but it was as if the All-Ireland final defeat knocked the heart out of them and they wouldn't even win a provincial title for another ten years.

I don't know how the Roscommon players view the 1980 final nowadays but deep down they must realise that they blew a great opportunity. It was as if they were so preoccupied with tying us down through whatever tactics they deemed necessary that they misread the situation completely after starting so well. Let's put it this way – Roscommon handed us that All-Ireland through a deeply flawed approach and did not recover for a long time.

Meanwhile, we continued on our all-conquering way, winning a fourth successive All-Ireland in 1981. It was all straightforward for us at that stage. We would ease ourselves gently through the League, check the date of the Munster final against Cork and set that as our first real target. It was the same in 1981 where we again beat Cork easily in the Munster final before thrashing Mayo in the All-Ireland semi-final to set up a final clash with Offaly.

Reaching the final represented progress on the previous year for Offaly and, while we won by 1-12 to 0-8, the margin flattered us. It took a late goal, a thundering effort from Jack O'Shea, to finally sink Offaly who were very definitely on the rise. We were without Spillane but Johnny Mooney was missing for Offaly after injuring himself when falling off a load of turf. He would be back in 1982 to play a major role in one of the most dramatic finals in GAA history.

With another All-Ireland title safely secured, we headed for a month-long adventure in Australia, Hawaii and San Francisco. God was in his sporting heaven as far as we were concerned. We had joined Wexford as the only team ever to win four successive All-Ireland titles, which they had achieved 63 years previously.

The difference was they had gone no further but, as we enjoyed our memorable trip around the world, we were already setting our sights on becoming the first five-in-a-row side. What's more, we were totally convinced we would achieve it. Nothing or nobody could stop us now. Or so we thought.

Testing the Testers

The minute I heard about the exam, I said, 'No thanks, not for me.' The notion of sitting down like a Leaving Cert student, being handed a set of questions about Gaelic football and told to write down the answers which would be returned to 'examiners' for marking was so foreign to me that I thought it was a joke at first.

But it wasn't. Still, I wasn't going to miss out on a chance to see what the opposition were up to so I went along to the coaching course in Gormanston College, listened to what everybody had to say, took some of it in, discarded much it and returned to Kerry vowing quietly to myself that I'd show them all we weren't the outdated, old-fashioned fossils we were made out to be.

It was Gerald McKenna's idea that I should attend the course in the first place. Mickey Ned O'Sullivan, who was fascinated by coaching methods from the first time he jumped out of the pram, was travelling up to Gormanston and McKenna, who was County Chairman at the time, suggested that I go with him. I doubt very much if McKenna had any more interest in it than me but, cute hoor that he was, he could always say that he had sent O'Dwyer along to see what the other counties were up to. The two main men doing the talking were Kevin Heffernan and Joe Lennon, both of whom had acquired certain reputations in Kerry. It was early in 1975, a time when Kerry football was as unsure of itself as Dublin and Heffernan were certain that they had hit on a winning formula which, in fairness, was the case. I had just taken over in Kerry and, while I had very definite views as to the direction I would steer things, there was no harm in listening to others, provided of course that they weren't going to mark me out of a hundred for reproducing on paper what they said.

Down had enjoyed a great decade in the 1960s and Joe Lennon, who played on the three teams that won All-Irelands in 1960, 1961, and 1968, had formed a very definite opinion as to where Kerry stood in the pecking order. Some time after the 1968 All-Ireland, when Down had again beaten Kerry, he implied that we were twenty years behind the times.

It was a fairly sweeping assessment, based I suppose on how Down and Galway had beaten us so often during the Sixties. Still, we did manage to win two All-Irelands in 1962 and 1969 and another in 1970 so I don't know where the notion came from that we were so old-fashioned. Yes, there were years when we simply weren't good enough but that's altogether different from portraying us as a county out of touch with changing times. Besides no county – and that includes Kerry – can have a monopoly on titles and good ideas. Lennon seemed to think we were losing ground at a ferocious rate around 1968, a theory that didn't hold up very well as Kerry went on to win ten All-Irelands between then and 1986. Not bad for a county out of touch.

It wasn't the last time that Kerry's obituary would be scripted prematurely and rather foolishly. It was comical to hear and read the nonsense being spouted after Kerry lost to Armagh and Tyrone in 2002, 2003 and 2005. Once again, Kerry were depicted as being old-fashioned innocents abroad who couldn't possibly match the tactical sophistication of the Ulster teams. Once again, it was pure rubbish as Kerry went on to prove. Why is it that if Kerry go a few years without winning an All-Ireland they're supposed to be losing touch, yet others can go decades without a title and nobody passes any heed?

I closed my mouth and listened in Gormanston, hoping to pick up some little nugget of information that might help me along in the new Kerry set-up. Without being in any way disrespectful to Heffernan or Lennon, I reckoned there wasn't much I could learn from either that I didn't know already. I wasn't being cocky or arrogant but I had played under some of the best brains in Kerry football, men like Dr Eamonn O'Sullivan, Jackie Lyne and Johnny Culloty, all of whom really knew their stuff. As for doing an exam and getting a certificate to prove how much you knew about coaching – it wasn't my scene. We had forgotten more about football in Kerry than most people ever knew so I wasn't in the mood for being tested by some blasted theory paper. On the morning of the exam, I said to Mickey Ned, 'C'mon to hell, let's get out of here.' Which we duly did.

The one thing I took away from Gormanston was a recognition that if Kerry were to overtake the Dublin team that had won the 1974 All-Ireland, we would need to be fitter than them. I had five PE teachers on the panel: Mickey Ned, John O'Keeffe, Ogie Moran, Jimmy Deenihan and Pat Spillane, all of whom would have been delighted to have an input into training but I never consulted them. It wasn't that I didn't respect their views but I wanted everybody to know exactly who was in control. There were times when I'm sure they thought I was pure mad but, to their credit, they never complained (not to me anyway) and they all bought into my way of doing things whether or not they agreed. Of course, it would probably have been a whole lot different had we lost the 1975 All-Ireland final.

Success justifies everything and once we won in 1975, we had a formula to work off. It would have to be tweaked from time to time but at least it showed that the basic model was right.

I had picked up an awful lot of ideas over many years and wanted to put them to the test with the Kerry squad. I was always interested in watching how other sports went about their training and had even visited Old Trafford at one stage to study Manchester United. Billy Behan, a scout for Manchester United and also a very shrewd coach, had set it up for me and I found it quite helpful.

Super fitness was at the heart of what I set out to do. I had trained Waterville teams over the years and, because we were operating from a much smaller panel of players than other clubs, we had to come up with something different. I saw real fitness as the way forward for Waterville and it worked to a large degree. When I took over in Kerry I opted for the same policy. However, the football wouldn't be forgotten about either while we were building up the fitness levels.

I recall playing under the great Dr Eamonn O'Sullivan who had a theory that if a squad didn't play that much football in training sessions, they would be fierce hungry for it on match days. It wasn't something I agreed with but it worked lots of times for Dr Eamonn and Kerry. Still, I believed that the football should be central to everything we did.

I also ran the life out of the squad in those early days. It had to be done if we wanted to not only reach Dublin's fitness levels but to actually surpass them. I had a young squad who were prepared to try anything which is why I picked most of them in the first place. There was no point sticking with the panel who had failed in the early 1970s, even if there was a chance that we might have won an All-Ireland with them in 1975. No, the plan was to go with the young lads and try to build a team that would stand the test of time. I had no idea that it would work out so spectacularly well but I was certain that the future lay with youth and was prepared to accept the consequences if it went wrong.

We trained 27 nights on the trot for the 1975 championship which was unheard of up to then. The late Tadhg Crowley, who was County Board Secretary at the time, was in Killarney one night and after watching the training he drove home to Tralee and told some friends that I had gone completely crazy.

'Horse or hound or man couldn't stick what they're at beyond in Killarney,' he declared. I could understand his reaction because we were training like no Kerry team had ever done before. If Dublin had raised the bar, we were going to lift it even higher, a lot higher.

We varied the training but never let up on the intensity. But then we had mostly young lads who were well able for it, even if they like to tell horror stories of the laps and the sprints and the dreaded wire-to-wire where they ran flat out over and back across the pitch.

The trick was to make sure the training was never boring and that's why I always regarded ball work as an essential part of every session. Even then we varied it. We played ground football where they weren't allowed to pick up the ball (it wasn't soccer because there was no off-side). We'd change to hand passing, then on to regular football, then a game without soloing and back to physical work again. I would take part in as much of the training as I could, especially in the early days, which was helpful as it brought me right into the heart of the action. We worked extensively on backs against forwards and, boy, were they tough sessions. Imagine you're a Kerry defender and you come up against Spillane, Sheehy, 'Bomber', Egan, Power and Ogie every night in training. Any wonder our backs went home with splitting headaches. Match days were simple after that!

Because I was actively involved in the sessions, it was easy to make corrections as we went along. I'd stop the play if things went wrong, assess the problem and try something else. It's a policy I took with me to Kildare, Laois and Wicklow, even if I was no longer taking an active part in the actual training. Still, I always believe in being right in the middle of it, rather than watching from a distance. That way, I'm involved and players know that I'm there, watching everything from close quarters.

Mind you, it can be a dangerous business, as I discovered during my second stint in Kildare. David Earley ran into me during a practice game in Newbridge one evening and I suffered a bad shoulder injury. It needed surgery but we were in the middle of the championship campaign and I had no intention of taking time off to get the shoulder repaired. As I said at the time, it would have been worse had it happened to one of the players.

I have always held that Gaelic football is a simple game. The trick is to get the fundamentals right, keep the game plan straightforward, play at the highest possible tempo and trust your team. Of course, all of it is dependent on players being properly fit because if they're not, then everything else falls apart.

There were so many brilliant players on the Kerry squad with which I started out in 1975 that once they were fully fit, the patterns created themselves. We kept it simple and direct, although we moved away from the traditional Kerry catch-and-kick style. Our failure to do that earlier probably cost us All-Irelands. There was very little change in our style during my playing days. Even when Down came along with a different system in the early Sixties, we ignored it to a large degree. Similarly, when the Galway three-in-a-row team moved things on, again we stood still. Not as still as Joe Lennon might have thought, but we did need to reassess what we were at.

I'm not saying we should have imitated either Down or Galway but we should have been more innovative ourselves. After all, we're pretty crafty in Kerry when it comes to thinking up new ideas. For most of my playing career we never trained for the League and didn't begin the championship programme until May. It worked often enough to convince Kerry people that it was okay but as other counties became more advanced we had to do something about it.

It was a natural evolution process, one that I oversaw myself because I was strong willed enough to do things my own way. I was self-taught and didn't care tuppence for what others thought. Nor did the Kerry players. They knew they were good and that we had the system in place to get the best out of them.

There were times when they believed I was insane but once we kept winning they were happy to go along with whatever I wanted. Naturally, some would have thought that I was unfair on them, but when you're dealing with so much talent it was inevitable that not everybody could be kept happy.

Take Paudie O'Mahony for instance. Paudie was the goalkeeper when we made the breakthrough in 1975 and had the rare distinction of not conceding a single goal in the four games it took us to win the All-Ireland. It was some achievement. He even saved penalties against Cork and Sligo.

He was a great goalkeeper but as the years passed he was overtaken by Charlie Nelligan who went on to become one of the best ever. Paudie seemed to think I was unfair to him and kept messing him about but that wasn't the case. I had to do what I thought was right for the team and once Nelligan got enough experience, he was number one. Paudie would have been first choice for years in most counties and in Kerry too if Nelligan hadn't come along. Paudie's Achilles tendon snapped during the 1976 All-Ireland final which allowed Charlie to get some big-time experience earlier than would otherwise have been the case. Paudie was back for the 1977 championship but Charlie was improving all the time and was first choice from 1978 on, something that Paudie didn't agree with which was understandable from his point of view.

There were lots of players in Kerry at that time who would have prospered in another county or another era in Kerry. I was often criticised for not introducing more fresh talent to the squad but I couldn't do it just for the sake of it. We had a special group whose standards never dropped. Neither did their appetites. So why should I change what was a successful formula?

Take the full-forward line alone. You could drive any type of ball in on top of Sheehy, 'Bomber' and Egan and they would win most of it. 'Bomber' was the final piece of the jigsaw in 1978 because he gave us so many options while the other pair were deadly finishers. Sheehy could look lazy on the ball but he had such unbelievable skill that, once he got possession, you knew that the chances were that he would score himself, lay it off or be fouled.

Egan was a marvellous man on a solo run. His ball control was amazing and he had an unbelievable knack of scoring crucial goals for us. There aren't many things I'd change about my days with Kerry but I still regret taking him off in the 1984 All-Ireland final against Dublin. It upset him greatly and I fully understand that. He had given so much to Kerry that he felt he deserved more than to be taken off in an All-Ireland final in front of 70,000 people. And he probably did.

I take full responsibility for replacing him but I'd have to say that I was coming under fierce pressure from the selectors. In the end, it was a collective decision, made because we were feeling a bit apprehensive after what had happened against Offaly in 1982 and Cork a year later. We were well in control against Dublin but were fearful of a kickback. Mick Holden was getting the better of Egan and we feared that he might inspire a revival so we decided to change tactics. We replaced Egan with Timmy Dowd and played him as a third midfielder which worked quite well as it reduced the pressure on our backs. The trouble was that we had sacrificed Egan which didn't go down well with him or the many who admired him.

It was a hard call, and probably unnecessary at it turned out. He never played for Kerry again which was a great pity. If Sheehy, 'Bomber' and Egan made up a deadly full-forward line, we had some talent in the half-forwards too. Spillane wore 12 but you might as well instruct an eel to doze downstream as to expect him to stay in an allotted spot. We didn't mind because he was at his most effective when he was given the freedom to ramble as he wished. He could be a fierce selfish devil with the ball but that was part of what made him such a great player.

When self-confidence was being handed out, Spillane wasn't just at the top of the queue, he was organising it as well. His ability to kick points from what looked impossible positions was a marvel to watch but in fairness he worked very hard at the skill. It might have looked as if it came easy to him, and it did, but only because of the time and effort he put into it. You wonder how many modern-day players work at that side of their game as much as Spillane did. Very few, I suspect.

If Spillane was high-profile, Ogie Moran was very much the understated member of the forward line. I don't know if any player in the history of the game was as good at getting on to breaking ball as Ogie and, once in possession, he used it consistently well. He always seemed to be in the right place at the right time, which wasn't accidental of course. It was down to his shrewd reading of the game, a natural asset that served him well throughout his career.

It was a remarkable achievement to win eight All-Ireland medals at centre-forward and, of course, I'm constantly reminded that he was on the wing for the two finals we lost in 1976 and 1982. It was probably a mistake to move him out of centre-forward, certainly in 1982, by which time he had established himself as one of the best of all time, but we wanted to accommodate Tom Spillane who was playing very well.

We felt that whereas Spillane wouldn't have been comfortable on the wing, Ogie could improvise quite easily. Much was made of it when we lost to Offaly but there wouldn't have been a word had Darby not got in for that famous goal. Having said that, we probably shouldn't have altered what had been a winning formula.

I always had great time for Ogie and his family whom I got to know very well over the years. He was a joy to work with although I'm not sure he thought the same of me after an incident in the 1979 Munster final against Cork in Killarney. We had left him off and played Tommy Doyle at centre-forward which wouldn't have pleased Ogie in the first place. We brought him in as a substitute in the second half and after six or seven minutes I got a complete brainstorm and decided to take him off. To this day, I don't how or why it happened. I beckoned Ogie to the sideline and naturally he thought I had some instruction for him.

I had Seánie Walsh warming up but Ogie assumed it had nothing to do with him. Anyway, I told him I was taking him off and he looked at me as if I had just grown two heads. It was as if he were

Happiness is winning an 8th All-Ireland title in 11 seasons.
I share the moment with Jack O'Shea after Kerry beat Tyrone in the
1986 All-Ireland final.

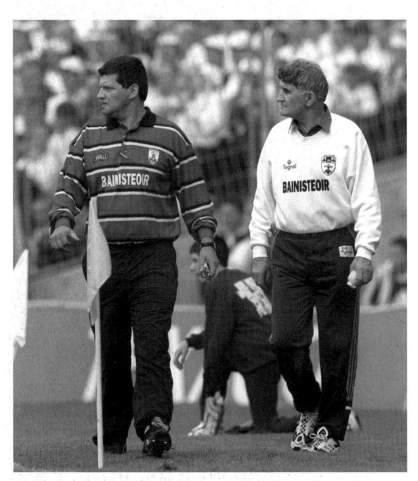

Not the maroon and white again! Galway caused me untold heartache as a player and manager, including the 1998 All-Ireland final where John O'Mahony led them to a famous win over Kildare.

Once more into the breach. I take charge of Laois for the first time in an O'Byrne Cup game against Longford in Portlaoise in January 2003.

'Well done, big man.' Joe Kernan did a great job with Armagh, including the 2003 All-Ireland quarter-final where they beat Laois.

Two old gunslingers watching the action. I keep a close eye on what that wily fox Sean Boylan is up to during a Laois v Meath championship clash in 2004.

Charlie Nelligan congratulates me after Kildare had beaten Kerry in the 1991 League quarter-final. Managing Kildare against my old Kerry colleagues was always an awkward experience.

I was a number 15 myself so I know what it's like. Tadhg Fennin gets an earful during the Kildare v Galway All-Ireland semi-final in 2000.

'What are we doing here, Páidí?' Two Kerrymen in charge of Leinster teams in Croke Park. Páidí had the last laugh as Westmeath beat Laois in the 2004 Leinster final replay.

I'm looking glum during the 1984 All-Ireland final against Dublin. There was no need to because we won fairly easily to clinch a special title as it was the GAA's centenary year.

frozen by the bewildering, not to mention inexplicable, decision to replace him. He was keeping an eye on a Cork player about 15 yards away as I'm telling him the bad news as he obviously thought it was some sort of mistake.

It wasn't.

'C'mon, Ogie, will you get off,' I roared. It was one of the few times I ever lost it with a player and why I did it to poor Ogie that day, I'll never know. Nor will he, because there was no rhyme or reason whatsoever to the decision. Gentleman that he was, Ogie just shook his head and toddled off, no doubt convinced that O'Dwyer had finally flipped. Thankfully, he didn't hold it against me!

Ger Power made the switch from wing-back to wing-forward for the 1978 season, largely because we felt he would have more to offer in a direct attacking role. He liked to sprint forward from left half-back too but wasn't as keen on man-marking so, when Jack O'Shea settled in at midfield, we could afford to drop Paudie Lynch back to number seven where he did a great job.

The move worked for Power too as he went on to become a highly effective right half-forward before being switched into the full-forward line. The range of versatility in that squad was unprecedented and has never been replicated since. Ogie, Power, Doyle, Tom Spillane, Walsh, Lynch and John O'Keefe could play virtually anywhere and frequently did. Power was a huge addition to the attack. He had searing pace which opened many a defence and also created space for the other assassins.

If midfield was a problem in 1977, it was settled quickly once Jacko and Seánie settled in. Jack was, without question, the best midfielder I ever saw. He had a Rolls Royce engine and so much natural skill and application that he needed no instructions. Off you go Jacko, and do your thing. He hardly ever missed a game from challenge to championship and it's a testimony to his unbelievable consistency that he won six successive All-Star awards.

The funny thing was that despite his natural athleticism, he didn't adapt well when we tried to turn him into a full-back, similar to what we had done with John O'Keeffe and Seánie Walsh. Jacko didn't like to be tied down to something as mundane as marking an opponent. He wanted the freedom of the park whereas the other two enjoyed the personal battle of wills and wits with full-forwards.

We blackguarded Seánie for a time, using him as a super-sub which he hated but it served us well. He was being compared with David Fairclough, who had the super-sub tag with Liverpool at the time and while it made snappy newspaper headlines, it was frustrating for Walsh but he kept his patience and was rewarded in the end. He would go on to become an outstanding midfielder before heading for full-back after Johnno left. He turned so many games from midfield that I have no doubt that, had we left him there, his partnership with Jacko would have been one of the longest and most successful in football history.

Walsh was a fantastic big day man. The bigger the occasion, the more you got out of him but he couldn't be bothered with the less important games. In fact, it was a complete waste of time trying to motivate him for an ordinary League game. We just let him get on with it, knowing that come the heat of Munster or All-Ireland final day, Seánie would deliver.

If Jacko was the best midfielder I ever saw, the same goes for Johnno at full-back. By their nature, full-backs have to be stoppers but it's how they go about it that distinguishes the really great ones. O'Keeffe did it with style and guile, using the head at all times. I doubt if any opponent would have a bad word to say about him. His duels with Jimmy Keaveney were worth the entrance money alone. He took it as a personal insult if he had to resort to fouling and I am convinced that very few defenders in the history of the game conceded as few frees as he did.

He had Tim Kennelly in front of him for years in what might be termed the ultimate central locking system. 'The Horse' was one powerful man, hewn straight out of the traditional mould of dominating centre-backs. Still, he adapted well to the new style we introduced in the mid-Seventies but did it in his own individual way. Suffice to say that when 'The Horse' thundered into an opponent, there could only be one winner. He later served as a selector with me which he also enjoyed immensely. It was tragic that he died so young but he will never be forgotten by those of us who came to know and appreciate him so much for the superb player he was.

And then there was the old dog himself – Páidí Ó Sé. If you were taking on a job for three men, all you needed was Páidí because he'd do the work of two. He loved the thrill of the challenge – the harder the better. He was a bit like Kennelly in that he was a throwback to the traditional Kerry footballer but Páidí adapted well to the changing times too. The trick with Kennelly and Páidí was to get them fully fit which took plenty of work (by them) early in the year but once they were primed for summer, they were mad for action. The tougher the challenge, the more they liked it.

Páidí had a fierce cute way about him which enabled him to make the switch, and not an easy one, from wing-back to corner-back where he excelled for years. Indeed, he would have soldiered on for longer if he had his way.

He was furious with me for not playing him in the 1988 Munster final against Cork but he would come to understand in his own management days that these are the sort of calls that have to be made. He wasn't picked for one simple reason – he hadn't been going well that year and a decision had to be taken. Naturally, when we lost to Cork by a point, the criticisms started, not just about leaving Páidí off but about the general direction the squad had taken. Páidí's fan club argued that he was so driven by the desire to beat Cork that he would have been worth at least two points (we lost by one!) while others felt that, instead of trying to hold on to the squad that had delivered so many titles, we should have made a lot more changes.

Even the late Liam Higgins, who was a selector at the time, sided with the latter view. Liam and myself had soldiered through many battles in our playing days and always got on well which was also the case when he became a selector, but we had our own opinions on how things should be done. He went on Raidió na Gaeltachta after the 1988 Munster final and let it be known that he was unhappy with certain aspects of the set-up. There were implied criticisms of me on the basis that I found it very hard to let older players go and that I showed too much loyalty to them. Mind you, I was being vilified in other quarters for not playing Páidí so it goes to show that whatever you do, somebody will be dissatisfied.

In hindsight, Liam may have been right but what was I to do? It wasn't as if we had a new crop of exceptional players ready to replace the older lads. Besides, many of the old guard were still going quite well. We only lost to Cork by a point in 1988 and even then the circumstances of our defeat were questionable as there was virtually no stoppage time played at the end despite the fact that play had been held up for a while after a bust-up which arose when Jack O'Shea was grabbed by the testicles in one of the meanest, nastiest fouls I have ever seen. It was most unlike Jacko to retaliate but he let fly that day and nobody could blame him. The row took a few minutes to sort out, but that time wasn't added on at the end and Cork held out. Had we snatched a draw, who knows what direction the Cork–Kerry rivalry of that era might have taken. The replay would have been in Killarney and we would have been mighty driven after the replay embarrassment of a year earlier.

As it was, Cork went on to dominate Kerry for six of the next seven seasons. It was inevitable, I suppose, that there would be some friction as the great Kerry team began to break up. I never had any problem whatsoever with Liam Higgins for speaking his mind and we always remained great friends. He said to me afterwards, 'Look Micko, I just expressed my opinion, nothing personal.' I have no doubt that was the case as, when it came to Kerry football, there was no more loyal or dedicated man than Liam, whose untimely death was a great loss to his family, friends and everybody who knew him.

If Páidí Ó Sé was upset with me in 1988, he would later come to know what's it's like to have to make unpopular decisions as a manager. He was always destined to go into management – it was only a matter of when and he got his chance at the end of 1995, at a time when Kerry people were thoroughly fed up being second best to Cork in Munster.

Just as I had been lucky over twenty years earlier when a smashing young crop of players came along, Páidí hit a golden streak too with the U-21 team that won All-Irelands in 1995 and 1996. Many of them would go on to anchor the team that broke Cork's stranglehold in Munster and start bringing senior All-Irelands back to Kerry again.

People will say that Kerry should have won more than two All-Irelands in the Páidí years between 1996 and 2003 which is probably the case but, then again, they were lucky to win in 2000 as Galway had a great chance to win the first game but wasted a late scoring opportunity when the sides were level.

That one might well have got away from Kerry but I have always felt that they would have beaten Galway in 1998 had they got past

Kildare in the semi-final. I'm even more convinced that they would have beaten Armagh in 2002 if Maurice Fitzgerald had been on the panel. I could never understand why Páidí didn't get more out of what I would regard as one of the truly great players of his generation. Kerry wouldn't even have been in the 2000 final if Maurice hadn't turned the two semi-final games against Armagh after coming on as a substitute, yet he didn't start the final. It was the same in 2001 when he was again left on the bench. It was frustrating for Maurice and bad for Kerry. He watched the 2002 All-Ireland final from the stands when I have no doubt that, had he been playing, he would have pilfered a few points off the Armagh defence in the second half when it dried up for the other Kerry forwards. Kerry lost by a point in the end, making Maurice's absence all the more galling for supporters and for him.

I have no idea why Maurice wasn't rated higher by the Kerry management at the time but I do know that if I had been in charge, his career would have been extended by a few seasons. Unfortunately for Maurice, and indeed Kerry football, Páidí saw things differently. Ultimately, everybody in Kerry lost, including Páidí, whose stubbornness on the Maurice issue became something of a black spot in his term as manager.

Typical though of the man, Páidí got straight back into management after being let go by Kerry in 2003 and while Westmeath seemed an unlikely port of call, that's where he found himself. What's more, he did a terrific job in changing the mindset of the county which, as I discovered in Kildare and Laois, is the first and absolute requirement in these situations.

He deserves enormous credit for the manner in which he steered Westmeath to a first Leinster title in 2004. I'd be the first to acknowledge that, all the more so since I had an up close and personal experience of that day as Westmeath beat Laois in the replayed final.

While Páidí's life remained firmly locked in football, Jimmy Deenihan took off in a different direction, winning a seat for Fine Gael in north Kerry and securing it every bit as tightly as he did the corner-back position for years. If ever there was a man who was falsely maligned, it was Deenihan. Stories went out that when Jimmy Barry-Murphy quit football to concentrate totally on hurling it was because he was fed up having Deenihan mauling him in every Munster final. It became something of an urban – and, indeed, rural – myth that Deenihan marked JBM by grabbing his jersey at the start of a game and releasing it only for the half-time break and at the final whistle.

The truth is a lot different. In fact, those allegations were a downright insult to Deenihan who was one of the best markers I ever saw. What's more, it was brain rather than brawn that made him what he was. He could be tough when the need arose, but there was much more to his game than putting opponents in a headlock and leaving them there for the day. Nobody judged angles better than he did, he was a lot quicker than he was given credit for and, most of all, he had a fantastic football instinct. As I have repeatedly said, his absence in 1982 cost us the five-in-a-row.

It wasn't that we didn't have good replacements, it's just that Deenihan was so damn cute when it came to being last man back. We were extremely lucky to have so many smart footballing brains on that squad, men who could figure things out for themselves and improvise accordingly. It's a quality I always looked for in players because if they have it, the rest usually falls into place.

Deenihan, Ger O'Keeffe, Paudie Lynch, Mick Spillane and of course, Páidí Ó Sé, were our corner-backs from the mid-Seventies to the mid-Eighties and while they all had different individual qualities, they shared one common attribute: sound judgement. Lynch and Ó Sé had plenty of experience further out too which was a great help, but as our options increased in the half-backs with the arrival of Ger Lynch, not to mention Tommy Doyle who could play front or back, we were spoilt for choice. Anywhere a vacancy cropped up, we were able to fill it with a real talent. When Johnno left and we switched Seánie Walsh to full-back, Ambrose O'Donovan came in at midfield where he did a fine job in the 1984, '85 and '86 All-Ireland wins. He even had the distinction of captaining Kerry to the title in the GAA's centenary year which was quite an honour. Then there were lads like Tommy Dowd, John Kennedy, Ger O'Driscoll and Willie Maher, all of whom contributed enormously to the overall package.

Despite the unprecedented levels of success achieved by Kerry, I came in for lots of criticism from elements in the county who claimed I had sold out on the county's heritage by exploiting the hand pass in the Seventies and Eighties. Joe Keohane, in particular, hated the hand pass game but my view was that we should make the most of whatever suited us best. We were so good at the hand pass that the GAA authorities changed the rules, presumably in the belief that it would even things up a bit which was pure daft. It didn't matter what style was in use, the Kerry team of the Seventies and Eighties would have prospered.

Even if they had gone back to the old Kerry style, they would have won All-Irelands too although maybe not as many as they did. In my playing days with Kerry, our games were based on the traditional philosophy that the 14 outfield players each had a sector to control. When a player won the ball, you kicked it as high and as far as you could into another sector where your colleague was expected to win it.

That was all fine when everybody played the same game because Kerry had the players to cope with individual battles. However, when Down introduced the possession game in the early Sixties and Galway built on it with their passing style, things changed. They changed even more dramatically in the Seventies when Dublin moved forward in a number of ways so we had to do something about it and, for a long time, quick, effective use of the hand pass was a key component in our game.

I could never understand the antipathy towards the hand pass. It ensured lots of scores which added considerably to the entertainment value of the games. Nobody ever left a game complaining about seeing too many scores, yet that seemed to be one of the reasons the hand pass rule was changed. The GAA outlawed hand passed goals which I always thought was a major mistake, but then some rules get altered for the silliest of reasons while those that should be changed are left as they are. For instance, where's the sense in the pick-up as we know it? It adds nothing to the game but it does create problems for players and referees as the border line between a legal and illegal pick-up is barely distinguishable. Everybody knows that but the GAA continues to insist on the daft requirement to get a toe under the ball, yet they have always been suspicious of the hand pass.

We exploited the hand pass to the full for as long as we could and we left nothing to chance in terms of what would be accepted. On one occasion, we invited Paddy Collins down from Westmeath to explain his interpretation. Paddy was the top referee at the time and we reckoned that if we could work out with him where exactly the boundaries were, it would stand to us on match days. It was a sensible move and I could never understand why others didn't do the same.

Pat Spillane would claim later that when Paddy left the session, I told the lads to have no fear about throwing the ball the next time he was refereeing one of our games but that wasn't true. I had great respect for Collins as a referee. He was always in control and wasn't swayed by anybody. Paul Kelly from Dublin was another excellent referee but his star waned after a controversial Kerry v Derry League semi-final in the early 1970s which was a great pity. The GAA had a history of not standing by referees who were involved in controversies which was very unfair.

Kerry referee Séamus Garvey ran foul of Meath for his handling of the 1964 All-Ireland semi-final against Galway and they childishly refused to play under him in a subsequent Grounds Tournament game. They actually withdrew from the tournament which was a fairly petty thing to do. I have no doubt it came against Garvey in the corridors of power which was unjust because he was a good referee.

Séamus Aldridge was another referee who I regarded highly. He was always in control and players knew exactly where they stood with him. He was very much his own man and didn't shy away from making the tough calls. Dublin might have a slightly different view of him after Sheehy's goal in the 1978 All-Ireland final, but I'm sure that even they would admit that overall he was an excellent referee.

It's important for players to have respect for referees but then respect is a two-way street and referees need to understand and empathise with players too. There's nothing more irritating for players than if they think the referee sees himself as a policeman out to catch them breaking rules rather than acting as a friend who is trying to steer them through the game with as little interference as possible.

For all that, I always encouraged my teams to respect referees because there's nothing to be gained by antagonising them. There were times, when Kerry were in their prime, that I felt that some referees took it upon themselves to even up games by being especially hard on us but I knew that if I complained, it might make the situation worse. Instead, we accepted it as one of the hazards attached to being a successful side over a long period. It was one we could live with. Well, most of the time anyway.

Offaly and the Five-in-a-Row

How many times have you looked back on some event in life which you thought was hugely important at the time, only to see it now as a distant speck of irrelevance? It happens quite a lot because the passing of time puts a completely different complexion on things.

Those of us who live much of our lives in the cocooned world of sport are probably guiltier than most of over-dramatising events. Take the 1982 All-Ireland football final. Much has been made this year about the 25th anniversary of the day when Seamus Darby's late goal wrecked Kerry's ambitions of becoming the first team to win five successive finals. It has become one of those 'where were you when Darby hit the net' moments. I know where I was!

I must have been asked ten thousand times about that goal, that game, that day and how I felt afterwards. That's understandable, I suppose, as there's no question that it was a moment that left an indelible imprint on GAA history. It wasn't just that Kerry failed to step through a door never previously opened but also the sensational manner in which we were prevented from doing so. This was the ultimate in theatre, involving a script that was altered dramatically just as the curtain was about to come down on the final scene.

So then, a quarter of a century on, how do I feel about what was certainly a momentous day in football? To be quite honest, I couldn't care less about it. It's long since past and, while it will always be part of football folklore, it doesn't matter to me anymore. I admit it wasn't always like that. I took the defeat very badly at the time. The entire Kerry camp was wrapped up in a self-centred world where nothing or nobody mattered except the five-in-a-row for which we were overwhelming favourites. Having it snatched away was hard to take, but so what? It was only a game of football.

That's why I'm not pining for what might have been. I'm quite prepared to revisit the background and the context to the 1982 All-Ireland but you won't find me trapped in some nostalgic time warp with my eyes filling up every time the game is mentioned.

In fact, this may come as a surprise but I have no doubt that if Kerry had won the five-in-a-row, we would not have won three of the next four All-Ireland finals. Completing the five-in-row would have taken over the county to such a degree that it would have been impossible to keep control of it. Besides, how could the players keep clear of the hype and the celebrations that would have accompanied the historic fifth title?

As it was, we were beaten again in 1983 so their careers entered a curious phase where they had to decide whether all their ambitions were realised. They decided they still had unfinished business to attend to so they redoubled their effort and came back to win another three-in-a-row. That would not have happened if we had won in 1982. It has often been suggested that, with a bit more luck, we could have won nine-in-a-row from 1978 to 1986. But it's also true that in slightly different circumstances we might not have won in 1978, 1980 or 1986 so we're thankful for what we got.

What if a super-confident Dublin side, bidding for the three-in-a-row in 1978, had tacked on a few more points when they were five clear and in control of the first half?

What if Roscommon had capitalised on their brilliant start two years later rather than reverting to a destructive game plan which they had obviously decided was the best way to disrupt us? What if Kevin McCabe had goaled that second half penalty in the 1986 final to put Tyrone nine points clear?

Those are three All-Ireland finals which might have gone the other way. It was inevitable then that luck would flow against us on certain days, as it most certainly did to some extent in 1977 and very definitely in the 1982 All-Ireland final and the Munster final a year later. That's life, that's football, that's over.

Granted, it didn't seem like that on the evening of 19 September 1982, or for some time afterwards either. I felt desolate, empty and lost. Most of all, I kept reviewing my own role in the whole affair, in particular whether I had done as much as I possibly could to get things right. Losing the Munster final to Cork by another late goal ten months later deepened the misery but it too passed.

And so it should because Matt Connor's serious car accident on Christmas Day 1984 put everything in perspective. It left Matt in a wheelchair for life but, typical of the man's iron strength of character, he never lost that wonderfully positive attitude that helped him become such a remarkable performer. I have always classed him as one of the greatest players of all time so wouldn't it have been a real pity had he never won an All-Ireland medal?

That he won it in such a historic final, which he helped shape to a huge degree, added to the magic of it all. The truth is that it was far more important that he won an all-Ireland medal than that Kerry won five-in-a-row. And when you look right through that Offaly team from Martin Furlong in goal, to Connor, Fitzgerald and the Lowry brothers, to dual star Liam Currams, Pádraic Dunne, Johnny Mooney, Gerry Carroll, John Guinan and of course to that damn heartbreaker, Darby, who could begrudge them their All-Ireland win? Not me anyway, although whether they deserved it in 1982 is another matter!

All these years later, I look back on the 1982 final as one that Kerry certainly had the capacity to win. It would be nice to be in the record books as the only five-in-a-row winners but the Kerry team of that era don't need that honour to prove that they were the best in GAA history.

In hindsight, we probably should have seen the 1982 result coming, maybe not in such a devastating finale but there were little indications that the pendulum was beginning to swing away from us. There are times too when fate makes a decision and isn't for turning, however much it's influenced.

Naturally, all that's ignored when you're living through it but when I look back, there were some signs that things were happening over which we had absolutely no control. They began as far back as August 1981 when Pat Spillane injured his knee. It was to be the start of a nightmare for him which went on for a very long time. He played the final few minutes in the 1981 All-Ireland final and we all thought that everything would be fine for the following year. It wasn't. The knee bothered him all through and he could rarely play a full game. When he did, he wasn't anywhere near his best because the knee was so badly damaged. The thing about Spillane was that he needed to be fully fit to make an impact. He could play anywhere but he needed room everywhere. His pace and endurance earned him space but, with the knee restricting him, he was never in a position to contribute at full power in 1982.

We brought him on at half-time in the final and he did okay but it wasn't the vintage Spillane we all knew. It's impossible not to think that if Spillane had been fully fit and playing for the full seventy minutes he wouldn't have been worth three or four points to us.

Equally important was an injury sustained by Jimmy Deenihan in a training session in early June 1982. An accidental collision with John Egan left Deenihan with a broken leg that would end his Kerry career. It stunned the whole panel into dejected silence and, even as the ambulance drove out of Fitzgerald Stadium that evening, the five-in-a-row dream went with it, even if we didn't realise it at the time. Naturally, I banished all such negative thoughts from my head but things were taking on a worrying look.

Deenihan was out, Spillane was half-in and half-out, while Sheehy's ankles and Power's hamstring were bothering them. Were the gods trying to tell us something we didn't want to hear? It grew even more ominous when Jack O'Shea and his family were involved in a car accident on the way to the Munster final. The car was a write-off but, thankfully, nobody was injured although the O Sheas were all badly shaken. Typical of Jacko, he never thought of withdrawing from the team. The show had to go on as far as he was concerned. He had also been troubled with an ankle injury so it was no surprise that he wasn't at his best against Cork. As a result, Kerry didn't fire fully either and we were lucky enough to get out with a draw.

We won the replay in Killarney by 12 points which convinced everybody that the Kerry machine was on full throttle again. Confidence soared even higher when we beat Armagh by ten points in the semi-final. It was a misleading result as Armagh wasted several chances in the first half.

It was the latest in a string of heavy semi-final defeats inflicted on Ulster champions. Confidence was so low in the north at the time, especially when their teams were facing Kerry, that their supporters travelled in very small numbers. Kerry fans didn't bother much with semi-finals either because they expected us to be in finals which accounts for the unusually small attendance of 18,000 at the Kerry v Armagh game in 1982.

Offaly had walloped Dublin in the Leinster final but were lucky to beat Galway by a point in the All-Ireland semi-final with a performance which was an awful long way short of what they delivered against us. Still, it created the perfect scenario for Eugene McGee and his team because nobody gave them a chance against us.

While Offaly were training away quietly in the peaceful surrounds of Ballycommon, we were facing unbelievable five-in-a-row mania. Every huckster got in on the act. Songs, poems, recitations, team photos, t-shirts, caps, towels, mugs. Wherever you looked or turned, people were cashing in. Everybody except the Kerry camp were at it which annoyed me greatly because all sorts of chancers were making money out of the players. There was also the fear that it could get through to the team. I arrived for training on the Thursday night before the final to find a fella selling five-in-a-row t-shirts outside the gate which infuriated me so much that I could barely control myself. There were even arguments over where the Sam Maguire Cup should be brought on the Monday night after the homecoming.

It was crazy stuff and, if all that wasn't enough, there was a row over our gear as the GAA tried to dictate what we could wear. Put it all together and the distraction tank was overflowing. However, there was absolutely no question of the team being over-confident. We always believed we would win matches but we never took it for granted. That applied most of all to the 1982 final which was always going to be a massive test against an Offaly team that had been built up carefully over five seasons.

Much was made afterwards of our decision to play Ogie Moran at wing-forward in 1982 whereas he had been at centre-forward in each of our previous five All-Ireland wins. It was simple really. With Pat Spillane out, his brother Tom came into the attack and did well against Cork and Armagh. He was more suited to a central role so we slotted him in at number 11 and moved Ogie, who was very versatile, to the wing. When we lost, it was pointed out that the years in which we hadn't won All-Irelands (1976, 1977, 1982) were also the seasons when we hadn't played Ogie at centre-forward.

That's a fact but it's also a coincidence. Playing Ogie on the wing had absolutely nothing to do with our defeat by Offaly. Nor do I blame the five-in-a-row hysteria, even if was hard to take. It might have made the lads a bit edgy but they were well used to pressure and this was merely a new form of it.

However, a number of other factors combined to weaken our position in the final. The absence of Pat Spillane and Deenihan, missed opportunities and some very debateable decisions by the referee left us vulnerable and then, of course, there was Offaly's growing maturity and sense of destiny that they had been chosen to thwart us.

Still, when we were awarded a penalty coming up to the three-quarter stage it looked as if we were on our way. A goal would have put us four points clear but Sheehy's kick was saved by Furlong. Mikey would be the first to admit that it wasn't his best penalty and Martin would probably be the first to admit that he was well off his line when the kick was taken. Referee PJ McGrath took no action and the chance was lost. However significant that incident was, it didn't settle the game. Our best spell came afterwards when we went four points clear with six minutes remaining.

It was at that stage that I believe the role of the referee became very important. I wouldn't suggest for one second that he didn't call the game as he saw it, but I have always believed that referees are unconsciously susceptible to what I would term the 'underdog influence'. It becomes easier for the 'underdogs' to win frees when they've fallen behind, not because the referee is biased but because he's human. It was something the Kerry team of that era encountered all the time but it usually didn't matter because we generally had plenty in hand. However, we didn't in the 1982 final so it turned out to be crucial.

As we defended the four-point lead, Seán Lowry won a free which Matt Connor pointed and, to this day, I have no idea why it was awarded. Even Eugene McGee accepted that it was a harsh call. Connor pointed a second free shortly afterwards and suddenly the whole scene changed as Offaly were within striking distance.

There's no doubt but we became nervous from there on. Instead of holding our shape and taking the game on, we funnelled back in an attempt to protect the lead. That invited Offaly on to us, eventually providing Darby with the goal chance. Did he push Tommy Doyle under the dropping ball? Ask yourself this? Why would Doyle totally misjudge the flight of a ball so badly that he didn't even make any sort of contact? Would he really have got it so wrong that the ball would drop gently into Darby's arms? That's not the Doyle I knew. Should it have been a free out? Of course it should have and nine times out of ten it would have been, but this was one-in-ten day.

However he managed to win the ball, Darby deserves enormous credit for his rasping finish past Nelligan. Even then, all wasn't lost as we had a chance to grab the equaliser but, typical of how disjointed we had become in the final minutes, we didn't take it. The five-in-a-row dream was over.

Even as Darby blasted the ball past Nelligan, my mind flashed back to that June evening when the sickening crack of Deenihan's breaking leg could be heard around Fitzgerald Stadium. Had he been playing in the final, his natural corner-back instincts would have taken him behind Darby under that dropping ball and the chances are that he would have broken it away, just as he did so often in previous finals. Here, after all, was a man who conceded very little to any opponent in the six finals in which he played.

It was impossible to spot any chink of light after the defeat by Offaly but, as time passed, I began to think that maybe it was a good thing for some of the players that they didn't win the five-in-a-row. The celebrations would have taken a heavy toll on anybody who wasn't prepared for them. Instead, we all had to face up to the reality that nobody is immune from disappointment.

If the players didn't believe it then, they were certainly left under no illusions in the following year's Munster final when they were hit by Darby The Second. The 1983 Munster final was a strange affair. Thunder in the morning, followed by heavy rain left Páirc Uí Chaoimh soggy and uninviting. A poor game followed, one where we seemed to have done just enough to win a ninth provincial title in a row when we took a two point lead into the closing seconds.

Enter the Darby factor. Only this time it was Tadhg Murphy who crept in behind our defence, seized a long range free and drove past Nelligan. Not again! Had we been hit by some evil jinx?

As is usual in Kerry, even after times of plenty, a championship defeat is regarded as a disaster. We had lost to two last second goals in successive years which, by any standards, was freakish but there were plenty of takers for the theory that I was to blame for both defeats. Apparently, I misread the situation in 1982 and allowed myself to become preoccupied by rows over gear. And when Offaly began their recovery in the final six minutes, I had failed to respond. As for the Cork defeat, you could take your pick from a long line of mistakes I was supposed to have made. Frankly, I didn't pay any attention to the criticisms, nor did I think of walking away.

The GAA was preparing for centenary year and I was determined to be part of it. Anyway, just because we lost to late goals in successive years didn't mean that there weren't a whole lot of positives living comfortably in Kerry. If we had held on against Cork in the 1983 Munster final, we would have won the All-Ireland. Cork had every chance of beating Dublin in the All-Ireland semi-final but, having put themselves in a great position, they failed to press on and were hit by a late equalising goal from Barney Rock. The replay was fixed for Páirc Uí Chaoimh where Cork made the stupid mistake of thinking that home advantage would generate a winning momentum. How wrong they were. Dublin destroyed them. We would have beaten Dublin and, given how Galway performed in the final, I'm sure we would have been too good for them also.

I didn't get the chance to put those theories to the test and instead found myself watching the 1983 final from the stands, already planning for 1984. I decided that our approach would have to be different. The practice of going through the League without formal training was abandoned because it was time to experiment, so instead we started back in October. We needed to freshen up the panel and, to do that, I needed to have a look at some new players in a competitive environment. For the first time in ages, the League was important to us, certainly in terms of promoting players to the front line. Besides, centenary year was coming so we wanted to win as much as possible.

The integration of new players with the old guard worked even better than I expected and we won the League, beating Down in the semi-final and Galway in the final. I was doing my best to con the media, playing the poor mouth and telling them that it would take quite some time to rebuild the team. I wanted Dublin, Cork and indeed all other aspiring contenders to believe that Kerry were a combination of aging players, who had won so much that they couldn't possibly be motivated, and untried newcomers.

The reality was somewhat different. What we had was a solid nucleus of remarkably gifted players, who were still hungry for success and were desperate to make amends for 1982 and 1983, and emerging stars like Tom Spillane, Tommy O'Dowd, Ger Lynch, Ambrose O'Donovan, John Kennedy and Willie Maher.

John O'Keeffe was gone so now it was Seánie Walsh's turn to show what a versatile character he was by switching from midfield to full-back, thus becoming one of the few players to have played at full-forward, midfield and full-back at the very highest level. Tom Spillane was relocated at centre-back in place of Tim Kennelly, Ambrose O'Donovan joined Jacko at midfield and Kennedy, O'Dowd and Maher were vying for positions in attack. Tommy Doyle and Ger Lynch were handed the wing-back positions while Páidí Ó Sé and Mick Spillane booked into the corners.

I suppose the biggest challenge was to convince the lads who had already pocketed five All-Ireland medals that there were more to be picked up. They had seen and done it all and it would have been easy for them to settle into the comfort zone because whatever happened, they wouldn't be blamed. Their great record in the 1975–81 era ensured them of a permanent place in Kerry folklore and if things went wrong in the 'second coming' it would be put down to a lack of talent in depth. Plus, of course, I would have been blamed for not blooding enough players during the glory days.

I would have liked to, of course, as there's nothing to keep a scene fresh like a few young buckos marching into the dressing room, making it clear that they couldn't care less about past achievements and that they were there to take somebody else's place. It was different in Kerry in the 1978–82 period. Plenty of new lads arrived on the scene but they weren't good enough to dislodge the established players who guarded their own particular kingdoms with fierce pride and determination.

I headed into the 1984 championship with a mixture of excitement and trepidation. I knew that, on paper at least, we had a fine team but would it gel on the big day? A 17-point win over Tipperary told us nothing but we put down a very clear marker in the Munster final against Cork with a 3-14 to 2-10 win. Okay, so we conceded too much but that could be addressed. The main thing was that the attack was back on form. Free from injury at last, Pat Spillane returned to his devastating best scoring two goals, Willie Maher added the third, John Kennedy kicked four points, while at midfield, Jacko and Ambrose were superb. Ambrose was captain in his first full championship year, a legacy of the system for appointing captains in Kerry. It wasn't easy for a young lad from Gneeveguilla who was only settling into the team to stand up in front of a dressing room full of heroic figures, but it didn't bother him in the slightest. He turned into a fine leader and an even better footballer.

Injury-ravaged Galway offered only token opposition in the All-Ireland semi-final, leaving us in another final against our old friends, the Dubs. And, as had been the case in 1975, they were reigning All-Ireland champions thanks to the 13-man show against Galway a year earlier.

The jigsaw pieces had slotted together neatly for us through the summer of 1984 but, just when it looked as if the picture was complete for the All-Ireland final, Sheehy's Achilles tendon packed in. I couldn't believe it. What was it about us that we always seemed to lose a key player for a final? This was a serious blow. Sheehy, who had scored 1-4 against Galway in the semi-final, was our ace free-taker, not to mention being a man who could poach a goal in the tightest of situations.

The restructuring plan involved a return to duty for Ger Power, who had been in and out of the team that year. Not many teams would have had the luxury of calling in a five-time All-Ireland winner, especially one who felt he should never have been out in the first place and was determined to prove it. The free-taking duties were transferred to Kennedy and the show went on.

No player should ever need extra motivation for an All-Ireland final but it's always nice when it arrives, especially from a most unlikely source, as it did in 1984. I always thought the *RTÉ Guide* carried the TV schedule with some light, fluffy pieces about various programmes but, for reasons that nobody could ever figure out, they decided to use the All-Ireland week issue to unload themselves of the most astonishing attack on the Kerry team.

The *Guide* wouldn't have been compulsive reading in the Kerry dressing room but news of that particular edition spread quickly, much to my delight. The team was described as 'a cowardly blend of experienced players, has-beens and a few newcomers'.

I thought to myself this should go down nicely with the lads as they head for Dublin! Furthermore, Tom Spillane was categorised as being 'the most glaring weakness and [Tommy] Conroy should give him a severe roasting'. Ger Lynch, who would be marking Hill 16 hero, Barney Rock, was classed as 'a nice footballer but a poor marker'. Tommy Doyle would have severe problems with Ciaran Duff too, it appeared.

Astonishing stuff and pure guff too! Describing a Kerry team – especially one that had so many proven winners aboard – as cowardly was like telling a rottweiler that he was an ugly mutt. The *RTÉ Guide* piece was the opinion of one person, and not a very informed one either, but I gave it a broader context, telling the players that this was what the outside world really thought of them. It wasn't, of course, but why spoil such a juicy line with the truth?

It was probably the first and last time that the *RTÉ Guide* found itself commissioned for motivation service before an All-Ireland final. We loved the insults but I suspect that Kevin Heffernan and his players weren't best pleased with the writer as they would have known how we were going to use the piece.

The centenary final was a disappointment for neutrals but a joy for Kerry, right down to every last 'cowardly has-been' in the dressing room. Dublin were unusually poor, scoring just 1-6 to our 0-14. The winning margin should have been much higher but we couldn't care less. Sam Maguire and the National League trophy would spend the centenary winter in their rightful place. The only blot on the season was the failure to win the Centenary Cup, a special knock-out competition which was introduced to mark the occasion. Still, we could live without it, until the following April that is, when we won the 1985 version.

It didn't matter a jot really but it was nice to win it so as to maintain the great Kerry tradition of having won every competition in GAA history. What's more, we hammered Cork in the final which made it all the sweeter. League or championship, minor, U-21 or senior, challenge or tournament, Kerry always get a special satisfaction from beating our neighbours so it was very nice to get the better of them again in a competition which only lasted a few years. Mind you, it's only half what they feel when they beat us. We won the 'Open Draw' final by 2-10 to 0-4 on a day when Ger Lynch was outstanding at left half-back.

A few months later we reinforced our superiority over Cork in a Munster championship that, with the exception of 1983, had developed into something of a pattern. Cork would stay with us until half-time only to drift away in the second half. Sheehy and the 'Bomber' scored the goals as we racked up another win, this time by six points. Still, there were signs that Cork were beginning to take shape which indeed proved to be the case as many of them would be aboard the squad that took over in Munster from 1987 on.

Having easily dismissed Ulster champions, Derry (1976), Monaghan (1979) and Armagh (1982), in All-Ireland semi-finals, we may have been a bit complacent going into the 1985 All-Ireland semi-final against Monaghan. A manager can lecture a squad all he likes about the dangers of taking anything for granted but if a mindset is in place, it can be very difficult to change. We had crushed Monaghan in 1979 but this was a very different side, carefully-built and shrewdly coached by Seán McCague. They had won the League title a few months earlier and had beaten Donegal, Armagh and Derry in the Ulster championship. McCague had them well-tuned for a game where probably nobody, other than themselves, reckoned they had a chance.

As events transpired, they most certainly had. In fact they led by four points at one stage as lads like Paddy Linden, a damn fine goalkeeper, Gerry McCarville, Ciarán Murray, David Byrne, Declan Flanagan, Ray McCarron, Eamonn McEneaney and, of course, the irrepressible 'Nudie' Hughes took us on with real confidence. It finished level in the end after McEneaney had pointed a long range free.

The replay was a fiery affair. 'Bomber' was sent off in the first half after retaliating on McCarville and Monaghan midfielder Hugo Clerkin was dismissed in the second half. We led by nine points at one stage in the first half and, while Monaghan battled back, we held them comfortably and won by five points.

The difference in the size of the crowd between the draw and replay was very interesting. Less than 22,000 turned out for the first game but obviously it looked very good on TV. That, plus the possibility of a Kerry defeat, helped swell the replay attendance to almost 54,000. There's no doubt that Kerry's dominant years had a negative impact on All-Ireland semi-final crowds. At one stage, it was even suggested that the two semi-finals be played together. It's difficult to imagine that being contemplated these days but it was different back then.

Once again, our great rivals from Dublin awaited us in the All-Ireland final. Astonishingly, it would be our seventh championship clash in ten years, but if we met seven times a month it would still be extra special. After our comprehensive win a year earlier, we were confident going into the final and Dublin did nothing to make us reassess the situation in what was an embarrassing first half for them. It was as close to humiliation as any Dublin team had ever come.

Jacko cracked home a goal from a penalty early on and then proceeded to dominate the entire park in one of those amazing performances he specialised in around that time. Any wonder he won the Texaco award for a second successive year? We led by 1-8 to 0-2 at half-time and when Timmy O'Dowd goaled 15 minutes into the second half, it looked like a landslide. However, we dropped our guard as John Kearns led a Dublin rally. Two goals from Joe McNally and a string of points and suddenly we were only one point clear. Losing to Dublin would have been bad enough but losing after being so far ahead would definitely have been regarded as treasonable in Kerry. Executions would have been swift and painful and no doubt my neck would have been first on the line. That prospect concentrated minds and we kicked three points late on to close the game out.

There was a nostalgic dimension to that game in that it marked Brian Mullins' final championship outing for Dublin. Mullins had been an incredible warrior ever since he burst on the scene in 1974 and had shown just how resilient he was by battling back bravely after being involved in a serious road accident when he was at the peak of his powers. As with many great careers, it ended in sadness as he never got into the 1985 final and was replaced by PJ Buckley.

We completed the three-in-a-row a year later after a campaign that very definitely flashed out signals that the end was nigh. Cork edged ever closer, losing the Munster final by four points, a result that flattered us, and we were made to look better than we really were by Meath in the All-Ireland semi-final. Seán Boylan's persistence had finally paid off and, in his fourth season in charge, Meath finally closed the long gap without a Leinster title. They were an imposing outfit, built around strong (physically and mentally) characters like Mick Lyons, Joe Cassells, Liam Harnan, Liam Hayes, Gerry McEntee, Colm O'Rourke and Brian Stafford. They hadn't fully matured as a team in 1986 but they were really putting it up to us in the semi-final until a dreadful mistake in the first half changed everything.

Ogie's lob into the Meath square should have been a routine job for such a big defence but amazingly Lyons, Cassells and goalkeeper Mickey McQuillan collided, allowing the ball to run to Power who tapped it into an empty net. Power winked at me at half-time, smiled and remarked: 'Christ, Micko, if they'd got me in a sandwich I'd be dead.' The thing was, they didn't. That was Power for you, cute as a fox.

We ran out seven-point winners but I wasn't happy. Meath's big time inexperience had been a major contributor to our success. We were beginning to rely on things to happen for us rather than making them happen. Tyrone had also reached the final which we were pleased to see because we had a good record against Ulster teams. In that era, the only way a Connacht or Ulster team could get to an All-Ireland final was when the semi-final cycle pitched them against each other. In fact, not since 1973 when Galway beat Offaly had a Connacht or Ulster team won a semi-final against Leinster or Munster opposition.

I knew that we were beginning to slip but I still couldn't see Tyrone beating us. Well, not until they were 1-7 to 0-4 ahead early in the second half and the referee is pointing to the penalty spot in front of Charlie Nelligan's goal. A whirl of emotions started to spin around my head. What if he scores? Nine points clear and just over 25 minutes to go? Can we pull it back? What can I do to make it happen? How have we found ourselves in this position? Surely Tyrone aren't that good.

Jacko had missed a penalty early on in the first half, blazing his shot off the crossbar, and now Kevin McCabe had a chance to strike for what could have been the decisive kick of the final. I say 'could' because in light of what happened afterwards, there's no reason to believe that we wouldn't have recovered even if he had scored a goal. His kick flew over the bar, leaving Tyrone seven points clear and us looking at the highest mountain we had come across in years.

Astonishingly, we outscored Tyrone by 2-11 to 0-2 from there to the finish. Pat Spillane, who gave one of his finest ever performances that day, began the revival with a point and followed up some time later with a spectacular flicked goal after he launched himself at a cross by Power, who was also involved in the second goal, a goal which Tyrone allege to this day should never have been allowed.

More specifically, they claim that it had its origins in a clash between Plunkett Donaghy and Power. Tyrone claim that Power fouled Donaghy before picking out Sheehy with an inch-perfect pass. Even then, Sheehy had plenty to do but he was the right man in a tight situation. He had no more than 18 inches of a target to aim at if he was to beat Aidan Skelton, but Sheehy's eye for precision was at its sharpest at times like that. The same applied to Peter Canavan, whose winning goal against Kerry in the 2005 All-Ireland final also needed an expert finish which he executed perfectly. That's the thing about instinctive finishers – the greater the pressure, the more they thrive.

Did Power foul Donaghy? Did Darby foul Doyle four years earlier? All that counted was the referee's view and it ended one-all for Kerry which proves, I suppose, that these things balance out over a period of time. Sheehy's goal wrecked Tyrone who were already in trouble having lost John Lynch, who was having a great game, with an injury.

Eugene McKenna, one of the best ever to come out of Tyrone, was also in trouble having suffered a recurrence of a leg injury which forced him off. It was a serious double blow to Tyrone, as was their failure to goal from the penalty. Still, it was an amazing comeback by Kerry. It was as if the lads called on every ounce of experience and determination to summon one last huge effort which ultimately won the day.

It was our eighth All-Ireland win since 1975 and, while there were some signs of decay around the fringes, nobody could possibly have envisaged what lay ahead. If every Kerry person at home and abroad had been asked after the 1986 final to name the next captain to lead Kerry to an All-Ireland title, none would have come remotely close. Which is hardly surprising since the lad in question was only 11 at the time. I'm sure Liam Hassett was watching the game with all the wide-eyed wonder of a young hopeful but he certainly wouldn't have thought that it would be all of 11 years before Kerry next produced an All-Ireland winning squad with him as captain.

I'm often asked if I knew the end was nigh after 1986. The answer is yes and no. Logic suggested that every great empire crumbled eventually and we were going to be no different. Many of the players had been winning All-Irelands since 1975 and simply couldn't keep going indefinitely. The wear and tear had taken its toll, leaving many of the team going into games carrying a variety of injuries.

Still, there was an enormous sense of pride in the squad and they had so much natural talent that they were able to improvise when things got tight. Most of all, their ambition levels never dropped which was remarkable. Even in 1987, when the great run finally ended, it had nothing to do with a lack of appetite or determination. They wanted success as much as ever but the bodies weren't quite up to the demands in the Munster final replay.

The main core of the team had been settled for so long that it was fierce hard for emerging talent to force their way into the side. I have no doubt that we lost another Kerry side in that era but what was I to do? Drop super players who were winning All-Ireland titles?

It was frustrating for those just outside the panel and many who would have prospered in other times faded from the scene. I knew exactly what was happening but was powerless to stop it. And when the time came that, as 'Bomber' put it, the circus was over, we were left with a team that had nearly all grown old together.

And there was I in the middle, trapped between a fierce loyalty to such fantastic men who had brought Kerry unprecedented glory and the need to move things on. It should have been my cue to quit. The right time for me to go would have been at the end of 1987 which, as history shows, was the natural breaking point. Trouble was, I didn't know it at the time.

People may think I'm mad but I still believe that if we had got past Cork in the drawn Munster final that year, we would have won another All-Ireland. We lost the 1987 League final by a goal to Dublin but it didn't bother us unduly as, to be honest, it was a reflection on the rest of the country that we were there in the first place.

League titles didn't mean much to us at that stage but, even without training or trying very hard, we nudged our way to the final where Dublin awaited us. Naturally, that stirred the passions but it was clear from early on when Ciarán Duff thumped home a goal that new Dublin manager Gerry McCaul had brought them much closer to championship tempo than we were. Not that I was bothered by that as we had the training schedule down to a fine art by then and it did not involve any sort of peak in April. Dublin won by a goal but wouldn't capture a Leinster title for another three years. Kerry, by the way, wouldn't win another Munster title until 1991 so the 1987 League final – for all its hype and competitiveness – counted for nothing in the context of things to come.

With the exception of Timmy O'Dowd for Willie Maher, the Kerry team that lined out in the 1987 Munster final against Cork in Páirc Uí Chaoimh was the same as that which won the All-Ireland ten months earlier. However, a number of significant changes had taken place in Cork. For a start, Billy Morgan had taken over as manager. Nobody had endured more misery against Kerry than Morgan from 1975 on and nobody had done more to try and break our dominance. There were so many days when he looked out from the Cork goal at defences that were left with splitting headaches as they tried to sort out what the Kerry forwards would do next but, however bad the result, Morgan was always back the next year, trying harder than ever.

When he took over as Cork manager at the end of 1986, we knew that he would not only bring a fierce determination to beat Kerry but also improve the organisation. His master stroke was to land Tompkins and Fahy. So, when we headed to Cork for the 1987 Munster final, it was clear that we were in for a different type of challenge than we had grown used to.

And how! Right at the end, we were two points down. We needed a miracle man, in which circumstances there was no more likely provider than Sheehy. He had been carrying so many injuries over the years that he would probably have quit in 1986 only for Austin Stacks winning the county title a year earlier which meant he would be captain in the following season.

He certainly played a captain's part in Cork that day, somehow managing to squeeze in along the endline before poking the ball to the net. After being hit by last minute goals in 1982 and 1983, we had finally got one of our own but this time it wasn't enough to win the game. Ger Lynch asked referee Pat Lane how much time was left and got the impression the kick-out would bring the final whistle but it didn't. Instead, Cork worked the ball downfield, drew a free and Tompkins pointed.

Sunday, 2 August 1987, has gone down in Kerry history for all the wrong reasons. It isn't recalled with any affection in the O'Dwyer household either. The Kerry v Cork Munster minor final had also finished level a week earlier so both replays were fixed for Fitzgerald Stadium. I had two sons involved in the minor game – Robert was at right corner-back and Karl was at right half-forward. A certain Maurice Fitzgerald was also on that team.

I watched as much of the minor game as I could but it didn't go well for Kerry who were beaten by four points. Early advantage, Cork.

It was a bad omen for the seniors, even if we didn't know it at the time. Nobody – and that certainly includes me – can explain how it all went so flat for us that day. Sheehy was such a reliable place kicker that when we won a free within striking range of the opposition goal, I never even thought about it. I would often look up the field to see where various players were and wait for the roar of the crowd to confirm another Sheehy point. It was different that day in Killarney. For some strange reason, the grass was cut bare to the ground so when he lined up his first free, he never rose the ball. He was using a pair of boots he borrowed from Ger Lynch which didn't help matters either. When Sheehy started missing frees, the alarm bells began to jangle. They clanged ever louder as the minutes passed and we couldn't score. Growing in confidence all the time, Cork racked up the points and got another boost a few minutes before half-time when Power was sent off. It took us 33 minutes to score our first point, an unthinkable situation for such a gifted forward line.

'Bomber' had a go at a free early in the second half and, as Sheehy remarked later: 'He didn't even get a good wide.' Dermot Hanafin scored a goal for us but Cork were so comfortable that it was never going to rattle them and they sailed home comfortable winners, 0-13 to 1-5.

Kerry scoring 1-5 in 70 minutes! If drug testing were in place in the GAA at the time, we would have had the entire squad tested. It was one of those strange, inexplicable days but I suppose it had to come. However talented and dedicated the group, they weren't machines who could turn on the power every time they went out. I was criticised afterwards for remaining in the dug-out rather than patrolling the sideline barking out instructions. The reality is that I had nothing to say. Everybody could see how flat the team was and there was no point in me showboating on the sideline.

These boys had turned games around before and would have done it again had there been any energy left in their batteries. There wasn't, so all we could do was endure the pain and get out of Killarney as quickly as possible.

Having said that, I remain convinced that had we beaten Cork the first day – and remember we were seconds away from victory – we would have won the All-Ireland. A mediocre Galway team would not have bothered us in the semi-final and we'd have fancied our chances against Meath in the final too.

All-Ireland finals are different to any other game. We had the experience and the guile and would have lifted our game for another mighty push. Bear in mind that Cork led Meath by five points in the first half of the final and actually should have been further ahead. They were slowly reeled in but if we had been there and opened a five-point lead, Meath could have grinded all they like but they wouldn't have worn us down.

I should have left at the end of 1987. The spell had been broken and it was time for a serious reassessment. I didn't quit because I was still enjoying it and, ever the optimist, I reckoned we could recover. At least that's what I told myself. I was wrong.

We never really fired in 1988. Sheehy and Walsh were gone; others were injured or struggling to find their form. The mixture of the old and the new was slow to come together, yet we still ran Cork to a point in the Munster final on a day when the only good news for Kerry was the emergence of Maurice Fitzgerald as a senior player. He kicked ten points but still finished up on the losing side.

The slide continued. We lost a League semi-final to Cork by six points in April 1989 and three months later they beat us again in the Munster final in Killarney. The pendulum had swung very much their way by now. We led by three points at the end of the first quarter but were eight down at one stage in the second half before eventually losing by three.

Cork were now doing to us what we had done to them so mercilessly for so long. The margins were smaller – although they increased dramatically in 1990 – but it was as if they knew they could take our best shot, stay on their feet and go on to beat us.

I couldn't stand that anymore. I knew as I left Páirc Uí Chaoimh on the evening of 23 July 1989 that my days as Kerry manager were finished for good. I laid low for a few days just to make absolutely sure that I wouldn't have a change of heart. I didn't. The Micko era with Kerry was over.

Coming Events and Long Shadows

Coming events are supposed to cast their shadows in advance, but if they did in the summer of 1985, I certainly didn't spot them. This was understandable enough, I suppose, given that they were happening in Kildare not Kerry. Still, they would have a big impact on me, Kerry, Kildare and Cork some years later.

Kerry were bounding along quite nicely, preparing to defend the All-Ireland championship. There were no obvious clouds on the horizon even if we hadn't qualified for the knock-out stages of the League. That never bothered me in the slightest, certainly not with the Kerry squad of that era. All-Irelands were their only ambition and if the League presented itself as a bonus in the spring, all the better. The County Board liked us to stay involved for as long as possible because it brought in revenue but in terms of getting ready for the championship, we didn't need the League.

Besides, in 1985 we won the special Open Draw competition which was introduced the previous year to celebrate the GAA's centenary year. We beat Cork in the final in April. Good! We always wanted to keep our great, big, ugly thumbs pressing down on them. League, championship, challenge or open draw, Cork had to be beaten because the more doubts we planted in their minds, the harder they found it to escape from our grip.

We didn't start our 1985 Munster championship campaign until late June, by which time Kildare had been eliminated in Leinster, losing fairly tamely to Meath. There wasn't anything particularly unusual about that back then as Kildare rarely seemed to do their talents justice on the big days.

A few weeks later, a row broke out between Larry Tompkins and the Kildare County Board over an airfare to New York. It might seem strange nowadays that something as trivial as an airfare for one player could spark off a controversy that would have a knock-on effect for years to come, but things were different in the mid-Eighties, certainly in Kildare.

Tompkins had returned from New York to play against Meath and, after Kildare lost, he headed back the following day. The County Board felt he should pay half the air fare; a decision he took serious issue with, and it was hard to blame him for that. Here you had one of the best young talents in the country playing in New York when he should have been at home in Kildare. But then Larry was a carpenter and work was scarce in Ireland at the time. Supporters' clubs and other back-up supports were unheard of in most counties so players were left largely to their own devices. And, in this case, that involved a remarkable talent becoming embroiled in a row over the price of an air ticket.

Tompkins would never play for Kildare again which was a disaster for the county and turned out to have serious implications at many levels. First, he set up home in Cork of all places (could we not have found a job for him in Kerry?) and was hugely important in changing the Cork panel's attitude and approach at a time when the great Kerry team was beginning to fray at the edges in 1987.

Second, his switch may well have been an influence on another Kildare man, Shea Fahy, who also joined Cork in 1987. Fahy was an army man, based in Cork and hooked up with Nemo Rangers and Billy Morgan. But I often wonder would he have continued to play with Kildare had Tompkins stayed there and the county had shown more ambition instead of getting involved in a petty row over an air-fare. I'm sure Kildare football fans wondered about it even more.

Anyway, Tompkins and Fahy switched to Cork where they made a massive difference. Cork beat Kerry three times and drew with us once in the championship between 1987 and 1989. By the time I stood down as Kerry manager, I was heartily sick of Tompkins, Fahy and Cork. I know that Cork people don't like to hear it, but the reality is that without the Kildare pair, Sam Maguire would have found another home in 1989 and 1990. Cork had some good players but they needed an inspirational talisman, the type who didn't entertain the thought of losing. Tompkins fitted the mould perfectly.

He was one of the best players ever to play Gaelic football. Not only did he have every skill in the game, he was also an exceptional leader. He had the heart of a lion, never knew when he was beaten and refused to accept defeat. Throw in his accuracy from frees and you have a truly great player.

Fahy was a fine midfielder who played a sensible, intelligent game. He won the Texaco award in 1990 after a great performance in the All-Ireland final against Meath and had the sort of presence that you always want in a team. He would have contributed an awful lot during my first stint with Kildare but I'm convinced that Tompkins was the man who would have won the All-Ireland for that squad.

Rarely, I suppose, has any county picked up two such outstanding talents in such easy circumstances as Cork did with Tompkins and Fahy. There were question marks at one stage about Tompkins' eligibility to play with Cork but once he joined Castlehaven that was sorted out. Cork couldn't believe their luck.

In soccer terms, they had acquired the services of two brilliant players, in their prime, without having to pay a penny. There was some unease around the country as to how Cork managed to secure the services of both, but the real question was why Kildare had been so appallingly careless with two of their most prized assets.

That they ended up playing for Cork was a terrible indictment of Kildare. You just don't let two proven stars walk out the door, certainly not if you're serious about being genuine contenders for major honours. It was different, of course, back then, as there was little contact between county boards and players except perhaps in the more successful counties. Still, that doesn't excuse Kildare for not making a better effort to hold onto two players who went on to change Cork's fortunes and, by extension, the fortunes of lots of other counties too.

Tompkins was only 24 years old in 1987 while Fahy was just a few years older. They were coming into their prime and were at the peak of their powers when I arrived in Kildare at the end of 1990. I would have given anything to have brought them back straight away but they were committed to Cork, who had just won the two-in-a-row with Tompkins the captain for the second one.

I knew we wouldn't get them back to Kildare at that stage, but a season or two later we made an effort with Tompkins in particular. Michael Osborne agreed with me that he could have made all the difference in the world to us and used all his persuasive powers in an effort to coax Larry home. At one stage, I thought we had him but, in the end, he wouldn't move.

He was still very sore over the way he had been treated by Kildare in 1985. Besides, he had a business in Cork and obviously felt his future lay on Leeside which it did because he still runs a pub there. Also, Cork were the dominant force in Munster, even if they lost to Kerry in both the 1991 and 1992 Munster semi-finals. However, they would come back to win three more provincial finals over the following three seasons, making it seven out of nine in the 1987–95 period. God, even writing that makes me go pale! It certainly wasn't a period that Kerry people recall with any fondness.

Tompkins had some serious knee injuries in the early Nineties but kept battling back every time. He missed the 1993 All-Ireland final against Derry, a game I have no doubt Cork would have won had he been playing. He was a real game-breaker which was why I was so sorry he wasn't available to me when I joined Kildare.

I often think back to how Tompkins and Fahy would have impacted on Kildare in the early Nineties. Apart from the Louth ambush in 1991, Dublin were the team that undid Kildare the most during that period. They beat us in the 1991 League final, the 1992 and 1993 Leinster finals and the 1994 first round.

That was a very good Dublin team, one that under-achieved by winning only one All-Ireland final, but if Kildare had Tompkins and Fahy, the balance of power would have switched our way. We might even have won an All-Ireland. With Tompkins and Fahy aboard, we most definitely would have beaten Dublin in the 1991 League final. We gave a away a silly goal early on, missed some makeable frees, kicked some bad wides and generally conceded little things which was down to inexperience at the highest level.

Tompkins and Fahy would have sorted that out straight away. If we had beaten Dublin that day, we would have had a right cut at the All-Ireland. Instead, we suffered a narrow loss which raised doubts in players' minds, especially when it came to playing Dublin over the coming seasons. Unfortunately, they never quite disappeared during my first spell in Kildare.

I'm not one to dwell in the past but I can't help thinking how Tompkins and Fahy had such a double impact on my managerial career. Kerry were slipping in 1987 but would still have beaten Cork if they didn't have the Kildare pair. And I believe we would have beaten Galway in the semi-final to set up a clash with Meath in the final.

We had beaten Meath by seven points in the previous year's All-Ireland semi-final. Psychologically, they would have found it much harder against a Kerry team chasing its ninth All-Ireland in twelve seasons than they did against Cork who hadn't been in the final since 1973. Certainly, there's every reason to believe that Kerry would have won the 1987 title only for the Tompkins/Fahy influence on Cork.

In 1988, Kerry lost the Munster final by a point to Cork. Take Tompkins and Fahy out of the equation and we would have certainly won. I know that this is all hindsight but it is important in a double context for me, first with Kerry and then with Kildare.

In effect, they broke my heart in two counties! I wonder do they ever regret not returning to Kildare in the early Nineties? I know both were settled in Cork but the prospect of achieving something with their native county must have held its attractions since nothing can ever match that special feeling of winning with your own people. We'll never know for sure what impact they would have had with Kildare between 1991 and 1994, but personally I'm convinced that things would have turned out a whole lot different if they were in white jerseys in those years.

A figure of around £400 (€508) was reputed to have been the cost of the disputed airline ticket which lay behind Tompkins' decision to quit Kildare. It might have looked expensive to the County Board in the immediate aftermath of a championship defeat in 1985, but it was nothing in comparison with what it cost Kildare football over the next ten years. Worse still, it turned out to be a winning Lotto ticket for Cork who were handed an extraordinary talent without even asking. And they claim Kerry is a lucky county!

In effect, what Kildare did was to export two of their finest and brightest without getting anything in return. For a county that has produced so many hard-headed businessmen, it's difficult to understand how they could have been so silly. I can't imagine that happening in Kildare today.

From the Mountains
to the Plains

It didn't end in tears but it wasn't exactly the happiest time of my life either. A strange, eerie feeling hung all around Croke Park which looked more like a building site than a sports stadium. High summer 1994, but already the shadows had lengthened on my first term as Kildare manager.

Once again, Kildare were playing Dublin in a first round Leinster championship replay and this time the pressure was really on. We had drawn the first game on a day it seemed that, somewhere high up in the heavens, somebody had decided that Kildare weren't going to get any breaks while I was in charge. We led by five points at half-time but Dublin came back to draw level as much through our inability to remain solid and secure as to any great outbreak of invention from them. Still, we looked to have finally shaken them off when Ken Doyle kicked the lead point just as the game ticked into stoppage time.

What happened next showed that Kildare still hadn't learned how to close out a game. John O'Leary, cute old fox that he was, took a quick kick-out and Dublin worked their way downfield while the Kildare supporters screamed at the referee to blow the final whistle. It didn't come in time and the ball was transferred to Charlie Redmond who kicked a long range equaliser.

There were two ways of looking at the result. It could have been regarded as Kildare's best performance against Dublin in the championship for several years or it could be seen as a lost opportunity. Actually, it hovered somewhere in between, but by the time we came back for the replay 13 days later, the pendulum had swung very much Dublin's way. It was as if the Kildare players had given it their best shot first time out but, having failed to finish the job, they were beset by negative thoughts.

In Kerry, we always think we'll win replays. So much so, that the opposition tend to very often think the same which is a great boost to Kerry. After all, if you walk with a swagger, people will assume you know where you're going. Unfortunately, such positive thoughts didn't fit easily into Kildare minds in the early Nineties.

Dublin took us apart in the first half of the replay and were nine points clear at half-time. There were days when I'd stood on the sideline in Croke Park watching Kerry destroy Dublin but now I was on the receiving end. I'm standing there, unable to do anything to change the flow, and wondering to myself was this what I had given the last four years of my life for? Long journeys from Waterville, non-stop training, planning, working, scheming and hoping, and now it had come to this.

Dublin were so superior in the first half that it looked like seniors v juniors. We improved after that and a Niall Buckley penalty goal helped cut the margin to three points but it was as close as we came and Dublin ran out fairly easy winners.

I couldn't wait to get out of Croke Park afterwards. The field of dreams looked dreary and uninviting. My Kildare adventure was over – for then at least – and I was convinced, at the time, that I'd never be back with them. Losing to Dublin for a third successive year was hard to take. Kerry had won so much against Dublin in the decade between 1975 and 1985 that I wouldn't be the most popular man in the capital. When I took over in Kildare, it was as if the Dubs saw it as payback time. I always felt that my presence in the Kildare camp was a huge motivator for Dublin which was fair enough. Also, they did have a very good team around then, but that didn't make three defeats in successive years any easier to take.

Dublin weren't the only ones happy to see Kildare fail to make the breakthrough. From day one, the GAA authorities took a jaundiced view of my involvement with Kildare, despite the fact that it helped to greatly increase interest, even in League games. For instance, a crowd of 44,532 – the largest since 1968 when Down beat Kildare – turned out for the Dublin v Kildare League final in 1991, so it was clear that the public had bought into the hype. Still,

I have no doubt that every time Kildare lost a major game some very important people in the GAA lit a candle in thanksgiving.

What disappointed me even more was the manner in which certain elements within the County Board had turned against me in Kildare. There had been a controversy after the 1993 championship over the appointment of selectors and maybe that was the time for me to go. But any time I thought like that, people I knew and respected insisted that I ignore the minority who were making more noise than sense. What did they want or expect from me?

I had given the job a crazy level of commitment, driving thousands of miles, day and night, up and down to Kildare. Even when I wasn't doing that or overseeing training, my mind was always ticking over trying to figure out how to get an extra edge for and from the team. There were days when I thought everything was in place only to have a few lads not quite reach peak performance, days too when we simply didn't perform or had no luck. But I would also be honest enough to admit that, after winning the 1991 League final, a very good Dublin grabbed Kildare in a psychological headlock and held them there. For all that, considerable progress had been made in Kildare in the 1991–94 period, yet some on the County Board and others in key positions with clubs seemed quite happy to dump all the blame outside my door with the message: 'Fix that Micko.' Maybe it was a Kildare thing at the time. Shift the blame without ever wondering why the county wasn't producing enough good young players to feed into the senior side.

Despite all the negativity, one thing kept me going. I always felt I had the backing of the players and the vast majority of Kildare people which was fiercely important to me. They remained warm towards me throughout and, while they were as disappointed as those of us inside the camp when things went wrong, they were sensible enough to know that there were no easy solutions to a malaise that had infected Kildare football for a long time before I ever arrived in St Conleth's Park. After all, it wasn't my fault that Larry Tompkins and Shea Fahy were down in Cork sporting red jerseys rather than wearing the Lilywhite of their own county.

When the final whistle sounded at the end of the 1994 replay with Dublin, I felt very low. I had come to Kildare with a plan and a mission in mind and, four seasons on, it hadn't yielded anything in terms of titles. I still believed in the squad but I felt that it was time to go. Anyway, even if I wanted to stay, I'm not sure it would have been greeted with much enthusiasm by the County Board.

I thanked the Kildare players in the dressing room afterwards and walked out the door into a posse of waiting journalists. I told them I'd be back in a minute and promptly headed for home. I have always been conscious of the responsibility to talk to the media after games but I just wasn't in the humour this time. For once, I had nothing to say. The journalists could draw their own conclusions as to why I had left so quickly and those of them who knew me well did. They knew my reign was over.

Some hours later, I rang the County Chairman, Jack Wall, and informed him that I was finished. It came as no surprise to him. I always got on well with Jack who was an outstanding chairman. He was extremely gracious that night too, which I appreciated. I got on with the County Secretary, Séamus Aldridge, too. Putting it at its most diplomatic, we didn't always agree on things but I had no problem with that. I always found him to be straight and direct; we knew where we stood with each other which is always a good basis for a relationship in any walk of life.

My first spell with Kildare really was an incredible rollercoaster. From those crazy days in early September 1990 when news of my impending move to Kildare first broke, to that forlorn Saturday in July 1994 when it ended on a disappointing low, there was rarely a dull moment.

But then that was always certain to be the case because, after being involved with Kerry for so long, everything I did was going to be scrutinised, analysed, dismantled and dissected. And, of course, misrepresented if it suited a particular agenda. Everybody had their say, from the cynics who claimed I was in it purely for the money, to those who wanted to see Kildare succeed, to those who were happy that they didn't in case I got any of the credit.

I didn't give a damn what anybody thought. All I wanted was to create something in Kildare, a county I always admired in football terms. I would do it my way and see what happened. That's always the policy I have operated in life and it hasn't served me badly. Worry about what others think or say and you'll wrinkle very easily and long before your time.

It has helped, of course, that my love affair with Gaelic football is based on a form of madness that I have never come remotely close to fathoming. What else, except a complete and blinding obsession, would convince me to take over in Kildare 14 months after ending such a long term in Kerry?

I genuinely thought that when I stood down in Kerry the week after Cork beat us in the 1989 Munster final, my days as a county manager were finished. After all those years when football consumed so much of my waking time, I planned to settle back to a more normal lifestyle at home in Waterville, play a lot of golf, buy a boat, lobster pots and fishing nets, and go into fishing in a big way.

All belonging to me had been in the fishing business, in particular my uncles, the Galvins, so seafaring was very much in my blood. So, of course, was Gaelic football but I thought at that stage that it would take second place to the fishing – for a while at least. And it would have too, if a few people in Kildare didn't have the daft notion that maybe they would try to lure me up there.

Kildare were going badly back then. They had lost a Leinster championship game to Wicklow by 1-7 to 0-6 in June 1990, a dismal result that looked even grimmer when Dublin easily beat Wicklow in the next round. The fallout in Kildare was quick and explosive. Pat Fitzgerald, a man I knew from his successful playing days with Offaly (he was on the team that beat Kerry in the 1982 final!), had been manager and quickly became the fall guy. I wasn't aware of it at the time, but the criticism he took at a County Board meeting was ridiculously unfair. You would think from some of the comments that he had done his best to wreck Kildare, instead of which he had put his heart and soul into what was a very difficult job.

His resignation led to a rethink about the direction Kildare should take. Early in 1990, a supporters' club had been set up which would turn out to be the first important step in a long journey of rediscovery. It included some heavy hitters on its executive, men such as Gus Fitzpatrick, Seán Conlon, Paddy O'Loughlin, Dermot Murphy, John White and Pat Mangan.

Best of all, it had Michael Osborne, the main man in Kildangan Stud, as its Chairman. Apart from being shrewd businessmen, they all shared a common passion for Kildare football and were driven by the sole motivation of doing their best to create a climate in which it could flourish.

Around the middle of August 1990, I got a few informal phone calls to see if I had any interest in taking the Kildare job to which I responded with an emphatic 'No'. Me? Go to Kildare? No thanks. There was golf to be played, businesses to run and fish to be netted. And if I had any time left over for football it would be spent with Waterville. Kildare could sort out their own problems.

Then Michael Osborne rang and started talking about the potential in Kildare. He had come to Waterville several times over the years to play in various golf classics so I knew him quite well. He asked if I would meet himself and his committee. I agreed, as much out of politeness and curiosity as anything else because I had no intention whatsoever of becoming involved with Kildare. Nevertheless, I found myself heading for the Dunraven Arms Hotel in Adare one evening in late August to meet this group of football-mad Kildare men who would try to convince me that things were beginning to look up in the county.

It wasn't an easy argument to make as Kildare hadn't won a Leinster senior title since 1956 and had even fallen out of the habit of reaching finals. Osborne and his committee painted a positive picture but I wasn't persuaded. Various names had been mentioned in the papers as possible successors to Fitzgerald and I wondered if they were asking me because they had been turned down by their first choices. They assured me that this was not the case. Nonetheless, I told them I wasn't interested but I would give them a hand to set up a system that might push things along. I felt that might get them off my case. It didn't.

In fact, I had fallen for the bait, even if I didn't know it at the time. I left the meeting still thinking that my only input would be to take a look at Kildare's structures and suggest a few areas which might be improved. However, they had spotted a weakness and were going to exploit it.

Michael Osborne rang early next morning and asked if I would give them six months. I met them again and they became even more persuasive. They had obviously sensed that I was beginning to weaken. Would I manage the team for even one season? The thought of travelling between Waterville and Newbridge didn't exactly fill me with delight but the bloody football bug had bitten again. Very deep too.

Logic was telling me not to take the job because of the time factor and the extent of the challenge with a team like Kildare whose confidence levels were low. Still, another little voice grew progressively louder: 'Go on, give it a shot. Sure the boats can wait – there will still be plenty of fish in the sea when you're finished with football. You had marvellous years with Kerry but they're over now. Why not see how you get on with a squad and a county that's down on their luck?'

Word spread very quickly that I was being linked with Kildare. Secrets don't last for long, even among the smallest groups, and very soon I was being hounded by the media. Some of my friends actually thought it was a wind up when they heard about the Kildare link. Waterville to Newbridge? Surely not – even for that lunatic.

Just as I have done all my life, I trusted my instincts and decided to take up the Kildare challenge. It might have looked like a strange time to join them but actually the reverse was true. The defeat by Wicklow had left the county numb with despair so things couldn't get any worse. I had also noticed that they had put some decent under-age teams together. They might not have won a whole lot but they had some good young players who would fit neatly into the evolving scheme once they matured.

It's important to look at where Kildare stood in pecking order at the end of 1990. They had won just two games over the previous five Leinster senior championships. They had even lost to Kilkenny in an O'Byrne Cup game in 1988 which was as low as it got for a county that prided itself on a fine football tradition.

The trouble was that the tradition had been established in the 1919–35 period when they won three All-Irelands and eight Leinster titles. All that followed was a Leinster title in 1956. They had won very little at under-age level either. A few months before I took over in 1990, Kildare lost a Leinster minor final to Meath by 13 points which wasn't exactly encouraging although, as things turned out, that team provided me with four lads who would develop into fine senior players: Glenn Ryan, Niall Buckley, Christy Byrne and Ronan Quinn.

So, while there was always a great interest in football in the county, the return was poor after the glory spell that ended in the 1930s. But none of that figured in my thinking when I arrived. My successes with Kerry obviously convinced Kildare people that the county was about to undergo a miraculous transformation because a huge crowd turned out in Newbridge for the county final between Naas and Clane. So did half the national media. In fact, there has probably never been a county final that attracted such widespread interest.

There was a carnival atmosphere in Newbridge and I couldn't have got a more rousing reception if I had just been elected Pope. All very nice but I knew how much hard work lay ahead. The sheer scale of it became apparent when we played Galway in a tournament game in Newbridge at the end of the month. A humdrum game between two ordinary sides, nobody could possibly have imagined how exciting the decade would eventually turn out for both.

Only a few hundred people turned out for that match, but a week later St Conleth's Park was heaving for our first League game against Leitrim. We were in Division Two but, judging by the number of media people around, the clash was regarded as the match of the day. Leitrim, who were in the early stages of putting a right good team together, harnessed the hype a lot better than us and won by three points. God, what had I let myself in for?

It turned out to be a temporary glitch as we picked up from then on which was encouraging because, apart from Leitrim, the group also included Tyrone, Derry, Mayo, Antrim, Longford and Cavan. It was during that winter that I began to realise just how fanatical the Kildare support really was. Even our furthest 'away' games were well supported. Some supporters travelled on the day, others made overnight stops, but either way it was clear that their love affair with football was the real thing. We played Kerry once or twice in challenge games too and it was remarkable to see how many people travelled from Kildare to Killarney. It certainly helped make the players begin to feel special which, in turn, raised their self-esteem.

We won five of seven games to finish in joint second place in the 1990/91 League. In those days, scoring averages or difference weren't used to decide who qualified or who were relegated when they had the same number of points. Instead, it went to a play-off which left us facing Leitrim again, this time in Navan. It was exactly what we needed. The more games we got the better, as it was important to keep building the momentum which we certainly did against Leitrim.

There were at least 7,500 in Páirc Tailteann for that play-off game, the majority of which came from Kildare, but it looked for a long time as if Leitrim would wreck the day. Indeed, it took a great second half performance to turn things around but, in the end, we won by six points to reach the quarter-final. Things were beginning to take shape much quicker than I had anticipated.

It was as if the gods had planned it all along because that win meant we would be playing Kerry in the quarter-final. For the first time, I would find myself up against many of the lads I knew so well. I would get used to it over the years but I felt extremely self-conscious coming out in Croke Park in Kildare gear for that League semi-final.

Managing against your native county is a strange sensation. The pull of your native place can never be eroded yet here you are, trying to plot their downfall. As was usually the case with League games, especially long-distance ones, there weren't many Kerry people there which made it a bit easier, but I still felt awkward. In fairness, though, I got a good reaction from the Kerry supporters. They understood the situation and knew that my presence in the Kildare camp was in no way a betrayal of my birthright.

There was a huge Kildare contingent present but then for months you could sense a rising tide of optimism all around the county.

It needed to be kept in check, of course. It was good to be making rapid progress but expectations can often outstrip reality. We beat Kerry by a point in a fairly nondescript game which got a lot more coverage than it warranted because of my presence in a rival camp.

The upward curve continued a few weeks later when Kildare beat Donegal – also by a point – to reach their first League final since 1968. Nobody realised the extent of the achievement at the time, but 17 months later the vast majority of that Donegal team were aboard the All-Ireland winning side so they were very much on the way up when we beat them in 1991.

The League final against Dublin proved a bridge too far for us. We gave away a disastrous goal to Vinny Murphy after seven minutes which left us chasing the game. Keith Barr was sent off near the end and while we pressed Dublin all the way to the line, they won by two points.

People have often said to me since that we would have been better off had we lost to Donegal in the semi-final as we could have retreated quietly back to the training ground and focused on the trip to Drogheda for the Leinster championship first round game with Louth. They may well be right but you have to play the hand you're dealt and we were very pleased to have got to a League final so quickly.

Louth had finished in third place in their Division Three group but, with home advantage, they were always going to be mighty tricky customers in the championship. We tried to get the game switched out of Drogheda, ostensibly on the basis that the capacity wasn't anywhere near enough to cater for the crowds, but, in reality, we felt that playing there was a huge advantage to Louth. Quite understandably, Louth resisted the move and insisted on their right to host the fixture. They knew that Drogheda was worth three or four points to them and they weren't going to concede that advantage.

Even then we should have beaten them. We led by five points with twenty minutes to go but Louth raised their game and applied ferocious pressure. They drew level with 15 minutes to go and in the end we were beaten by a point after Stefan White fired home a late goal. Total disaster!

There were huge question marks over the legality of White's goal as the move that led to it started with a throw-in around midfield. But just as referee Paddy Collins went to throw up the ball, Séamus O'Hanlon grabbed it from his hand and began the build-up that led to the goal. In my view, play should have been stopped for a proper throw-in.

There were shades of Séamus Darby's late goal in the 1982 All-Ireland final and Tadhg Murphy's strike for Cork in the 1983 Munster final about White's score. I was beginning to wonder if I was destined to spend the rest of my days being caught by bloody late goals.

It was claimed afterwards that Kildare were over-confident going into the Louth game. That's pure rubbish. We knew exactly how tough they would be and planned accordingly. A key setback that day was the absence of full-back John Crofton through injury. His stabilising presence was badly missed but, even without him, we had enough chances to win.

Losing to Louth wrecked our season. There was no 'back door' to resurrect us so all we could do was walk away and start thinking about the next year which, I must admit, seemed an awful long way off as I drove home to Waterville that June evening.

Inevitably, the Louth defeat led to some criticism of me in Kildare. The early euphoria had waned and been replaced by a view (certainly among the more pessimistic wing) that, while some progress had been made in the League, it was a question of 'the same old Kildare' in the championship. That was unfair but clear thinking and balanced judgements aren't exactly plentiful after a county is knocked out of the championship, especially when expectations are raised. Still, I had failed in my first championship which was hard to take, especially given the circumstances.

I decided to not even think about the future for a while but Osborne kept contacting me with the same message: 'Whatever you do, don't leave us now.' He obviously suspected that I might be having second thoughts. Michael wasn't the type of man to take no for an answer. His enthusiasm from day one was so infectious that you couldn't ignore him. He was a pure fanatic.

When I arrived in Kildare, he started naming lots of lads that I should take a look at. There wasn't a player in any grade, in any club in Kildare, he didn't have a view on. My phone would ring on Monday morning and Michael would be on the line telling me excitedly about some player he had seen in a club game over the weekend and why it might be a good idea if I took a look at him.

We were both of the view that it didn't matter whether a player was from a senior or junior club. If he was good enough, he deserved a chance. Some people seem to think that unless a player is from a senior club, he won't make it with a county panel which is plain daft. A player's club is decided by where he was born so why that would have anything to do with his talent is beyond me. Osborne shared that philosophy which is why he regularly brought players from junior clubs to my attention.

His judgement was first class, although we often disagreed about players. Still, he was at his happiest when discussing Kildare and its footballers. He always had this remarkably upbeat way about him and never seemed to harbour a single doubt about Kildare's ability to make the breakthrough.

It was no surprise that the racing boys brought him over to Dubai to head up the operation because he was full of ideas and had the energy and the commitment to see them through. Above all, he had great integrity. His passing left a huge gap in the lives of all who knew him and I don't think that Kildare people ever fully realised how much he did for football in the county.

Tommy Carew, Jack Donnelly and Fr Moling Lennon were my first selectors, men who knew their stuff too, while I always loved talking to Pat Mangan because he always made great sense and was as good a judge of a player – whether from Kildare or elsewhere – as you'll ever get.

As ever though, I made up my own mind on players. I would take myself over to the bank on the side opposite the stand in St Conleth's Park and watch club games on my own. I always had a fair instinct for assessing a player, probably because I was at it all my life. Waterville was a very small club where, at times, we might be drawing from less than twenty players so we had to get the best out of each and every one of them. It wasn't like the big clubs where there were lots of options and choices.

The Waterville experience made me very conscious of the need to squeeze the very best out of every player I came across in Kildare where the pick wouldn't be as wide as in Kerry. It was the same in Laois and even more limited in Wicklow.

When I came to Kildare, they had a mixture of experienced lads like Paddy O'Donoghue, John Crofton, Sos Dowling, Seán McGovern, Bill Sex and Martin Lynch who had been around for a while, as well as some good young lads like Glenn Ryan, Niall Buckley and Anthony Rainbow.

Eyebrows were raised when I brought young Rainbow into the panel. He was as thin as a jockey and didn't look physically ready for senior football but he had marvellous potential. He was tough and wiry; he had pace and determination. He had plenty of guts too and when the whole mixture came together with a bit of coaching, it didn't take him long to establish himself. The fact that he has survived so long at the very highest level is proof positive that he was a very special talent.

I often wonder what would have happened in 1991 if the 'back door' had been open. It's quite possible that Kildare would have resurrected their championship ambitions but, as it was, we were gone by mid-June and had to sit back and watch from afar as the Dublin v Meath saga unfolded. I always felt that Meath were vulnerable after the four games against Dublin. Wicklow had a great chance to beat them but were held to a draw and lost the replay. While Meath went on to win the Leinster title, I believe they were weakened in Leinster after the epic battle with Dublin.

Louth had the beating of Laois in the semi-final but were held to a draw before losing the replay. I'm convinced that, had Kildare got past Louth, we would have beaten Laois and given Meath a right good rattle in the final.

Losing to Louth changed everything in my first year. As usual, a few people had a go at me at a subsequent County Board meeting, claiming that it was a case of one step forward, one step back. I could understand their frustration because, believe me, it wasn't half as intense as what I was feeling myself.

The next three seasons are easily described – Dublin beat us every time in the championship. That was hard to take. Beating Dublin was always a high point during my days with Kerry but I simply couldn't find a way around them in the championship during my first spell with Kildare.

We reached the Leinster final in 1992 and 1993 but lost both. In 1992, which was Kildare's first Leinster final appearance since 1978, we opted to play against a fairly stiff wind in the first half. I reckoned that if we could hold Dublin to a reasonable lead at half-time we would come on strong in the second half because whatever shortcomings the team might have had, a lack of fitness was not among them.

I was criticised afterwards for telling our captain, Martin Lynch, to play against the wind in the first half if he won the toss but it was a calculated decision, which unfortunately didn't come off. Dublin powered up their momentum very early and were nine points clear at half-time. We battled back in the second half, just as I knew we would, and cut the gap to four at one stage but couldn't complete the task and eventually lost by six points.

Dublin did us again early in 1993, in a League quarter-final. So, by the time we headed into the championship, we were beginning to get a bit desperate. It showed in our first game where we were incredibly lucky to beat Wicklow. We had whipped them by 14 points a year earlier so maybe there was a hint of over-confidence in the camp. Whatever the reason, we were stuck to the ground in the first half and came in at half-time trailing by nine points. I remember walking off the pitch and thinking to myself: 'What sort of a bloody fool am I? This crowd have no heart, no soul and no future. And now they're going to embarrass themselves, Kildare and me.' It's hard to be positive when the scoreboard is flashing up 2-7 to 0-4 in favour of an opposition that was walloped a year earlier.

I'm normally quite calm at half-time, even when things aren't going well, but I let rip that day. I told them they were a bloody disgrace and that if they didn't do something about the situation, they could never raise their heads in Kildare again. I was more dismayed than angry. How could such a talented bunch of players allow themselves to be humiliated? This wasn't about tactics or theories. It was about temperament and a sense of self-worth.

In fairness, their response was emphatic. Lynch hit two cracking goals and, while Wicklow hung on doggedly, we won by two points. Just as well because had we lost, the whole lot of us would have been strung up on the Curragh. And rightly so.

We hammered Offaly in the semi-final which was satisfactory on the day because it showed what Kildare were capable of but it also brought some concerns. History has repeatedly shown that a team is better off to scrape through a semi-final and reserve the best for the final. I experienced that in both Kildare and Laois where we looked great in semi-finals but didn't repeat it in finals. That was certainly the case in 1993 when, once again, Dublin beat us in the Leinster final, this time by four points.

Dublin led by seven points at one stage in the second half and, while we rallied and put a fairly respectable look on the scoreboard, the truth was we had come up short against them once again.

What's more, we hadn't scored a single goal against them in a League final and two Leinster finals.

It was very satisfying for the Dublin manager, Pat O'Neill, who had suffered at Kerry's hands as a player during my spell in charge. I had a run-in with him one day during a League game in Newbridge when, it's fair to say, we had a fair and frank exchange of views!

He told me to go back to Kerry, or words to that effect! I gave as good as I got but it showed just how intense the rivalry between Kildare and Dublin had become. I had a lot of respect for O'Neill as a player and manager. He persisted with that Dublin team until they won an All-Ireland in 1995.

Paddy Cullen, another marvellous character, had been in charge in 1991 when Dublin beat us in the League final and were damn unlucky not to have beaten Meath in any of the four games in the Leinster championship. Would Dublin have gone on to win the All-Ireland if they had beaten Meath? It's very possible, in which case Cullen would have been a hero. Instead, it was made very uncomfortable for him after Dublin lost to Donegal in the 1992 final. Dublin people couldn't accept losing an All-Ireland to Donegal so somebody had to shoulder the blame and unfortunately for Cullen, he was first in line. He stood down and O'Neill took over but it would be another three years before Dublin won the title.

One All-Ireland was a poor return for a Dublin team that won four successive Leinster finals. However, it was a whole lot more than Kildare won so by the end of 1993 confidence was beginning to drain away from our camp.

A dispute over selectors followed which wasn't helpful but, to be honest, things were beginning to unravel anyway. We could have done without meeting Dublin so early in the 1994 championship but once we didn't put them away in the drawn game, we were in trouble and they made no mistake second time around.

Much had changed in Kildare during my first stint but the bottom line remained the same. We had failed to win a Leinster title and failed to match Dublin who had taken over from Meath as the pacesetters in the province.

Nobody actually said it to me, but the view in Kildare seemed to be that although they had a reasonably good team, they wouldn't progress any further under my guidance. I didn't share that jugement because I still had great faith in the core of the squad but the repeated failures against Dublin had drained our momentum.

I don't know what would have happened if I had indicated that I was prepared to stay on but I had no intention of finding out. My days of long journeys between Newbridge and Waterville were over, temporarily at least. Although, as I headed home after losing to Dublin in 1994, the thought of returning to Kildare at some stage in the future never arose.

It was back to the Waterville club for me, while Kildare entrusted the next two seasons to Dermot Earley Sr.

Unfinished Business

There's only one thing worse than being half mad and that's fully mad, a condition which probably afflicted me when I agreed to return to Kildare at the end of 1996.

What else could it be? They hadn't exactly wailed for days when I motored home in July 1994. In fact, I had taken a few verbal slaps at a subsequent County Board meeting where some delegates accused me of, among other things, various crimes against football such as not studying the opposition in sufficient detail, of not using the ball enough in training, of not attending club games in Kildare and of not changing the panel more regularly.

Most of the gripes were personally motivated and, in fairness, several delegates spoke in my favour but the reality was that by the end of the 1994 campaign I no longer had the backing or support of the entire county. However, the players were still behind me which was the important thing. Still, when I was asked after the 1996 championship if I would be interested in taking over again I was, to say the least, surprised.

Things hadn't gone very well in my absence. Kildare lost to Louth in the 1995 Leinster championship, a defeat that seemed to have a huge impact on the county's psyche. That match was supposed to be revenge for Louth's smash-and-grab raid in Drogheda in 1991 but instead it turned out to be a tame surrender in Newbridge.

The game was played on a Sunday evening in an experiment for 'live' TV. There was a strange atmosphere in St Conleth's Park, almost as if neither side could figure out how and why they were playing such an important game at such an unusual time. The standard was poor throughout and, while Kildare led by four points at one stage in the second half, Louth rallied to win by two.

Kildare kicked some awful wides, especially in the closing minutes, and looked like a team that had only come together just before the throw-in. I was working as an analyst for RTÉ and hated what I saw. I still had a great affinity with the Kildare players and was sorry to see things go so terribly wrong. It was tough on Dermot Earley too because expectations had risen after a decent League campaign which included that most elusive of prizes for Kildare, a win over Dublin.

It got no better for Earley and, a year later, Kildare fell again at the first fence in Leinster, losing to Laois by five points. Morale was very low in the county after that so they decided it was time to look in my direction again. Besides, with interest in the county team having dropped, the apathy was reflected on the club scene, leading to a serious reduction in income.

That was in marked contrast with the bulging coffers which accompanied my first spell there. All boats in the county had risen on the tide of the early Nineties when Kildare reached two Leinster finals and a National League final but they had dropped back down again. I suspect some senior figures in the County Board reckoned I would help the financial side of things if I managed to lift the scene after the disappointments of 1995 and 1996.

It would have been easy to tell them where to go when they came knocking. Why was I back in demand now when just two years earlier they didn't seem remotely concerned when I left? The answer, I suppose, lay in the harsh reality that whatever signs of progress there had been during my first spell, the following two seasons had been terribly depressing.

The main reason I agreed to return was because I still retained great faith in the players. I had worked with most of them in my first spell and knew at first hand how committed they were. They had always done what I asked of them and almost all had remained loyal to me. Indeed, in the intervening years, I constantly found myself drawn to everything that was written about Kildare and on match days their result was among the first I listened out for. You don't spend four seasons with any group without building a special bond.

I also figured that standards had evened out, not just in Leinster but nationally too. I knew that if I could harness Kildare to their very maximum, they had a fair chance of achieving something. John Crofton, Pat McCarthy and Pat Dunny were my selectors as we set out on an adventure that would provide me and, more importantly, Kildare with some thrilling experiences and no little success.

There's a defining game in the development of most teams and I have no hesitation in saying that the 1997 Leinster quarter-final clash with Laois fitted into that category for Kildare. In fact, it may well have been the greatest victory I ever presided over in my many years as a manager.

An exaggeration? Not really. Consider the context. Kildare hadn't won a first round championship game for a few seasons and were up against a Laois team that had beaten them comfortably a year earlier. If that weren't enough to leave Kildare feeling brittle, they were dealt a shocking blow in the first ten minutes when both Martin Lynch and Johnny McDonald were sent off.

I don't know what the on-line punters would make of it nowadays but I doubt if anybody would have put a bad cent on 13-man Kildare to beat Laois. In fact, it looked as if we would be beaten out the gate and home to Newbridge. With two of our full-forwards gone, Pádraig Graven had to play across the line on his own and, in fairness, he did it very well. He also hit one of those special days with his free-taking, hitting the target with a range of kicks. We needed Graven to be on song that day and he sure was.

Every one of the 13 Kildare men were brilliant, but Glenn Ryan rose above all to produce as good a centre-back performance as I have ever seen. He was inspirational. Left, right or centre, he went in search of work and responsibility and stood so defiantly against the Laois attack that he broke their hearts and spirits. It was as if he was inviting them on to him and then knocking them back. The more they challenged him, the more he responded. It was thrilling to watch.

If that wasn't enough, he slotted a penalty kick past Fergal Byron early in the second half and also kicked two points. We won by 1-11 to 1-7 in what was unquestionably the making of that Kildare team. I have always regarded it as one of the most special occasions in my managerial career because it was a victory very much from the heart. I was privileged to stand on the line and watch a weakened team develop into heroic figures, especially since they had been the victims of whispering campaigns about a lack of real courage when the pressure came on.

It would be remiss of me not to acknowledge the team that won that day as there is no doubt they changed the course of Kildare football.

Christy Byrne; Davy Dalton, Ronan Quinn, Sos Dowling; Anthony Rainbow, Glenn Ryan, Ken Doyle; Niall Buckley, Willie McCreery; Eddie McCormack, Declan Kerrigan, Tom Harris; Pádraig Graven, Martin Lynch, Johnny McDonald.

Substitute: Martin Ryan for Tom Harris.

If Kildare had lost that game, there would have been no Leinster titles for them in 1998 or 2000. That game changed everything and, as it happened, we might have won the Leinster title later on that season but for a Meath team at its dogged best. It took three games and four hours to separate the sides and, in the end, Meath made it through by two points.

We had more than our fair share of chances to beat them, not least in the first replay when we led by six points at half-time in extra-time. It was a sizeable advantage but then Meath substitute Jody Devine hit the most glorious 15 minutes of his career.

Jody would be better known as a running, ball-carrying forward than a finisher but on this particular day it was as if his kicks were radar-directed to the black spot on our crossbar. He kicked four points and Meath added three others to lead before another substitute, Paul McCormack, fisted the equaliser for us.

The tie was beginning to take on the same texture as the Meath v Dublin saga in 1991, only this one ended a game earlier. It turned out to be a controversial affair in which four players were sent off with one decision leaving us particularly aggrieved.

Davy Dalton was dismissed midway through the first half for a foul on Brendan Reilly who, in fairness, took a heavy knock. However, it was completely accidental but the referee, Pat O'Toole of Longford, deemed it otherwise and sent Dalton off. Dalton had called the referee's attention to Reilly's plight and was very upset by the incident which he has always insisted was an accident. Losing Dalton unhinged us and we never really got going in the wet conditions which suited Meath better.

The three games took their toll on Meath who, due to injury and suspension, were without several regulars for the Leinster final where they lost to Offaly, who themselves were beaten by Mayo in the All-Ireland semi-final. If we had beaten Meath in the first game – or even the first replay – we could have gone a long way. However, I think we would have suffered the same fate as Meath had we got through in the third game. It had been an exhausting series of matches so whoever won was going to be extremely vulnerable against Offaly.

After the heroics against Laois and in the first two games against Meath, it was disappointing not to reach a Leinster final but when we analysed the balance sheet, we were very much in profit in terms of getting a settled team, all going in the same direction and with a considerable sense of purpose. With a few new players and some minor adjustments, I knew we would be a competitive force in 1998.

Not everybody shared the view. There were still some people in Kildare who claimed that the team would never make the breakthrough under me but, as ever, I didn't give a damn what anybody thought and, even as the 1997 season wound down, I couldn't wait for 1998 to start.

Apart from the harder edge and greater sense of resolve that Kildare had shown in 1997, there were other reasons why I was confident that there would be further improvement in 1998. Dermot Earley Jr was maturing into a dynamic young player who would provide us with extra options in the midfield/half-forward area while we also acquired the services of Brian Lacey from Tipperary, who was playing for Round Towers, and my own son, Karl. Also, Brian Murphy from Cork, who was playing for Clane, was beginning to show good form.

Lacey was a real find. A tough, tenacious corner-back, he had a great campaign in 1998 and finished up with an All-Star while Karl got the right corner-forward award. Seeing that rumours seemed to accompany me wherever I went, there were plenty stories of how I had poached Lacey from Tipperary. Again, untrue. It was his call. He had joined Round Towers and obviously felt that he might as well take his chance with Kildare as well. In fairness, it was a tempting situation. He knew Kildare had good prospects of making the breakthrough and he wanted to get a shot at the big time which wouldn't have been available in Tipperary. Only the very small-minded would begrudge him that opportunity. Kildare were linked later with another Tipperary man, Declan Browne, and I have to admit that I did suggest to Lacey that he should ask him if he was interested in joining us. What an asset he would have been. Nothing ever came of it, however, as Declan didn't want to leave Tipperary under any circumstances.

Karl's arrival in Kildare came about because of the way he had been treated in Kerry. He had been discarded from the county panel after Clare pulled off their famous win over Kerry in the 1992 Munster final and had never got another chance. He was one of only a few players left off the panel after that game which was very strange because he certainly wasn't the only one responsible for the defeat.

He played some wonderful football for UCC and Waterville later on but he never got a recall for Kerry which was wrong. People will say I'm biased – which I am – but if he was good enough to win an All-Star award in 1998, was he not good enough to be on the Kerry team prior to that? I can't help thinking that the O'Dwyer name and the Waterville tag didn't help his cause. It didn't help my other sons, John and Robert, either. It's awkward for a manager when his sons are pushing for places on the team because if he picks them, he's accused of bias. Yet, he has to be fair to them too. It's a difficult balance to strike.

I was long gone from Kerry by the time Karl forced his way onto the senior team but I always felt he was looked at in a different manner to others. It was certainly very odd that he was discarded so ruthlessly after 1992. As the years passed, it became clear that his Kerry days were indeed over but, like anybody with a bit of ambition, he was still keen to play inter-county football. It provided me with the ideal opening to acquire a player who had a lot to offer.

I knew he could do a fine job for me so I suggested that he should try to get a teaching job in Kildare, which he duly did in Rathangan. He joined the local club which made him eligible to play for Kildare, a move that worked out great for him, me and Kildare.

Mind you, not everybody approved of the move. In Karl's first League outing for Kildare against Cork in February 1998, the reaction from a small section of the crowd in Newbridge was downright hostile. They obviously thought that I had brought him in just because he was my son. They saw him as a Kerry reject who would get into the Kildare team ahead of some local players because of who he was.

The reality was a lot different. He was still only 28 and, if right was right, he would have been on the Kerry panel so he had plenty to offer Kildare. He wasn't fully fit when he first joined us, which accounted for his indifferent performance in his first game, but I knew that he could bring plenty to the team once he was properly tuned up.

Still, it was uncomfortable for me standing on the sideline in Newbridge listening to people behind me throwing barbed comments in my direction any time Karl made a mistake. It was hard on him too because he knew he wasn't being judged in normal terms, but rather as the son of the manager who was also an outsider. We expected the initial bad reaction and we knew that the only way to win people around was for him to perform to the level we both knew he could. As the weeks passed and he improved, the mood changed and he came to be accepted as an important part of the attack. He scored in every game in the 1998 championship so he certainly played his part in turning the season into something special for Kildare. I'm sure he would have preferred to be on the Kerry team but when, through no fault of his own, it didn't happen, he was dead right to press on with his career elsewhere.

He enjoyed some great years with Kildare and nobody could argue that he didn't make a serious contribution. Despite that uneasy first game in which we lost to Cork by a point, he settled in well during the spring of 1998, a period in which we solidified quietly without actually showing our hand for the championship.

After coming so close to Meath in 1997, I knew that things were coming together quite nicely so I wasn't in the slightest bit disappointed when we failed to make the League quarter-finals. We won six of eight games, as did Down and Cork but they both had a better scoring difference than us and took the quarter-final spots. Fair dues to them. I was happy to slip quietly out of the competitive scene in mid-March because there was a championship campaign to be plotted.

The scene in Leinster – and indeed nationally – was beginning to change around then. Kerry were reigning All-Ireland champions but there was a feeling that they won a fairly handy title in 1997.

They didn't even have to beat Cork in Munster as Clare took care of that in one of those big upsets that happen from time to time.

Cavan came through in Ulster for the first time in many years but the All-Ireland semi-final occasion got to them. They did well for the first half against Kerry but fell away after that. Kerry went on to beat Mayo in an All-Ireland final remembered for Maurice Fitzgerald's excellence but again, they didn't have to do anything particularly special as Mayo (not for the first or last time) under-performed on the big day.

Leinster was wide open going into 1998. Dublin were in transition; Meath were solid but beatable; Offaly had won the League for the first time but had their weaknesses too, as had Laois. So, from where I looked at it, Kildare had a right good chance against any of them. I didn't know at that stage that Galway were regrouping and would arrive, virtually overnight, to be the biggest problem of all.

Still, Leinster was the first aim for the year and, if Kildare succeeded there, we'd take our chances with the rest. The jigsaw was coming together. The question was, could we complete the picture?

Breakthrough and
Breakdown

So, what would I do differently if I could rewind the clock to Sunday evening, 30 August 1998, after Kildare had beaten Kerry in the All-Ireland semi-final? I'd round up the whole Kildare panel, herd them onto a blacked-out coach under the Hogan Stand and tell the driver to head for Dublin Airport.

There, I would purchase tickets for some quiet, comfortable getaway spot with good sports facilities where we would spend the next few weeks preparing for the All-Ireland final. We would arrive back on the Friday before the game and stay in a quiet hotel for the next two nights. Trips home to Kildare would not be allowed.

Okay, so all that was never going to happen but it gives an indication of the concerns I had from the second Michael Curley blew the whistle to end the semi-final. Suddenly, everything had changed. If the whole of Kildare had blasted into orbit after the Leinster final win over Meath, it was no more than a docking station for the next big adventure which presented itself with the All-Ireland semi-final win.

It was always going to be so. The sheer passion for football in Kildare is so intense that it was inevitable that pride, emotion and expectation would grow into an unstoppable force. It would take on such a crazy momentum of its own in the run-up to the final that there was absolutely no way of controlling it.

Kildare people simply couldn't wait for Sunday, 27 September to dawn, having spent the previous few weeks in a wild and wonderful whirl where normality was suspended.

And who could blame them? The record books showed that Kildare had won four All-Ireland and eleven Leinster titles prior to 1998 but they were all from a different age. The last All-Ireland had been won in 1928 and the Leinster title hadn't been captured since 1956.

So when the 42-year drought ended in 1998, it was natural for Kildare people to expect that part of the heavenly deal also included Sam Maguire's return after seventy years. I knew that it was never going to be that simple.

But then there was nothing simple about 1998, an amazing year that Kildare people will remember for as long as they live and one that gave me incredible personal satisfaction on a number of fronts. From New Year's Day, I had high hopes that something special would unfold, a view perhaps not shared by the more sceptical wing of the Kildare support who felt the team would continue to come up short.

Even if I wasn't living in the county, I was there often enough to pick up the vibes. The vast majority of Kildare people believed in what I was doing but others muttered about training the team like horses who would gallop all day but who lacked the finishing spurt at the end. In other words, they doubted my tactical approach.

That didn't bother me in the slightest because clearly they didn't understand the reasoning behind the way I had the team playing. Every coach wants to adopt a direct gameplan, moving the ball as quickly and fluently as possible into the scoring area. But he needs to have the players to implement it, which I didn't in Kildare, so I had to devise a system that suited the players I had.

It was built on the highest possible level of fitness which enabled us to play a methodical possession game, working the ball from any part of the field and, hopefully, arriving in a good scoring position. It was painstaking and called for great patience and precision, but it was by far the best tactic for that Kildare team.

Of course, they had some exceptionally talented footballers but they had even more outstanding athletes who were prepared to work as hard as was required to get their fitness levels to a point where they could sustain their efforts at full force from start to finish.

There's no doubt that we exploited the hand pass to the full but it wasn't our only ploy. Besides, other teams used the hand pass too. All the talk after the All-Ireland final was of Galway's direct style but

Gerry McDermott, who was doing statistics for us at the time, had figures to show that they used the hand pass just as much as us.

Our attack didn't have that many natural finishers but we did have lads with a great work ethic and an understanding of how to work the ball methodically and accurately into a scoring position. I knew after 1997 that we needed to sharpen the attack which was why I was so keen to get my son Karl on board. He had a good football brain, was well able to make space for himself and never lacked the confidence to have a shot at goal. Once he got fully fit and formed an understanding with his new colleagues, he was always going to be a considerable asset.

The best natural finisher I came across in Kildare was Johnny McDonald but I wasn't able to get the level of commitment from him that was required and he faded from the scene. It was an awful pity because he was a fine talent with a natural scoring instinct but you need more than that to make it at the highest level. I don't know if Johnny ever realised how much skill he had or how much he could have achieved. I always regarded it as a great loss that he didn't put himself in a position to contribute as much as he could to Kildare football during those exciting years. If he had bought into what we were doing, he might well have been the final link in a long chain. Unfortunately, he didn't and there was nothing I could do about it.

After coming so close to beating Meath in 1997, it was natural that expectations would be high for the following year although I suspect that the general mood around Kildare darkened when we were drawn against Dublin in the first round of the Leinster championship.

Would it be 1991, '92, '93, '94 all over again? Some might have thought that way but not me. The past is always a different world. Whatever you're doing in life, you start from today. By all means bring experiences with you and use them to your advantage, but never allow them to become negative influences.

Yes, we had failed against Dublin in the early 1990s but so what? This was a new era and a fresh opportunity. Besides, the longer any sequence goes, the more likely it is to end and, given that Kildare hadn't beaten Dublin in the championship for 26 years, I was convinced that the break was about to come.

And so it did, albeit by the tightest of squeezes with a draw and a one-point win. Kildare were a fair bit better than Dublin in both games but didn't exploit it on the scoreboard. It was probably down to the psychological hangover of losing to Dublin so often but it worked out in the end, even if we did get a right scare in stoppage time in the replay when a Declan Darcy goal cut our lead to a single point.

Surely, we wouldn't be caught again. We weren't. I could sense a hardening of Kildare's resolve and they held out for a crucial win. It was their first over Dublin in the championship since 1972, the year I played in my last All-Ireland final. Beating Dublin was a huge triumph for the whole of Kildare and, quite naturally, it raised expectations again and they continued on the upward curve when Laois were well beaten in the semi-final.

Kildare v Laois games tend to be tight but this was unusually comfortable for Kildare who won by 11 points to set up a rematch with Meath in the final. A really big day was fast approaching. Kildare had lost eight Leinster finals since the 1956 success which some saw as a negative but which I regarded as irrelevant.

This was a new, confident Kildare who felt very much at ease with themselves. To hell with it, man, it was time to deliver! And they did on 2 August in a game that lived up to all the hype. The Meath team of that era – in fact of most eras – was fiercely resilient and doggedly defiant. They had an unreal ability to claw their way back from seemingly impossible situations. So much so that it became a double asset in that, even when the opposition opened a decent lead, they tended to start looking over their shoulders, waiting for the Meath surge. In a sense, opponents invited it to happen which it regularly did.

We experienced it in that Leinster final too when, after leading by three points with eight minutes left, we allowed ourselves to be pinned back and, before we knew it, Meath had drawn level. There was a time when Kildare teams might have seen that as a sign that the gods were against them again but this lot were different and when Brian Murphy, who had come on as a substitute for the injured Declan Kerrigan, cracked home one of the most vital goals in the county's history, the Leinster famine was over. We added two more points to win by 1-12 to 0-10 and begin one of the biggest parties any county has ever seen.

For once, the rub of the green had gone Kildare's way. Meath had Brendan Reilly sent off with twenty minutes to go and they lost Trevor Giles to injury which definitely made our job easier, although there was such a sense of determination in the side that day that I believe they would have coped with anything. It was typified by a brilliant early save by Christy Byrne which made a bold statement of intent on behalf of the whole team,

Keeping the balance between allowing players to enjoy their success while maintaining a clear view of the challenges that lie ahead is always difficult, but it was next to impossible in a football-mad county like Kildare that hadn't won anything for so long. It was something I wasn't used to either because winning Munster titles with Kerry was never seen as anything more than a stepping stone to the All-Ireland. The Munster trophy was never paraded around the streets of Killarney, but then everything is relative and the scene was very different in Kildare which was obvious from the homecoming after the Leinster final and in the days that followed. It was difficult to take it all in but, from my perspective, I would have to say that I got more enjoyment out of Kildare's Leinster title in 1998 than I did from all my successes as a player and manager with Kerry. I would also regard it as the number one achievement in my career.

All the talk about how I was in Kildare for the money and how I had got things wrong in my first stint there became totally irrelevant. And yes, there was a huge sense of personal satisfaction in watching my son play such an important role in Kildare's breakthrough. His career with Kerry had completely run aground so it was great for him and the rest of the family that he proved himself good enough in another county in a different province. Not that we ever doubted it, unlike those in Kerry who shamefully closed the door on him in 1992 and never let him back in.

Having finally reached the All-Ireland semi-final after such a long absence, I suppose it was inevitable that Kerry would await us. Not only that, they were All-Ireland champions! And they were managed by a certain Páidí Ó Sé, a man who, shall we say, was known to me! They were the last team I wanted to meet, not because of their all-round strength but because it left me in an awkward position.

Nobody ever had more pride in the green-and-gold than me, so finding myself plotting against it in an All-Ireland semi-final posed a whole new challenge. All the more so, since Karl was also facing a huge personal test against a team he felt he should have been part of.

There was only one solution for both of us. We had to block out the past and focus purely on what we wanted to achieve. No doubt, there were people in Kerry who regarded me as a traitor but that was their problem. Anyway, business is business and I owed it to the Kildare squad who had worked so hard, and to the Kildare public who had backed me, to do absolutely everything in my power to beat Kerry. For those few weeks, I had to be a Kildare man to my very soul, after which I could revert to being a Kerryman in charge of Kildare, which is a different class of person altogether.

Managing the hype after the Leinster final was almost as demanding as preparing the team. There were four weeks until the semi-final which gave us a chance to settle back into a controlled routine, even if it had to be played out in a whirl of publicity and anticipation. However, we ran into a problem which was to prove very damaging to our prospects of winning the All-Ireland.

Niall Buckley picked up an injury which ruled him out of the Kerry game and proved mighty slow to clear afterwards. We compensated for Buckley's absence against Kerry by switching Dermot Earley to midfield and bringing Ken Doyle into the half-forwards. Earley was having an excellent campaign, while Doyle was one of those wonderfully versatile players you could slot in virtually anywhere.

Buckley was a fierce loss but by now there was a maturity about the team that enabled them to compensate for the absence of any one player. It was when we lost more than one and had others carrying niggles, as happened for the All-Ireland final, that the lack of real depth in the squad began to show.

Our game with Kerry was a marvellous contest. We led by a point at half-time, extended the advantage to five in the third quarter, only to see it cut back to one after John Crowley poached a goal. Brian Lacey was doing a superb marking job on Maurice Fitzgerald which gave us a great psychological lift and, even when Crowley's goal went in, there was no panic in our ranks. We went three points in front again but Maurice cut it back to one as the final seconds ticked away. It looked like one of those games that would end in a draw but we held out amid unbearable tension.

We got a lucky break with five minutes left when Denis O'Dwyer flicked the ball to our net. However, after what seemed an interminable consultation between Michael Curley and his umpires, the goal was disallowed. Naturally, we were convinced that the officials were right but, in fairness, it was a marginal call which probably decided the match. And yes, if we had a goal disallowed in similar circumstances, I would have been very disappointed.

Kerry, as you would expect, didn't complain about it afterwards. They take the breaks when they go with them and accept it when they don't. I felt self-conscious as I walked into the Kerry dressing-room to say a few words afterwards. Páidí had visited the Kildare dressing room and joked about how I had come back to haunt him. It was tough for him but he was very gracious.

I wanted to hit the right mood in the Kerry dressing room but it wasn't easy as I looked around and saw Páidí with such great players as Maurice Fitz, Séamus Moynihan, Darragh Ó Sé, Declan O'Keeffe, John Crowley and Dara Ó Cinnéide all sitting there with devastated looks on their faces.

I can assure you that I was in no way gloating. I said my piece and left, hoping they understood how I felt, even if I wasn't quite sure myself. However, I'm convinced of one thing. If Kerry had won that day, they would have beaten Galway in the final. They were far more experienced than Galway, having won three Munster titles and one All-Ireland in three seasons, and that would have counted.

Don't get me wrong – that was a fine Galway team who would have gone on to win All-Irelands anyway, but I don't believe it would have been in 1998 had Kerry been in the final.

If keeping the lid on things was difficult after the Leinster final, it was totally impossible once we reached the All-Ireland final. Kildare had been a pressure cooker all summer and now the lid blew off completely. We had beaten Kerry, Meath and Dublin, the All-Ireland winners from the three previous years, something which hadn't been done for a very long time. It was only natural that the supporters began to assume nothing could stop the march to the title.

Fields, buildings, roads, offices and houses became shrines to Kildare football as the supporters embraced the county team like never before. In a sense, the players were smothered by the sheer scale of the interest. It was utterly impossible to live in Kildare at that time and not be affected by the hype. I would have loved to take the squad away from it all but it wasn't really an option so we had to work away as best we could.

We had plenty to occupy us too. Buckley's injury was proving a lot more troublesome than we initially thought and then, to add to our problems, full-back Ronan Quinn had a groin problem. The combination of both would cost us the final. I was concerned too about the manner in which Kildare people were dismissing Galway. It was as if Galway were regarded as mere facilitators in our march to the All-Ireland, a role I knew damn well they wouldn't act out.

I had endured enough bad days against Galway to realise that they're a big-day county who never lack self-belief. Granted, they disappointed in All-Ireland finals in the 1970s and again in 1983 but this was a new set-up with an experienced manager in John O'Mahony. Worryingly too, they had enjoyed a quiet, low-key passage to the final which made them extremely dangerous.

They were actually quite lucky to have progressed so far, having come mighty close to losing to Roscommon in the drawn Connacht final in Tuam. Roscommon led by a point late on and could have won a close-in free which would have secured victory when Gary Fahy appeared to touch the ball on the ground. However, in a stroke of luck which any team needs in a championship campaign, referee Séamus Prior adjudged that Fahy had been fouled and awarded a free out. Galway worked the ball upfield and won a free which Niall Finnegan pointed.

The replay was just as tight, going to extra time before Roscommon gifted Michael Donnellan the goal that settled the tie. Derry had won the Ulster title and travelled down to Dr Hyde Park to check out their prospective All-Ireland semi-final opponents. They were so dismissive of what they saw that they had a right good party that night. They were convinced that Galway were several notches below them and quickly removed all worries as they set about enjoying themselves on the overnight stop in Sligo.

Three weeks later, Galway demolished Derry far more comprehensively that the five-point winning margin suggests. For all that, it was impossible to convince Kildare people that Galway would be anything more than willing participants in the Lilywhite coronation. Kildare were 4/9 favourites and there wasn't much money going on Galway at 9/4. Well, not in Kildare anyway.

The whole scene had gone daft in Kildare. There were even suggestions that house prices would rise in the county if they won the All-Ireland on the basis that its new-found status would attract more people to live there. That was the sort of crap we had to endure and those of us who were trying to keep some sense of perspective knew we were fighting the ultimate in losing battles.

The media honed in on Kildare like never before which meant we were in the papers, radio and TV every day. That was exactly what John O'Mahony and Galway wanted. They could play the role of wide-eyed innocents coming to Croke Park to enjoy the day when, in reality, they were in the perfect position as outsiders.

I was constantly reminding the Kildare players of the need to remain as detached as possible from the hype but I'm not sure I got through. When lads are living in an environment where everybody is telling them they're about to be crowned All-Ireland champions, it's next to impossible for them to remain unaffected.

And all the time we had the Quinn and Buckley worries. If that wasn't bad enough, Glenn Ryan did himself some damage while out for a walk on a golf course on the Friday before the final. God almighty, who had we upset so badly that everything started to come against us?

I couldn't believe it when I heard that Ryan had a problem in his lower back and thigh. He was the rock, the anchor, the captain and the inspiration. We needed him at full power yet here he was, two days before the All-Ireland, barely able to move. If it was anybody else except Ryan, I might have thought that nerves were getting to them but that would never have been the case with him. The man had the heart of a lion so, if he said he was injured, I knew it was true.

I am usually able to find positives in even the worst of situations but not this time. In fact, once I heard the devastating news that Ryan was in trouble, serious doubts set in. There was a limit to how many hits we could take and, as the injuries piled up, I realised we were rapidly running out of options. I phoned a good friend of mine in Leixlip who I knew had backed Kildare heavily and suggested that he should lay it off. Our luck really had taken a drastic series of turns for the worse.

Ryan would eventually be passed fit to play but there was no way he could be the dominating figure he had been all season. We also decided to gamble on Buckley which I still regard as one of the biggest selection mistakes I ever made. 'Nuxer' was one of the most naturally talented players of his generation and a great asset when fully fit. He couldn't train much in the weeks before the All-Ireland but we took a chance that his skills would carry him through the day. It was the wrong call. We had beaten Kerry without him and should not have started him against Galway.

I suppose we were influenced to some degree by Quinn's absence at full-back. We didn't want to go in without two key men so we leaned towards playing Buckley in the hope that it would work out. It didn't. We started him at midfield alongside Willie McCreery but it was clear from early on that he was struggling. We moved him to left half-forward later and brought Earley to midfield but that didn't work out either. Buckley should have been well able to give Galway captain Ray Silke a hard time but he made no real impression.

It was tough on Buckley because, at full fitness, that would have been his stage. Instead, he couldn't impose himself on the game which was very frustrating. We should never have put him in that position. Brian Murphy, the man who kicked the crucial goal against Meath in the Leinster final, would have been a better starting option with Earley going to midfield. We brought Murphy on in the second half and he made such a difference that I deeply regretted not starting him.

With Quinn missing from full-back, we opted to bring John Finn back from right half-back and replace him with Sos Dowling. We were criticised afterwards for putting Sos on Michael Donnellan who had burst onto the scene as one of the real finds of that era.

Sos had been the regular corner-back but had lost out to Ken Doyle for the final. However, when Quinn pulled out and Finn had to move to full-back, we decided to leave Doyle in the corner and start Sos in the half-backs. I still believe there was nothing wrong in that. Donnellan did cause problems but he would have troubled anybody that day. The move he started in the left corner-back position, and continued up the field with a series of passes and returns before setting up a point, is still shown regularly on TV as one of the great GAA moments of modern times. It undoubtedly was but it's ridiculous to claim that it wouldn't have happened if somebody other than Dowling had been marking Donnellan.

There were lots of other Kildare players on the field as Donnellan went on his run so why didn't they intercept him? Anyway, after all that we came back to lead quite comfortably just before half time so all this talk of Donnellan's run defining that All-Ireland is pure rubbish.

I don't want in any way to take away from Galway who were a fine team, but that final was decided by the injuries to Quinn, Buckley and Ryan. If we had Quinn at full-back, Finn in his usual wing-back position, Ryan in full flow at centre-back and Buckley at the peak of his powers at midfield, we would have won. There's absolutely no doubt about that. But then luck had held Galway's hand all year and it sure as hell wasn't going to let go in the final.

Instead, we had to improvise all over the place. No team could afford to take a triple hit like that and show no ill-effects. Still, we put ourselves in a great position when we led by 1-5 to 0-4 coming up to half-time, having settled down after a slow start and Galway going three points clear.

Galway shaved a point back just before the break which was important as it gave them an impetus that they carried into the second half. There's no point trying to deny it – they destroyed us in the third quarter. Pádraic Joyce's goal set the scene and with Ja Fallon kicking some great points from left and right, they raced into a five point lead.

We still had chances to get back into the game. Brian Murphy and Dermot Earley came mighty close to scoring goals which would have changed everything but it seems Galway's name was on the title from a long way back. Maybe even as far back as when they got that crucial free out against Roscommon in the drawn Connacht final.

It's easy to play the blame game when you lose. I was blamed for putting Dowling on Donnellan, the impact of which was totally exaggerated. Besides, we switched Anthony Rainbow onto Donnellan and it didn't make any great difference. I was blamed too for leaving Martin Lynch in at corner-forward where he was having a thin time against Tomás Mannion. Lynch had been our best player in that championship but it didn't go for him in the final so there was no point in bringing him outfield. It was just one of those days for him when nothing went right. Undoubtedly, if Buckley had been fully fit and playing well, Lynch would have thrived because 'Nuxer' was a great deliverer of the ball who had the ability to lay a 50-yard pass on a colleague's chest. We badly missed that in the final.

You can analyse that final – which incidentally was one of the best for a very long time – all you like, but it still boils down to the fact that injuries, as opposed to tactics, undermined Kildare. I'm not trying to belittle Galway's success in any way because any team that wins an All-Ireland deserves it but, unfortunately for us, we just weren't in a position to do ourselves justice on the biggest day of all.

It wasn't the first day, or indeed the last, that Galway thwarted me. Two years later we met them again – this time in the All-Ireland semi-final – and lost out again. I was really angry after that game because I felt we had been the victim of a dreadful refereeing decision by Paddy Russell which cost us the game. It was all square with 15 minutes to go when John Finn slid in on Michael Donnellan near the sideline. It was a wet day so players could expect some leeway, especially when there was no malice as there most certainly wasn't with Finn's challenge.

However, he had been booked earlier and Russell sent him off on a second yellow. I was fuming because it was a total over-reaction by the referee, one that left us a man down. I was also angry with John O'Mahony who seemed to me to be telling Donnellan to stay down after the challenge. I don't know if that influenced Russell but he looked on the incident in the worst possible light and dismissed Finn. It was a bad call. The referee should have taken the conditions into account. Besides, Finn was anything but a dirty player but he still didn't get the benefit of the doubt. Donnellan caused all sorts of problems from there on and we lost by three points which was very frustrating.

What made it all so infuriating was that we had worked incredibly hard to get to the All-Ireland semi-final, having played no fewer than five games in Leinster. We were desperate to make up for 1999, a season which passed us by completely. It was a total anti-climax after 1998 and, despite reaching the League quarter-final, there was no time during that season when I felt the mood or the application came anywhere near the previous year. And once again, we were crippled by injuries.

We lost League games fairly heavily to Monaghan and Meath but still managed to squeeze into the quarter-finals where we were walloped by Dublin. They led by 11 points early in the second half and, while we pulled back two goals, they were always comfortably in control. It was a sign of things to come. The listlessness continued into the championship where Offaly sensed that we were there for the taking in the first round. They beat us by four points, leaving a long idle summer ahead which was such a contrast to the previous year.

There was speculation that I would quit but I didn't think about it all that seriously because I still believed in the squad and reckoned that if we could fire up the enthusiasm again, and escape from the injury curse, we were as good as any other team in Leinster at least. I felt, however, that the scene needed to be spiced up and decided to change my selectors. John Crofton, Pat McCarthy and Pat Dunny had done a great job over the previous few years but there comes a time when you need new voices around you.

It's never easy to tell selectors that they're not required anymore but when you take a manager's job you have to be prepared to make the hard calls. I would have kept McCarthy on, but with the other two gone he felt it wouldn't be right to stay on board. Crofton was very put out by my decision which I could understand but I had to do what I thought was right for the team. Dunny accepted that it was time to freshen things up which was the sole reason I made the changes in the first place.

JJ Walsh and Paddy Byrne came in and I have to say they brought a new energy to the scene which showed up very prominently in the 2000 championship. It was a very enjoyable summer as the camp was bouncing again and, after 1998, they knew the levels they could reach.

Louth tested us in the quarter-final but we got home by three points before Offaly staged a late rally to grab a draw in the semifinal. We won the replay despite conceding two early goals to set up another Leinster final with Dublin. As ever, it was a tense affair which also ended in a draw, setting up a memorable replay.

If ever anybody wanted proof of how much steel that Kildare team had, it came in the replay. Dublin produced a near-perfect performance in the first half and looked to be out of sight when they led by six points at half-time. Then, in an amazing turnaround, Dermot Earley and Tadhg Fennin scored two goals in the first two minutes of the second half. Few ever thought they would see the day when Dublin would score a single point in the second half against Kildare and end up comprehensively beaten.

There was no great mystery to the revival. It wasn't as if we swallowed any magic potions at half-time, nor did I do the Alex Ferguson 'hairdryer' act. Quite simply, we hadn't performed in the first half so it was a question of quietly and calmly trying to convince lads that they could have a right good go at winning if they got their own game in order.

I have to admit I didn't quite expect such an early blitz but once it came, there was no way back for Dublin. The manner of the victory added another dimension to our self-esteem and I genuinely believed that we had a marvellous chance of winning the All-Ireland. I still believed it with 15 minutes to go against Galway but Finn's dismissal changed everything, not just that day but into the future as well.

It was to be our last big fling. Meath beat us in the 2001 Leinster championship and Sligo dumped us out of the qualifiers. A year later, Dublin beat us by two points in the Leinster final. We did much better than many people expected but there was a whole new momentum about Dublin in Tommy Lyons' first year as manager and, while we pushed them all the way to the finish line, they were that bit sharper.

Lifting beaten provincial finalists for a qualifier tie is always very hard and Kildare certainly weren't right for the subsequent clash with Kerry. We managed to score just 1-5 and lost by double scores. It was the end of an era for me, one that had provided me with many memories and much satisfaction, while at the same time leaving a nagging feeling that the job hadn't been completed. The All-Ireland had eluded us and, while two Leinster titles in three seasons after such a long famine was a measure of success, it couldn't disguise the continued absence of an All-Ireland title.

It just wasn't to be, it seems. Too many little things went against us, things over which we could have no control.

Hijacked on the Home Run

❛Are you sure Laois are playing at all? Sure, where are all the people? All I can see is green.'

I'm walking up from Portlaoise town towards O'Moore Park with Declan O'Loughlin and his son Billy on a pleasant summer Saturday in early July 2002 and there's hardly a Laois jersey or a splash of blue to be seen anywhere. Laois are down to play Meath in a third round All-Ireland qualifier on a double header with Kerry and Fermanagh but, for all the locals seemed to care, it might as well have been a challenge game in January.

There's green everywhere, which is understandable because of Kerry, Meath and Fermanagh playing, so the blue and white of Laois should have stood out, especially since this was a home venue. And it would have, had there been much of it around. Which there certainly wasn't!

'Do Laois supporters not wear their colours?' I asked. 'For God's sake, Declan, what sort of a crowd are ye at all?'

'Ah, there's no confidence around here right now. No one seems to think we have a snowball's chance in hell of beating Meath,' replied Declan rather gloomily. He had suggested that I accompany him to the games, and with Kerry playing too it was a grand idea. In hindsight, I suspect that he might have had other plans hatching in his mind but he didn't mention them to me. Not that day anyway.

But then he couldn't. I was still in charge of Kildare, busily preparing for the Leinster final against Dublin eight days later. Kildare were chasing their third Leinster title in five seasons and I was quite confident they would win it. Even so, I had made up my mind that it would be my last year with them but I can honestly say that the prospect of moving to Laois – or anywhere else for that matter – had never crossed my mind. The plan was to step away from football, for a while at any rate.

I had known Declan O'Loughlin from his playing days with Laois in the late Seventies and early Eighties, a period in which Laois were unlucky not to win a Leinster title. He often came down to Waterville to play golf and over the years we had become friendly. After I took over in Kildare, I came across him quite a lot, either in his hotel in Portlaoise, on the golf course with Arthur French, another good friend of mine who had played club football with Declan in Leixlip, or on the football circuit.

Anyway, as we approached the ground that Saturday afternoon I was still commenting on how few Laois colours were around. Even those who were wearing them seemed to have a 'hang-dog' look about them, almost as if supporting their county was a chore to be endured rather than an occasion to be enjoyed. There weren't fifty Laois jerseys to be seen which I thought was unbelievable for a county with such a fine footballing tradition. Besides, Laois had been doing so well at under-age levels in the previous few years that I couldn't understand why they hadn't made more progress at senior level.

It was more frustrating for the Laois players and management than anybody else because of the widespread view that there was plenty of talent in the county. Sensing my surprise at the apathy which clearly existed among the Laois public and which wouldn't have gone unnoticed by the squad as they entered the ground, Billy O'Loughlin popped up with a bold statement.

'Mick, you're going to see some of the best young players in the country here today,' he remarked triumphantly.

Kildare manager or not, I couldn't miss the chance to mention the homeland.

'I know, sure aren't Kerry playing?'

'Not Kerry. I'm talking about Laois,' he replied.

As events transpired he was right, even if the Laois players did their best to heavily disguise it that afternoon. Meath beat them out the gate, eventually winning by 11 points. It could have been twenty.

Laois started well but kicked some awful wides in the first ten minutes, and from there on you could see the confidence and the will to succeed draining away from them. It wasn't a pretty sight. It was as if they didn't have the heart for the battle when Meath raised the stakes. You'd have to feel sorry for their manager, Colm Browne, as solid a wing-back as ever played the game and a man who put his heart and soul into his two terms as Laois manager. But, for whatever reason, it didn't happen for him.

Laois didn't score for over twenty minutes in the second half and if their support base was low to start with, it was virtually non-existent by the final whistle. The loyal minority who remained had fallen into a depressed silence while others had made their way back into town long before the end.

I kept a close eye on the Laois players when things were going against them and didn't like what I saw. Some of them were hiding, clearly hoping that the ball wouldn't come their way. You spot the signs very quickly when players are doing that. They run into positions where they know the ball won't, or shouldn't, come and then throw their hands in the air as if totally frustrated when it doesn't. That way, it looks as if somebody else is to blame.

'Look at me. I'm making the runs. I'm trying but the rest aren't responding.' It's a pure con trick but you see it all the time. There were plenty of bad runs and hands waved by Laois players that day as they allowed the life to drain from their season.

There was absolutely no reason why Laois should have been so flat and switched off. They had lost to Offaly by just one point in the Leinster quarter-final and, as Kildare discovered in the semi-final, Offaly were mighty dogged. It took all our will to squeeze them out, eventually getting through by a point after extra time in a cracking replay down in Nowlan Park on a Saturday evening.

Whatever the background or the reason, Laois were woeful against Meath and a little incident at the end offered a clue as to their mindset. The second that referee Paddy Russell blew the final whistle, a Laois forward – I'll spare his blushes by not naming him because he went on to be a really committed player for me – took off from inside his own 14-yard line.

I thought at first that he couldn't wait to get to the dressing-room after such an embarrassing defeat but no, he had other things on his mind. Instead, he galloped a full eighty yards to swop jerseys with Graham Geraghty. Meath had lost to Dublin in the Leinster semi-final a few weeks earlier but were still one of the glamour sides, on the back of a great run during Sean Boylan's second coming in the 1996–2001 era.

Geraghty was one of the highest profile players in the game and was obviously classed as a superior being by this particular Laois forward who wanted his jersey so badly that he was prepared to run half the length of the field to get it. This, after losing so badly! It looked bloody pathetic.

I couldn't help wondering at what stage he had decided he was going to trade jerseys with Geraghty. Before the game? When the pressure came on in the first half? During the long, boring second half? Or was it just a spontaneous thing right at the very end?

It didn't matter a damn because the fact that he was prepared to make such an effort for something so trivial when he had hardly won a ball all day suggested that he saw Laois as second class citizens who should be glad to touch the hem of Meath's garments. The question was – how many of his colleagues thought the same way? Did they all feel inferior to Meath? If so, they had a serious problem. Still, it wasn't mine. Not then anyway.

'What was that, Billy, about seeing some of the best young players? If they're that good, they're doing a mighty good job at hiding it. God almighty, that was shocking bad,' I remarked as we left the ground. To be honest, I thought Laois were brutal.

The O'Loughlins weren't happy, but then no Laois person could have been. Later on that evening, Declan's wife Liz remarked that people would have seen me at the game, sparking rumours if the Laois manager's job fell vacant. I have been well used to rumours all my life and didn't give a damn about a few more, but she was right. A few weeks later, after Kildare were knocked out of the championship, a story appeared in the *Irish Independent* linking me with Laois.

I had indeed been spotted at the Laois game with the O'Loughlins and some inspired guesswork had kicked in. The *Indo* added a two to another two which didn't actually exist at the time, but in fairness they came up with the perfect four, even if it wouldn't add up for a number of weeks. It was good detective work.

After leaving Portlaoise that evening, I put Laois out of my mind and went back to planning Kildare's bid for the Leinster title. Unfortunately, it wasn't to be successful and, as fortune would have it, we were drawn against Kerry in the fourth round of the All-Ireland qualifiers 13 days later.

It's very hard for a team to pick itself up after losing a provincial final, especially one played in front of a full house in Croke Park. They're coming in off a low while the team they're playing in the qualifiers have put a string of victories together. Kerry had lost to Cork in the Munster semi-final a full five weeks earlier and had spent the intervening weeks pumping up their confidence levels with wins over Wicklow and Fermanagh. Okay, so they would be expected to beat both but by the time they came to play Kildare, they had put in a solid month of hard work, interrupted only by what turned out to be target practice against Wicklow and Fermanagh. By now, they were a completely different force to the one that lost to Cork. The qualifiers had given them a chance to restart their season and when that sort of opportunity is presented to a county like Kerry, they don't waste it.

I had a bad feeling heading for Thurles on the last Saturday in July. Kerry had full wind back in their sails while Kildare were flat after losing out to Dublin at the end of a tough Leinster campaign. Kildare battled hard but lacked sharpness and resolve and Kerry won by double scores, 2-10 to 1-5.

The press surrounded me in the dark tunnel in Semple Stadium immediately afterwards, asking if I was finished with Kildare. My replies were vague as I didn't think that was the place to make an announcement, but I could see that the more experienced reporters sensed that they wouldn't be talking to me as Kildare manager again. I think the Kildare players knew it too.

I had completed ten seasons with Kildare in two stints and felt I had no more to give. They probably felt like a change too. The All-Ireland title had remained tantalisingly just outside our grasp but there had been plenty of good days which we would all remember. Now though, it was time for me to move on.

Someone wrote afterwards that Laois were waiting with roadblocks to intercept me as I left Kildare but it wasn't quite like that. Shortly after I let it be known publicly that I was finished with Kildare, I spoke to Declan O'Loughlin and he asked me would I have any interest in the Laois job which was vacant after Colm Browne stood down. I was totally surprised.

Quite honestly, I had never thought about it. Declan talked about the fine, under-age teams that Laois had produced over previous years and how they should be just about ready to mature into really good seniors. I couldn't get the awful performance against Meath out of my head but at the same time, it was clear that football was strong in Laois. Their under-age structure was obviously very good so the talent had to be coming through.

Some time later, Declan came down to Waterville and we played a round of golf. He kept on pressing me about the Laois job and we were joined later by his brother Tom who was on holidays in the area. Tom, the then Laois Football Board Chairman, was equally enthusiastic about getting me to take over. So too was Jim McDonnell, another great Laois football man. They were in the ideal position to move things forward at official level if I decided to have a go, which I eventually did.

Not that I had much choice. I was already feeling the withdrawal symptoms as the bloody addiction that has tied me to football all my life kicked in. It had to get its fix and Laois would provide it. It was going to be a big challenge but I felt ready for it. And so, after talking to Arthur French and a few other close friends, I found myself telling Declan O'Loughlin and Jim McDonnell that I would take on the job.

It was to be the start of another adventure, one where I came across some great characters. None more than Tom Scully, the man I called my 'bodyguard' because wherever we went, he was there. He provided all the fruit for the squad free of charge and would do absolutely anything to help the cause.

To be honest, I think Declan and the other lads were a bit surprised when I agreed to join up. All I had done up to then was listen to them and ask the odd question but I had given no clear indication that I was going to go back into management so soon. They had talked about the amount of young talent that had come through the Laois minor teams from 1995 onwards. I liked the sound of that. In that age group between 1995 and 1998, Laois had won two All-Ireland titles, lost another final, won three Leinster titles and lost another final. It was a fine record and certainly pointed to a county that had an excellent under-age system.

Not that I have never been one to overvalue minor success. Winning an All-Ireland minor title is a snapshot in time as to how a particular set of U-18s are doing. You can win a minor title with an evenly balanced squad of players who might never progress to senior standard and lose one with a team that has ten superb talents, who will make great seniors, and five who aren't quite up to it.

Besides, a minor team covers one year only, whereas a senior team is drawn from players whose ages span a decade or more. The senior scene is so much more demanding and complicated that you would want to be very naive to read too much into minor success. Let me give you an example of how unreliable minor form can be. In 1970, Galway beat Kerry by a point in an All-Ireland minor final replay. Both looked very good teams over the two games and it seemed likely that they would each go on to produce lots of fine senior players who would exert a major influence for years to come.

Many of them did, but not from the winners. In fact, John Tobin and, to a lesser extent, Michael Rooney were the only two Galway lads to develop into really good senior players whereas Kerry turned out several famous names.

Ger Power, John Egan, Paudie Lynch, Jimmy Deenihan, Ger O'Keeffe, Paudie O'Mahony, Mickey Ned O'Sullivan, John Long and Batt O'Shea were all on that 1970 Kerry minor team. Most of them went on to enjoy spectacular careers on the great Kerry senior team that came together in the mid-Seventies. Why did so many of them make it while the Galway lads didn't?

Some 24 years later, Kerry beat Galway fairly easily in the All-Ireland minor final. Looking at both teams in the 1994 final, you would think that far more of the Kerry lads would develop into good seniors. No so. Mike Frank Russell is the only one still on the panel while the other two who made it at senior level were Barry O'Shea and Denis Dwyer.

Meanwhile, several of the Galway team went on to be excellent seniors, including Pádraic Joyce, Michael Donnellan, Derek Savage, Tomás and Declan Meehan, Paul Clancy, John Divilly and Richie Fahy. I have good reason to remember those boyos as they did more than their share to wreck Kildare's All-Ireland ambitions in 1998 and 2000.

That's why I'm never overly impressed with talk of great minor teams in any given year. Lads are still maturing and can be completely different, both as players and individuals, a few years later. However, in Laois's case, they had done so well over an extended period that it was fair to assume that, even allowing for the inevitable fall off, a decent number would come through to be seriously competitive at senior level.

I was a bit concerned about how Laois hadn't won an All-Ireland U-21 title. It looked to be the next logical step when you have had a string of good minor teams but it didn't happen, whereas Westmeath had built on their 1995 All-Ireland minor win by adding the U-21 title four years later.

Like everybody else, of course, I had heard stories about how the young Laois lads were wined and dined and treated as heroes after winning the minor titles. A bad mistake. But then it would only happen in a county starved of senior success. Nobody is more easily led astray than a minor footballer who is held up to be something really special. How can he know that he's merely at the beginning of the long trek to becoming a senior player when he's told as a minor that he's a real star? Unfortunately, it happens all the time and promising careers get lost in bars, nightclubs and other pursuits which pop up in front of young lads in these bountiful times.

From what I have heard, the Laois minors of the late Nineties were nearly put on the same pedestal as some of the great football names from the county such as Tommy 'Boy Wonder' Murphy or Bobby Miller. What a joke! And what a disservice to the young lads! Was it any wonder they indulged themselves if adults kept backslapping them?

I made up my mind that if I took the job, a quick fall to earth was on the agenda for anybody who had delusions about their own ability or status. Once I let it be known that I was prepared to take the Laois job, things moved fairly quickly. The Football Board backed the idea, as did County Chairman, Dick Miller, who I would subsequently find to be a great man to work with.

And so on Monday, 16 September 2002, I was formally ratified as new Laois manager by the County Board. Was I apprehensive? Not a bit. I had no idea what the future held but isn't that part of the wonderful charm of life? The past gives you memories and experience but the next challenge is what keeps you going. Tomorrow is always a new day. I would apply the same basic principles that had worked in Kerry and Kildare and see how Laois reacted to them. If they worked, fine. And if they didn't, so what? Better to try and fail than to remain on the sidelines and never know what might have happened.

Laois hadn't won a Leinster senior title since 1946, an awful long time for a proud footballing people who had seen their great rivals Offaly drive home through the county so often with All-Ireland and provincial titles. Offaly had won three senior All-Irelands and ten Leinster titles since 1970. And if that wasn't bad enough, Offaly hurlers had hit the jackpot too. God, it was all so hard to take in Laois and who could blame them?

Kildare's re-emergence in 1998 further added to their sense of frustration. It was as if all their neighbours had struck oil while they continued to hit the hardest rock. Now they were turning to me to see if I could change their luck. I didn't know if I could but I would certainly work on changing their outlook because as it stood, there was absolutely no chance of making progress. There would have to be a change of mindset because, on the basis of what I had seen in that qualifier tie with Meath, the players were so mentally brittle that a shout in the dark would startle them.

Shortly before I took over, Laois were being quoted at 40/1 to win the 2003 Leinster title. By the time the first ball was kicked in the championship, they were down to 7/1. A fair wad of money had gone on them, much of which I suspect had come from Laois pockets. The county was beginning to believe in itself again. Either that or they believed that if I could do something with their great rivals, Kildare, I could make progress with them. I had no idea whether their confidence was well-founded but it would be some fun finding out.

The Transformation of Laois

Here's a strange thing. In the ten seasons I spent with Kildare, we only met Laois twice in the Leinster senior championship. I didn't come across them at all in my first stint in 1991–94, but we clashed twice in 1997–98.

The first – a Leinster quarter-final at Croke Park in early June 1997 – turned out to be a defining game for that Kildare team as they had to play with 13 players for nearly an hour after Johnny McDonald and Martin Lynch were sent off. Kildare would have been expected to collapse under such a heavy burden but instead they dug in for what was one of their finest hours. It took a special strain of resolve to survive that day, but they not only survived but won by a handsome four points.

A year later, Kildare beat Laois far more comfortably in the Leinster semi-final. Naturally, I wasn't paying much attention to Laois at the time except in terms of the threat they posed to Kildare. Anyway, by the time I took Laois out for their first competitive game in January 2003, the squad had undergone several changes although Fergal Byron, Michael Lawlor, Chris Conway, Ian Fitzgerald, Colm Parkinson, Kevin Fitzpatrick and Beano McDonald were all still there so there was a good strand of experience.

I had three initial aims when I took over in Laois: get the squad fit, motivated and self-confident. I'm not for one moment casting aspersions on what previous Laois managers had done but, just as I had done in Kerry and Kildare, I made up my mind that everything would be done my way. That policy had served me well so I wasn't going to abandon it in Laois. I would listen to others and weigh up what they said, but in the end, the calls had to be mine. It's the only way for a manager to operate. He who carries the can should be the only one allowed to put holes in it.

Given that he had played such a key role in my decision to join Laois, Declan O'Loughlin was an obvious choice as one of my selectors. Besides, he had played with Laois for years, knew the scene well and was convinced that with the right application and approach, things could be turned around. Gabriel Lawlor also came in as a selector. He too was a good choice as he had done a great job with minor teams, knew the lads well and was very ambitious for Laois.

I got to work quickly with the squad and set about putting down a solid platform. I started the famous running regime, driving lads as hard as was humanly possible, and sometimes even beyond. I wanted to make sure that, come spring and summer, there would never be any question of being let down by a lack of fitness. I'm not suggesting that was the case previously, but I wasn't taking any chances. I'd drive them like dogs and see who stood up to it.

Players have enough to contend with in big games without wondering if they're going to have the stamina to survive. Nothing draws the spirit and resolve from a player like feeling that he's up against a fitter opponent. That's especially true of players in counties who aren't used to success. They are carrying enough psychological baggage without that so I was determined that the squad would be so fit that they went into every game believing, even if it went on for five hours, they would still be galloping like steeplechasers at the end.

In fairness, the players bought into the new demands and expectations very quickly. Their commitment was every bit as intense as anything I had experienced in Kerry or Kildare. Laois might not have looked too closely at the Kerry model but they would definitely have felt that if Kildare could win two Leinster titles and reach an All-Ireland final in three seasons, they were entitled to harbour similar ambitions. Actually, probably even more, given the amount of young talent Laois had produced over the previous seven years. I have no doubt that the progress made by Kildare over the previous six years was an inspiration to Laois. If my neighbour can do, then so can I. That might not be a scientifically sound assessment but if it works, who cares?

Inevitably, there was a level of interest far and above the normal when we finally headed into action in an O'Byrne Cup game against Longford on the first Sunday of January 2003. It was a bitterly cold day but a crowd of around 2,000, nearly all from Laois, turned out at O'Moore Park. I don't know what miracles they were hoping to spot but all they saw was something they had grown quite familiar with – a Laois defeat. It's amazing how much store people can put on games in early January. Win or lose, they're pre-season warm-ups, no more and no less. The same thing happened for Wicklow's O'Byrne Cup games in January 2007 which were shown 'live' on TV. It gave the county a lift but it didn't tell me a whole lot I didn't know from watching lads in training.

I wasn't in the slightest bit perturbed by the defeat against Longford. In fact, if anything, it suited us because it meant we could return to training for the month of January well away from the fuss, the fans and the frenzy. By the time we were to hit the National League road in early February, things had taken shape very nicely.

Luckily, Laois had won promotion to Division One the previous year (they had beaten an Armagh team in the Division Two semi-final that would go on to win the All-Ireland) which meant we would have seven high-quality games in two months. Things had gone well in training but I never envisaged it would transfer so quickly to what was a very demanding schedule against Meath, Fermanagh, Mayo, Down, Sligo, Cavan and Kildare.

Amazingly, we ended up winning five and drawing the other two against Down and Cavan. It was as close to perfection as we could have asked for, even if I could have done without the last game against Kildare. We needed to win to make sure of a place in the semi-finals, while they had to win to give themselves a chance of avoiding relegation.

I was delighted with the Laois win but sad for Kildare, as the last thing I wanted was to have contributed in any way to their relegation. I had enjoyed some great times with them and would have much preferred not to have been in the same League group. And I most definitely didn't want to be playing them when the relegation door was springing but, Sod's Law, that's exactly what happened.

Still, we had ourselves to think about so it was business as usual against Kildare. We won by five points to top the group and crown an amazing two months. Things got even better when we beat

Armagh by three points in the League semi-final. Armagh were reigning All-Ireland champions so nobody gave Laois a chance but they produced an excellent display, especially in the closing quarter when they wore Joe Kernan's lads down which was some achievement even in a League game. All those laps of the pitch in training had clearly worked! What's more the players were thinking and acting like winners.

I have to admit that I was surprised by the rapid progress made that spring. I was also a little worried in case it left players with an inflated view of their status. The supporters were already talking of Leinster and All-Ireland titles and, however hard you work to dampen the sense of euphoria, it can get through to players. I saw it happening in Kildare after the 1998 Leinster final and feared the same might happen in Laois, even at that early stage of the team's development.

I would have been quite happy with a mid-table finish that year but instead Laois found themselves heading to Croke Park for a first League final appearance in 17 years. Waiting for us was a Tyrone team that was developing into the best ever produced by the county.

Taking on Tyrone, who had won the League title in 2002 and who were driven by an incredible obsession after not doing themselves justice in the subsequent championship, was always going to be a very tall order for a Laois team who, despite remaining unbeaten in eight games, was still learning its trade at this level. Still, playing Tyrone was a challenge we were really looking forward to although I have to admit I had serious concerns on another front.

The game was to be played on 4 May, just a week before we were due to play Wexford in the first round of the Leinster championship. Now that's the sort of planning that would leave you tearing your hair out. A team works very hard to reach the League final and are rewarded with just one week to refocus for the first round of the championship.

It doesn't happen anymore but it shouldn't have happened back then either. If Laois had beaten Tyrone, it would have sparked off celebrations all around the county and while the players wouldn't have been part of them, they couldn't have ignored what was going on around them either. Laois had fallen victim to that type of euphoria when they won the League title in 1986. They had a month between the win over Monaghan and a first round Leinster championship meeting with Wicklow in Aughrim but, according to what I heard afterwards, they allowed themselves to become totally distracted. Wicklow sensed what was going on and laid an ambush for the visitors which produced a spectacular upset.

As it happened, I didn't have to worry about League celebrations in 2003. We had massive support in Croke Park for the final – it was the biggest League final attendance for nine years – but the Laois fans were left frozen in disappointment as Tyrone won by ten points. It was a salutary lesson for the Laois squad, one which I'm convinced did a lot to make them much tougher mentally for the Leinster championship ahead.

With Peter Canavan pulling strings that our lads couldn't even get their hands on, Tyrone didn't concede a score for more than twenty minutes and while we put on a spurt before half-time, they were all-the-way winners, 0-21 to 1-8.

Would it be 1991 all over again, when Kildare lost the League final in my initial season and then crashed out of the Leinster championship at the first fence? Wexford had won promotion from Division Two and were a rapidly emerging force so we had genuine concerns all that week. It would have been disastrous for Laois had they lost because confidence would have dipped alarmingly. I'm not sure how much energy they would have mustered for the qualifiers and the last thing I wanted was to be in O'Moore Park facing a repeat of what happened in 2002.

Luckily for Laois, Wexford didn't really fire on the day. Ian Fitzgerald settled things down with a goal early on and we generally held the upper hand in what was a poor enough game, redeemed it must be said by the point-kicking exhibition from Beano McDonald who landed some beauties to take his final tally to six from play. Laois won by 12 points which was a mighty relief.

Great rivals Offaly were up next. Laois hadn't beaten Offaly in the Leinster championship since 1990 and while the match was in Portlaoise, many people were convinced that this was where our season would hit a major roadblock. And it very nearly did. We were in serious trouble when Offaly led by two points late on. You could almost sense that the Laois supporters, who had grown accustomed to seeing Offaly edge home in close finishes, were preparing for the worst. There was a time that the Laois players might have been undermined by similar negative thoughts but they had travelled a long way that spring. They had come to understand the power of self-belief which certainly came to their rescue on this occasion.

The game was ticking into injury time when, in a last desperate effort to save the day, a high ball was hoisted into the Offaly goal area. Kevin Fitzpatrick made a superb catch and off-loaded to Michael Lawlor who blasted the ball to the net. Suddenly, we were in front.

Offaly supporters – and indeed some media commentators – argued afterwards that Fitzpatrick threw the ball to Lawlor (he didn't of course!) but even if he had, we would have taken it. After all, I deserved a break against Offaly ever since 1982 and the Séamus Darby incident. At least, I felt I did, and maybe the gods did too.

Ciaran McManus kicked the equalising point from a '45' deep in stoppage time but I wasn't in the least disappointed. Yes, it would have been great had we won in such dramatic circumstances but, on balance, we probably had more reason to be grateful for another chance than Offaly did as they had led for most of the way.

That would be Tom Kelly's last game at right full-back. We switched him to centre-back for the replay in Tullamore and he remained there from then on. If Laois had put in the foundations during the League and the first two championship games, the replay against Offaly was the day we built something more substantial.

Taking them on in Tullamore was a tall order for a squad that was still coming together but the confident manner that they tackled the challenge was hugely encouraging. Ian Fitzgerald and Beano McDonald did most of the damage in attack and we ran out deserving winners, 2-10 to 0-13, in a much improved, if still far from convincing, performance.

Despite the win, I was deeply unhappy afterwards. I don't think we got a single free inside Offaly's '45' metre line and, to make matters worse, Ian Fitzgerald and Paul McDonald were sent off for fairly harmless offences. I let fly to the media afterwards, berating those responsible for taking the physical dimension out of our games. Laois v Offaly should have been a manly encounter – instead, as far as I was concerned, it was turned into a game for pansies by an overly-strict interpretation of the rules by Cavan referee Brian Crowe. The media were delighted with my outburst, turning it into big headlines but it wasn't designed for that purpose. I felt frustrated over what I regarded as a diluting of the great game that is Gaelic football and believed that it was easier to have a go from a position of strength after winning.

I heard afterwards that Tommy Lyons and the rest of the Dublin management team had made the June Bank Holiday Monday journey to Tullamore to size up their opponents for the Leinster semi-final and while we had gone fairly well, I suspect they had no great fears as they returned home.

Dublin were the reigning Leinster champions; they had come within a point of eventual champions, Armagh, in the previous year's All-Ireland semi-final and had beaten Louth with almost embarrassing ease in the first round in 2003. Laois hadn't beaten Dublin in the championship since 1981 so it felt like history was bearing down on us.

Ever since my early playing days, I have always loved taking on Dublin. I had faced them as a player and manager with Kerry and as a manager with Kildare, and now I was taking Laois into a big adventure against the Dubs. I could feel the buzz and, more importantly, I could sense that the players felt it too. They were getting ready to step up. I felt that man-for-man, we had the players to beat Dublin so it was then a question of getting our system right and making sure we set the agenda.

There's always a swagger about Dublin teams in Croke Park so if you show them too much respect, they'll destroy you. You've got to be bold and confident, stare them straight in the eye, take them on, make them think, give them headaches, disrupt their pattern and, for God's sake, don't allow Hill 16 to become a factor. In 2003, Laois were perfectly primed to do all of that.

We won by 0-16 to 0-14 after a marvellous contest. We never let them take the initiative and were clearly the hungrier side. Fergal Byron made a few great saves in the first half which inspired the team and with Pádraig Clancy and Noel Garvan dominating midfield for long stretches, Dublin struggled.

Having said that, they kicked 16 wides but in fairness to our defence where Tom Kelly and Joe Higgins were superb, they pressurised the kickers so much that finding the target was always going to be difficult. Dublin battled desperately all the way to the nerve-wracking end, cutting a five-point deficit down to two, but we held on for a very special victory.

There was a real edge to the game but we had expected that because both sides believed that the winners would go on to win the title. Players clashed as they made their way down the tunnel at half-time and, from what I was told, it was pretty nasty for a short time. By the time I got to the dressing-room things had calmed down, although some of the lads were very angry over what had happened.

Someone had given Joe Higgins a clatter which wasn't a good idea as Joe is well able to look after himself. As others became involved, things got completely out of hand. Declan O'Loughlin, no shrinking violet himself, was knocked over as he tried to calm things down. I didn't see the incident because I had another little bit of business to attend to.

When I got to the dressing room, there was lightning flashing in O'Loughlin's eyes as he demanded: 'Where the hell were you, Micko?'

'Giving a bit of a bollicking to the referee if you must know – just making a point or two to him.'

'F*****g typical, we're in here in a war and you're out there bollicking the referee.'

'Yeah, but it might do more good in the end.'

Now there's a lot I would have done for Laois or any other team I was ever involved with, but wading into brawls in a tunnel was not included and certainly not at that stage of my career. I'd leave that to others!

Maybe Dublin had decided to try and soften our lads up a bit but if they did, it failed because we were really fired up in the second half and fully deserved to win. Laois were back in the Leinster final for the first time since 1991.

Now, could we take an amazing season a stage further by winning the Leinster title for the first time since 1946? Who would have thought that Laois would find themselves in such a lofty position less than a year after that dreadful All-Ireland qualifier against Meath? In fact, even back in early January, when Longford beat us in the O'Byrne Cup, there had been whispers of 'same old Laois' doing the rounds.

It was inevitable, I suppose, that when Laois got through to a Leinster final in my very first season with them, Kildare would be waiting on the other side. It's as if the gods take pleasure in throwing up that sort of scenario. Kildare had won the Leinster title for the first time in 42 years in 1998 and who was waiting for them? You got it – Kerry! Now I'm with Laois and who's on the other side? Kildare!

Incredibly, Laois and Kildare hadn't met previously in a Leinster final since 1946. By any law of averages that was a long wait. I was only ten years old at the time and now here I was, some 57 years later, trying to preside over Laois's next provincial win. And me a Kerryman, having arrived in Laois by way of Kildare. A strange world or what?

Kildare had problems going into the game. Anthony Rainbow and Karl Ennis couldn't play and Glenn Ryan didn't start. And if that wasn't bad enough, they had a midfielder, Alan Barry, sent off on a second yellow card offence after just four minutes. New Kildare manager Pádraig Nolan was furious with the referee and I couldn't blame him. In my view, sending Barry off was totally unnecessary but it wasn't long before we felt the full brunt of the harsh regime implemented by Meath referee Séamus McCormack.

Kevin Fitzpatrick mistimed a challenge on Tadhg Fennin near the Hogan Stand sideline and to our utter consternation he was sent off on a straight red card. I still regard it as one of the most unfair decisions I have ever come across in my many years as player and manager. There was absolutely no malice or intent in Fitzpatrick's challenge. A free against him would have been adequate punishment, a yellow card would have been harsh but it was absolutely ridiculous that he was sent off.

Fitzpatrick is as fair a player as you'll find, yet there he was in the dug-out a quarter-way into his first senior provincial final. What's more he knew that, because he was sent off on a straight red card, he would miss the All-Ireland quarter-final if Laois qualified. He was devastated. His dismissal seemed to upset the rest of the team too and Kildare had cut a six-point deficit down to two by half-time.

I wasn't particularly worried, as we had shown against Dublin that we would last the course, however long or grinding it became. We made it easier on ourselves – or at least it looked that way – when Beano McDonald and Ross Munnelly scored early second half goals to set us up with a 2-9 to 0-8 lead. Kildare hit more problems when Mick Wright was sent off but, to their great credit, they refused to yield. In fact, they battled back with remarkable courage to draw level with ten minutes left but we finished the stronger. Points by Donal Miller, Ian Fitzgerald and Barry Brennan saw us home. Remarkably, all of our 2-13 total had come from play which may well have been a Leinster final record.

I have been often asked to compare the feelings I experienced after Laois's Leinster final with Kildare's success five years earlier. They were different, I suppose, because my son, Karl, was on the Kildare team that made the breakthrough in 1998. That made it very personal and very special, but I have to admit that it was pretty emotional too to watch Ian Fitzgerald waving the cup to the thousands of Laois supporters in 2003. Fitzgerald was the perfect man for the job. He had been excellent all through the season and was always prepared to do whatever it took to lead by example. Unfortunately, he began to pick up injuries from there on which badly restricted him. That was a big loss to Laois because, at his best, he was a real asset.

One major difference between the Kildare and Laois provincial breakthroughs was the time it took to achieve them. I was in the second season of my second stint with Kildare by the time we won Leinster in 1998. In effect, it came at the end of my sixth season, whereas I had success in Laois just nine months after taking over. Kildare were a much slower burn and by the time we finally won Leinster, I knew every pocket of the county inside out. Many of the players had soldiered long and hard too, so there was a huge sense of satisfaction for them.

It all happened so quickly in Laois that it came to be taken for granted more quickly than in Kildare. That made things harder for me when success wasn't replicated over the next three seasons.

Still, I have always been a man to enjoy the moment and the sheer delight on the faces of the Laois public on the night the Leinster cup arrived back in Portlaoise was something I will always remember. The overall sense of liberation didn't seem quite as obvious as in Kildare, but then Kildare is a bigger football county with a much higher population. And boy, did Kildare people know how to party! Laois were good at it too but even as the celebrations started among the public after the Leinster final win, I knew they had to end for the players.

An All-Ireland quarter-final beckoned and big Joe Kernan and his regrouped All-Ireland champions from Armagh were heading towards Croke Park. Monaghan had stunned an injury-ravaged Armagh side in the first round of the Ulster championship in May but by the time they lined up for the All-Ireland quarter-final, they had beaten Waterford, Antrim, Dublin and Limerick in the qualifiers. What's more, they hadn't conceded a single goal, a record they maintained against us.

Of all the provincial champions, ours was the toughest quarter-final draw. Galway got Donegal (and lost), Tyrone drew Fermanagh, while Kerry were paired with Roscommon.

With all due respects to Donegal, Fermanagh and Roscommon, none of them could compare with Armagh.

The All-Ireland quarter-final turned out to be one of those games where an edge in experience provided the cutting difference, especially in the final quarter. It was level for the ninth time at 0-10 each after fifty minutes but Armagh were that bit cuter and more clinical from there on and won by 0-15 to 0-13. Our great adventure was over for 2003 and, as events transpired, Laois wouldn't revisit those peaks again during my stay there.

I have always remained convinced that, had we got an easier draw in the quarter-final, we would have had a real cut at the All-Ireland title. We were learning all the time but we could have done with another game before facing an Armagh side that, as well as winning the 2002 All-Ireland title, had also won three Ulster titles, since 1999. They had real hard-edged experience, something we lacked at that stage.

Donegal pushed Armagh all the way before losing the All-Ireland semi-final. I would have loved to take on Donegal,

Fermanagh or Roscommon but luck checked out on us in the draw. It also ran out on Armagh in the All-Ireland final against Tyrone when they had Diarmuid Marsden sent off in very controversial circumstances as the game headed into a crucial phase in the last quarter. He was later exonerated by Central Council but that was no consolation, either to him or Armagh. Such are the narrow margins that often decide games, something Laois would come to understand over the following seasons.

There was a huge feelgood factor in Laois towards the end of 2003. After the disappointment of previous years, it almost seemed like a miracle that they were Leinster champions with a relatively young team that had a lot more to give.

Maybe too much was taken for granted after the rapid surge in 2003. Fate has a tendency to turn against you very quickly and it certainly took a dislike to Laois from 2004 onwards. The squad had remained largely injury free in 2003 but it was very different in the following seasons. Indeed, there were times when I began to wonder if I had annoyed the entire population of black cats or walked under too many ladders while breaking mirrors on Friday the 13th.

Nonetheless, it was important to savour a season that I found very fulfilling from a personal viewpoint. Working with a squad where the improvement is visible virtually every time they play is one of the most satisfying feelings for any manager, and that was certainly the case with me in 2003.

From a position where the Laois public were so apathetic that only the committed minority bothered to turn out for a championship game in Portlaoise in July 2002, to the Leinster peak in such a short space of time was as dramatic a transformation as any county has experienced for many years.

Laois lost just two of 15 League and championship games in 2003, one to Tyrone, who won the double, and the other to Armagh, All-Ireland runners-up. I was glad I had answered the call when Laois came knocking after I left Kildare, but I wasn't to know at the time that I had enjoyed my best season with them. It would never be quite the same again.

The Heath Accord

Life is both too short and too precious to dwell on regrets. It's easy and, at times maybe even comforting, to look back and say: 'I should have done that differently.' It's a pointless exercise though because, however much the world has changed, you can't alter the past.

It's like analysing a game on TV using video reruns to justify an opinion. You can prove just about anything with a video. Player A didn't make the right pass; player B should have made a different run; player C should have been closer to his opponent. It's the way modern TV analysis has developed in all sports and, to be honest, it can be shocking boring at times.

I was never a great man for the video. Yes, I've looked at reruns of games but only to check a specific aspect of play. I never allowed it to dictate or shape my thinking in any way. I'd much prefer to trust my experience and instinct any day. The tape will show you what happened, not why it happened. You have to work that out for yourself, whether you're a manager or a player. You have to think on your feet. By all means, use whatever expertise is available but ultimately a manager should rely on his own judgements. If he's right, he'll succeed in getting the best out of his players which is all that can be expected. If he's wrong, then he shouldn't be in the job in the first place.

But whatever you do, be decisive. Back your conviction and stick by it and move on if it doesn't work out. Having said that, there isn't a person alive who doesn't feel they would change a few things if they got the chance.

I enjoyed most of my time in Laois but, looking back on it now, I feel I should have done a few things differently. For a start, I should have quit at the end of 2004 but when I didn't, I definitely should have walked at the end of the next season. I was very close

My son Karl, who made a huge difference to Kildare, and Dermot Earley Jr, a great player when in full flow, are in jovial mood at a training session in Newbridge.

Another one bites the dust in the fractious Kerry v Roscommon All-Ireland final in 1980. I'm sure Dermot Earley Sr, who was a very sporting player, had nothing to do with this incident but he and I would always disagree over Roscommon's approach to the game. I remain convinced they ruined their chances of winning through an overly physical approach.

Alone with my plans. I love the sea and the fishing. It's a great way of getting your thoughts together. All the better if you land the big one as well.

Tom Spillane seems a bit weary of it all during a Kerry training session. There was no better man to come alive on match day.

I help Glenn Ryan, a great player and an inspiring captain, to raise the Leinster trophy after Kildare's win in 1998. Séamus Aldridge is pleased too.

It's gone boys. No smiles in the Kildare dug-out as the 1998 All-Ireland final with Galway draws to a close.

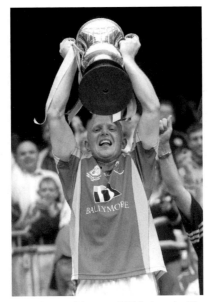

A historic day for Wicklow as Tommy Gill hoists the Tommy Murphy Cup after scoring a dramatic late winning goal in the final against Antrim in August 2007.

I'm normally cool on the sideline but I got very animated during the Laois v Tyrone All-Ireland qualifier in 2006. Cork referee John Geaney is in the firing line on this occasion.

Never say never. I seem to be waving goodbye to the Croke Park dressing rooms after Laois's defeat by Mayo in the 2006 All-Ireland quarter-final. Nine months later I was back with Wicklow.

TV cameras in Aughrim in early January. It's the start of a new era for Wicklow as we line up before the O'Byrne Cup clash with Carlow in January 2007.

*I'm not a superstitious man but I got into the habit many
years ago of always having a match programme in my hand
during a game. I'd feel lost without it.*

Dublin and the rare oul' times. Jimmy Keaveney, a wonderful player and a great character, reminisces about the famous Kerry v Dublin battles after I was inducted into the MBNA Kick Fada Hall of Fame in 2007.

My great pal Arthur French, who deputised for me as Wicklow manager during the 2007 Tommy Murphy Cup campaign, looks even more delighted than me after the thrilling win over Antrim in the final.

If the hat fits! Kevin Heffernan and I are pleased with ourselves after being awarded Honorary Doctorates from UCD.

to calling it a day in October 2004 but allowed myself to be persuaded to stay on, and much the same happened at the start of 2006.

I have to be honest and admit that after 2003, things were never quite the same in Laois. Maybe too much was achieved too quickly. Attitudes changed inside and outside the panel. With the exception of a crazy week in October 2004, the players continued to give great commitment (the vast majority of them anyway) but they probably began to think that if they could progress from such a bad situation in July 2002 to Leinster champions a year later, the upward curve would continue of its own accord.

It never does. The second year is more difficult on two fronts. First, players have to realise that it takes a greater effort to advance from where they are than it took to get them there in the first place, and second, the opposition have become more clued in to your strengths and weaknesses.

That's why the year after making a breakthrough is notoriously tricky. And it certainly was for Laois in 2004. We had an added problem in that the supporters were convinced that the only way was up and on to an All-Ireland title. Just like that. The All-Ireland minor successes had whetted the appetite to such a degree that there were people who felt it was Laois's right to win the senior title. Bring it on. Clear the streets of Portlaoise – Sam is coming to town in September.

Apart from the change in attitude, inside and outside the panel, and the increased expectations, another very important change took place in 2004 – Laois ran out of luck. It never returned in my time with them. The frustrating truth was that from 2003 on, we hardly ever went into a big game with a full squad. We were ravaged so much by injuries that there were times when I had to play lads who weren't 100 per cent fit.

Having said that, we should have retained the Leinster title in 2004 and we only had ourselves to blame for failing. We beat Meath quite easily in the semi-final to set up a final clash with the surprise packet of the year. At the start of the campaign, you could have named your own odds against Westmeath getting to the final. But then the great warrior himself, Páidí Ó Sé, was in charge and suddenly Westmeath's whole outlook changed as they went on a great run.

There's no doubt that Páidí's arrival in Westmeath brought a huge lift to the county. He had been a winner as a player and a manager and proceeded to inspire a very positive mentality among the Westmeath players. There are begrudgers who claim that Westmeath's success under Páidí was pure fluke which is rubbish. The facts show that prior to his arrival in Westmeath, they had never won a Leinster title. Nine months later, they were champions. And it wasn't as if they had an easy run either as they had to beat Offaly, Dublin, Wexford and Laois. How many other teams in the country, let alone Leinster, would have done that?

Fair play to Páidí – he sparked off something that changed the course of Westmeath history. It was bizarre really when you think of it. I had soldiered with Páidí for years in Kerry and then met as managers in 1998 when Kildare played Kerry in the All-Ireland semi-final. Six years later, we clashed as managers again, only this time I was with Laois and he was with Westmeath. You'll find Kerrymen everywhere, it seems.

I had serious concerns over Westmeath going into the Leinster final. What's more, I did my best to convey them to the Laois team but a mood of confidence had engulfed the county to such a degree that it was inevitable it would get to the players. Westmeath's three wins in the championship already that season had sent their self-belief soaring. Also, that particular team would have felt that they had nothing to fear from Laois because Westmeath had done well against Laois at under-age level over the previous eight years, beating them in a replayed minor final in 1995 and a U-21 final in 1999.

Laois broke very quickly from the blocks on Leinster final day and were three points up at the end of the first quarter. Maybe Laois lads thought it was all going to be very easy but suddenly the pattern changed and Westmeath kicked back and played some great football. In the end, we were lucky to scrape a draw when Chris Conway pointed deep in stoppage time.

Having survived with a late point, we should have had a psychological edge going into the replay and we would have had only for a stroke of bad luck (boy, did it start flowing in from there on!) in the days before the replay. We lost Conway to appendicitis which was a serious blow, one that probably cost us the game.

Again, we started well but allowed Westmeath back into the game and this time they did serious damage. They led by six points a quarter of an hour into the second half and seemed set for an easy win, but in fairness to our lads they battled back and cut the lead to three points with ten minutes left.

We were still three short in stoppage time when an incident that defined our unlucky season flashed before us at the Railway End. Beano McDonald put Kevin Fitzpatrick through on the Westmeath goal and it looked as if he couldn't miss. Fitzpatrick is a level-headed fella, the sort you'd back in a situation like that. Unfortunately for Laois, not this time. Maybe he was trying to be too precise in where he placed the ball past Gary Connaughton, or maybe the gods had decided it was going to be Westmeath's day, but whatever the explanation, he drove the ball just wide of the post. Our get-out card had been wasted.

It was a fierce disappointment but, at the same time, how could anybody begrudge Westmeath their first Leinster title? I certainly didn't but I was irritated at the manner in which Laois had blown a marvellous opportunity to win a Leinster two-in-a-row for what would have been the first time since the 1930s. We could make all the excuses we liked about injuries but it was also a fact that a certain level of arrogance had infected the camp. Westmeath weren't regarded in quite the same way as Dublin, Meath or Kildare would have been which was unforgivable.

People can blame me for not having the players' heads right but there's a limit to what you can do. Experienced players should always be alert to the dangers of over-confidence but I would have to say that on the basis of how the two games against Westmeath unfolded, it was clear that quite a few Laois players felt they were owed another Leinster title.

After losing to Westmeath, we had to prepare for a fourth round All-Ireland qualifier clash with reigning All-Ireland champions, Tyrone, and I knew it was a hopeless case. It was so unfair to ask a team that had lost a provincial final to play a qualifier a week later but we had to live with it. In the end, we died with it too because we were wiped out by Tyrone. They led by 13 points after the first half and, while we had cut the deficit to six by the three-quarter mark, Tyrone took off again and eventually won by 14 points. It could have been a lot more.

If that wasn't bad enough, Beano suffered a horrible ankle injury which ruled him out for a very long stretch. It summed up the way things were going for us at the time.

One of the most frustrating experiences in sport is when you feel you have under-achieved. I definitely thought that was the case in the 2004 championship which maybe explains why I wasn't in the best of humour going back into training in October. After a few nights back, I was in even worse form because it was beginning to look as if only a few of us gave a damn. Just six players turned up for training one night in Portarlington, and only a handful more the next night.

The Portlaoise contingent was tied up with the Leinster club championship and I had no problems with that because I have always believed that if the county champions go well, it lifts the whole scene. Some others had injuries and various excuses but I still couldn't tolerate having just six players at a training session. Did the rest think I was a complete fool? I took a look at what was going on and said to myself: 'To hell with this, it's the end of the road.'

I rang Dick Miller and told him I was packing it in. He was stunned. 'You can't,' he said, 'We've started something here. We have to finish it.'

'Dick, tell that to the players. If they can't be bothered turning up for training, I'm not going to waste my time. Are they happy with one Leinster title? That seems to be the case. If they are, that's fine. I'll be off and do a bit of fishing.'

It was claimed afterwards, of course, that the reason I wanted out was to take over in Dublin, but they were completely separate issues. Dublin or no Dublin, I wasn't going to run a halfhearted ship where players turned up when it suited them. I called the shots, not them.

A few crazy days followed. They were as confusing to me as anybody else because I was unsure what to do. I needed time to work it out but, as luck would have it, a County Board meeting took place in the middle of the uncertainty. The delegates were totally confused and, God knows, it was hard to blame them. They passed a vote of confidence in me but if I was to go back, I needed more than just the backing of the Board. I needed to know that the players were not only behind me, but would continue to buy into the way I was doing things.

I asked Dick, who kept reassuring me that the players wanted me to continue, to get the squad together but not to let anybody know whether or not I was turning up. The meeting was arranged for The Heath clubhouse on a Tuesday night.

I arranged for Dick to pick me up and drive me to The Heath. When we swung in towards the clubhouse, I couldn't believe my eyes. Word of the meeting had obviously spread and it seemed that every media person in the country had turned up. Arc lights, TV cameras, microphones and tape recorders by the dozen greeted us as we got out at the back entrance of the clubhouse. It was unreal. There would hardly have been a bigger media presence outside the Dáil if the government was about to fall.

Earlier on, Declan O'Loughlin had asked one of the TV guys what on earth they were doing turning up in such big numbers for something that really wasn't of earth-shattering national importance and he replied, 'Micko's box office. It's as simple as that.'

Really? I must say I didn't feel like that as I headed in to meet the players. How the hell had things reached this stage? We were all so immersed in what was going on that we missed the funny side of it, but it must have been a comical sight. The curtains weren't even pulled so the journalists had their noses pressed to the windows and, while they couldn't hear what was being said, they were trying to work out from the body language how things were going. I heard afterwards that lads were even taking bets as to the outcome. The biggest money was on me leaving, which would have been the right call if I got any bad vibes from the players.

I knew what I wanted from them and I didn't have long to wait to discover that it would be forthcoming. They wanted me to continue as manager. They also promised one hundred per cent commitment, exactly what I needed to hear.

I left the meeting with Dick without giving a clear indication of whether or not I was going back. Declan had to face the media pack and he did a great job in clarifying everything without actually explaining anything. A vintage performance! He should be in the diplomatic service.

It's well known that a good thunderstorm clears the air and that was certainly the case in Laois. The squad knuckled down to training and that was the end of the matter. Of course, it shouldn't have been necessary to threaten to quit in the first place but unfortunately it was. In hindsight, I should have held to my initial decision at that stage and left. Trust hadn't been broken, but it had been damaged and would never be quite the same again.

We were lucky to survive in Division One in 2005, winning three of seven games and finishing just above the cut-off point. Not that I was particularly bothered. Regaining the Leinster championship and putting up a real challenge for the All-Ireland was the sole target, one that was very nearly wrecked in the very first Leinster game. Offaly deserved to beat us, and should have, but they were caught by a last minute goal from Ross Munnelly.

And then we went and walloped the daylights out of Kildare, 0-21 to 0-9, in the semi-final. Nice on the day, but winning a semi-final by twelve points should carry the starkest of health warnings. It can make a team feel too comfortable about themselves while it makes it easy for the opposition to stoke the motivational fires. Dublin had a much tougher call against Wexford in their semi-final, giving them the perfect entrée to a cracking final.

And so it turned out in front of a crowd of 81,025, a record up to then for a Leinster final. God, how that game still rankles with me. An awful first-half performance left us five points down at half-time but a much improved second half had us two up with five minutes to go. Dublin pulled one back and then got a very debatable free which, to his credit, Mossy Quinn pointed.

It still looked as if we would get a draw out of it but Dublin were awarded a '45' which never should have been because the ball hadn't crossed the line when Joe Higgins picked it up. Even then, the kick wasn't taken from opposite the point spot where the ball was adjudged to have gone out. But Quinn held his nerve and found the target for what proved to be the winner.

I was never one for whinging when any of my teams lost a game, and I'm not doing it now, but there's no doubt that some very close calls went against us in the final minutes of that Leinster final.

Dublin have a distinct advantage playing in Croke Park. Because of the population in the city and surrounds, they will always have bigger support than the opposition which means that referees are subjected to constant pressures. Every referee sets out to be fair and neutral but they're all human so there's always the risk that the sheer volume of sound coming from the Dublin supporters will exert an influence. It might be very small but even the most marginal of calls are crucial in close games. Dublin definitely got the rub of the green in that final and ultimately it proved decisive. For the second year in a row, Laois had lost a Leinster final by one score.

We got back on track with a qualifier win over Derry, but after a good start against Armagh in the All-Ireland quarter-final, it turned flat for us and we were well beaten in the end. It was the third season in a row that Laois's All-Ireland ambitions had ended against an Ulster team. From my perspective, there was nothing especially significant in that since the opposition was Armagh (twice) and Tyrone, who just happened to be two of the best sides in the country. Others, it seems, saw it differently, claiming that our training methods and general preparation were outdated. Pure rubbish. But why spoil a good theory with anything as boring as the truth?

The trouble is that once a theory – however hair-brained – starts doing the rounds, it gathers momentum. This particular one obviously found its way into the Laois dressing-room too as it gradually became apparent that the players had doubts, not about themselves mind you, but about how they were being prepared. After twenty years as a manager and following so much success with Kerry, Kildare and indeed Laois, my methods were being queried. Sure is a strange world.

The Erosion of Trust

It isn't in my nature to walk away from a challenge and Laois very definitely represented one serious challenge at the end of 2005, but I still should have left. A year earlier, the reason I considered leaving was the lack of interest in training – now it was far more serious.

The truth was that my authority was being undermined from within and I should never have stood for it. Laois had won a Leinster final and reached two others which had been lost in the cruellest of circumstances. Yet, instead of seeing the glass as half-full many Laois people seemed to regard it as three-quarters empty. They had damn short memories.

What's more, it appears the three-quarter empty feeling was all my fault. Defeats by Armagh in 2003 and 2005 and Tyrone in 2004 raised doubts among Laois supporters – and players too, I have to say – about my training methods, my selections and my tactical approach. It seems I was out of touch with modern trends and demands. Never mind that I had been training teams since my teenage days or that my record with Kerry, Kildare and Laois suggested that I managed to get some things right over the years. Times had changed and now Mickey Harte and Joe Kernan were the managerial Messiahs whose methods had to be copied.

Good luck to both of them, they achieved things with Tyrone and Armagh that neither county had ever done before and you certainly won't hear a begrudging word from me about either of them. I don't know Harte very well but would have come across big Joe for more years than either of us care to remember.

A marvellous player with a big heart, he did more than his fair share to lift the Armagh load during bad times in the 1970s and 1980s before going on to lead Crossmaglen Rangers to All-Ireland glory. He did the same with Armagh and, while as a Kerryman I was disappointed with the 2002 All-Ireland final, I was pleased that when we were beaten, it was a county like Armagh that finally landed the big prize. I was happy too for Joe who really is one of the great personalities in the game.

Harte has had great success with Tyrone too, so full credit to him. The All-Ireland successes by Tyrone and Armagh have guaranteed this decade a permanent place in GAA history as one of the breakthrough eras, but it doesn't mean that every team that lost to them got it all wrong. And it certainly doesn't mean that in a short a space of time I was overtaken by the northern boys and left behind with outdated ideas.

However, that would appear to have been the feeling in the Laois camp in early 2006 when the Laois players got together and declared that what we had been doing in training wasn't going to take them any further. They demanded a change in the system, claiming that it was vital if they were to put themselves in a position to win the All-Ireland title. They didn't think they were physically strong enough and kept referring to the Ulster way of doing things.

They didn't say it directly but there was only one interpretation to take out of it. As far as they were concerned, the type of training that that had stood to me for years was out of date. John Doran, who had worked with me as trainer in Kildare and Laois, had gone back to Kildare so now there was a vacancy.

A change of direction in training wasn't the only thing the players wanted – they also pressed to have a psychologist brought in to get their mental approach right. God almighty, how did I manage all down the years!

It was at that stage that I should have said goodbye, thrown my gear in the boot and headed out of Laois. I still regard it as weakness on my part that I didn't head for home. I told Dick Miller what I was thinking and he got to work on persuading me to stay. Once again he succeeded, even if was against my better judgement.

I shouldn't have allowed him to influence me. My systems were okay in 2003 when Laois won their first Leinster title in 57 years and there was nothing wrong with them in 2004 or 2005 either. It's easy to look for excuses when you lose but it was unfair to blame me for the failure to win the Leinster titles in those years, which is effectively what happened when the players questioned my training regime.

We all make mistakes and I have never tried to cover up mine. But there are times when, if you're to be truly honest with yourself, you have to look in the mirror rather than at somebody else when you're trying to find out why something went wrong. I certainly felt at the end of 2005 that some mirrors wouldn't have gone amiss in the Laois dressing room. Instead, they were being turned in my direction.

My response to the doubts raised over our training methods should have been short and sharp. My way or no way – take it or leave it. Instead, I agreed to allow another trainer be brought in. Gerry Loftus was chosen and he set to work immediately.

He did a very good job too. He is an exceptionally fit man and he ran an excellent training programme. The players seemed very happy with him and I reckoned if they felt good about themselves and what they were doing, it would show in their performances. However, the fact that my authority had been questioned should have set my alarm bells ringing. However good Gerry was, he did nothing that I felt would advance the team any more than I had.

Not once in my 15 seasons with Kerry or my ten with Kildare had the players queried anything I did. Not to my face anyway, and as for what anybody said behind my back, well I couldn't care less. A bit of back-biting is no harm, it happens in every camp. It would have been easy for the Kildare lads to raise doubts when I came back for a second time. They might have thought: 'If we didn't succeed under him for four years, why should it be any different this time?' But they didn't. In fact, they bought into it straight away and the lads who had been there in my first stint redoubled their efforts.

I was annoyed by the inference in Laois that my methods weren't good enough but, having given Dick my word that I would stay on, I stood back on the training ground and let Gerry get on with it. Besides, I had plenty to occupy me and it wasn't all pleasant either. We tipped along quite nicely in the 2006 League, actually topping the group after losing just one game (to Meath by a point) to qualify for the semi-final against Kerry in Killarney.

And then the fun started. Yet again, we had been ravaged by injuries so we looked to the U-21 team. They hadn't been training with us because they were in the middle of their own championship campaign and had qualified for the All-Ireland semi-final. But as our injury problems increased, I looked for a few of them.

They were told by the team management that if they played for the seniors they would be left off the U-21 team which put them in an awkward position. We started the two Colm Kellys (Stradbally and St Joseph's) against Kerry but took them off at half-time because we would never have heard the end of it if we played them for the full 70 minutes. We didn't play Donie Brennan but he got caught in the crossfire because he was among the first to let it be known that he would play for the seniors if we wanted him. He was even dropped from the U-21 panel for a few days while the two Kellys were told they wouldn't start the All-Ireland semi-final against Cork.

It was crazy stuff. The senior team should always be number one in every county. By all means, facilitate other grades but they should never be allowed to dictate. The Kellys and Brennan were put in an impossible situation which was totally unfair on them.

My job was to try to win the League semi-final, and in normal circumstances I wouldn't have called them up but we needed them because of the injury blitz. They were getting calls on the way to the game with Kerry asking them not to play. What were they to do? I kept saying to myself: 'This is all wrong. Has this county gone off the rails completely?' To be honest, things were beginning to fall apart.

To make matters worse, we were well beaten by Kerry. Given the injuries and the sideshows, not to mention that Kerry were going well, it was hardly a surprise that we didn't function. Still, we had six weeks to the start of the championship which I felt was long enough to get things back on track. We beat Carlow to set up another crack at Dublin, a crucial meeting for both sides. The hype was unreal in the build up but sadly, for us, the day turned into a total disaster. After a bright enough start, we were smashed out the gate and half way back to Portlaoise. I could hardly bare to look at the scoreboard as Dublin piled it on, winning eventually by 3-17 to 0-12. It was the biggest championship defeat I had ever experienced as a manager.

We lost Pádraig Clancy with a shoulder injury in the first half and it was quite amazing the impact it had. We fell apart without him. It was claimed afterwards that Dublin had targeted him and that he was taken out unfairly but I wouldn't hold with that. Yes, it was a late tackle but these things happen. Nine times out of ten, no injury would have occurred but, typical of the way things were going for us at the time, this was the one in ten. With Clancy gone, Dublin took over around midfield and went on a scoring spree. Laois had hit rock bottom – it was back to the worst of the bad old days.

I was disappointed with the response of the Laois players after Clancy's departure. Yes, he was a key figure but they were experienced enough to improvise without him. Instead, it was as if they accepted that it was a lost cause and just went through the motions.

Loyalty to players has always been a high priority with me. I have never emerged from a losing dressing room and blamed them for defeat. I didn't do it after Laois's hammering by Dublin in 2006 either, although it was mighty tempting. They had asked for a change in the training setup which they got. In fact, they were granted anything they asked for within reason, yet when Clancy went off, they folded as meekly as against Meath four years earlier.

I had put the players first all along and, in return, they were to give absolutely everything on the pitch. They didn't do that against Dublin. Clancy's injury was a setback but it was no excuse for the subsequent collapse. Everything was geared to proving that we really should have beaten Dublin in the 2005 Leinster final but instead we allowed them to dictate all over the field.

While all this was unfolding, I stood in front of the Hogan Stand asking myself: 'How did I let this happen?' It was a horrible, empty feeling, definitely the worst I experienced with Laois and far more painful than anything I had ever gone through in Kildare.

Somebody once said that the biggest mistake you can make when things are going badly is to assume that they won't get any worse. They very definitely can and they did for Laois within a few hours of the Dublin defeat when we were matched with Tyrone in the All-Ireland qualifiers.

Bloody hell! What was it with Laois and Ulster teams? We simply couldn't avoid them. Tyrone were by far the toughest opponents we could have got. Hell, they were the defending All-Ireland champions who had been blown off course by Derry in Ulster due to an injury blitz.

However, it had gradually cleared up and, while they struggled against Louth before winning the round one qualifier in a replay, it was clear they were beginning to come together as a serious force again. Still, we got a lucky break with a home draw. Hallelujah! The All-Ireland champions were coming to O'Moore Park.

On the evening of the Tyrone game, I knew we were facing a real crisis. We had one chance to rescue the season and I was determined that this time, I would take sole charge of everything. I was angry with myself for not retaining more control all season and for not trusting the instincts that had served me well for so long.

The critics crawled out from under their stones whispering that I was over the hill and that I was no longer capable of managing a team in the modern era. All groundless crap but, however long you're in the game, you're judged by your last outing which, in fairness, was as disastrous as they come.

Still, I would have expected that my record over the years might have granted me some degree of immunity from the sort of nasty, personal attacks that is sadly creeping into GAA coverage these days. But no, I got it on a number of fronts. I was yesterday's man trying to survive in today's world. It was as if I personally had allowed Dublin to rampage through Croke Park and should now be preparing for another humiliation at the hands of Tyrone.

It was time to assert myself and to stand up for what I believed in. I didn't know how we would fare against Tyrone but, by God, I was ready to give it a right go. Before training on the following Tuesday, I told Gerry that I wanted the squad to myself that night. They needed to know that I was still very much in charge and wasn't in any mood for humouring them. By Jaysus, did I run the life out of them!

They weren't happy but I didn't give a damn. After the way they had performed two days earlier, their credibility rating wasn't registering very high with me. A few players remarked to Declan O'Loughlin that we were 'back to the same old thing' again. He told them bluntly that I was having a session like that to get things moving. He was in no humour to entertain complaints either. In fairness, some players came back to him later and admitted that it was exactly the right thing to do.

I don't think I ever felt more motivated for any game than I did for Tyrone. After such a dreadful performance against Dublin, it was as if my whole managerial career was flashing in front of me. I simply couldn't preside over another shocking performance. The players knew their reputations were on the line too because if they flopped against Tyrone, they would have been right back to 2002 when even their own people thought nothing of them after the heartless effort against Meath.

The mood in the Laois dressing room before the Tyrone game was as tense as anything I have ever come across. Lose today and the season is over. I'm gone as manager and I have no doubt that some players would have made their final appearances too. It was that crucial.

If I was critical of the players for the way they folded against Dublin, I have to say it was inspiring to be involved with them against Tyrone. They simply weren't going to take no for an answer when Tyrone came back at them with the help of the strong wind in the second half. Laois led by three points at half-time but, having played with the wind and having missed a whole lot of chances, the lead looked dangerously inadequate. And it would have been, had the team not been in such a driven mood. I told them that the lead was more than enough if they wanted to win the game badly enough. Clearly, they did.

I don't think I have ever been more animated on the sideline than I was in the second half. I wandered across the line a few times too and while I knew the 'eye in the stand' was watching, I didn't give a tuppenny damn. This game just had to be won.

At one stage, I ran on to the field and grabbed Noel Garvan and shook him hard as I let him know in no uncertain terms what I expected of him. He looked at me and I could see him thinking to himself that I had gone mad altogether. Mind you, he caught the next high ball so I didn't care what he thought of me.

We won by 0-9 to 0-6 – our season had been rescued, our sanity restored. We went on to beat Meath in Navan and Offaly in Portlaoise to qualify for an All-Ireland quarter-final against Mayo. Deep down, the burning ambition was to get another crack at

Dublin which would have come our way had we beaten Mayo. God, we wanted Dublin so badly!

Trouble was, we lapsed back into our sloppy ways against Mayo and blew a great chance of reaching the semi-final. We led by two in the drawn game before giving away a couple of cheap points. We looked tired and switched off in the replay and were chasing the game – in vain as it happens – all day.

At the end, every photographer and camera man popped up in front of me to get a shot of me leaving the Croke Park pitch for what they believed was the last time. Little did they – or indeed I – know that I'd back there with Wicklow nine months later. I didn't feel any particular emotion other than disappointment at losing the Mayo game. I was asked, of course, if I was finished as a manager and I gave the perfectly truthful answer that I didn't know. My Laois days were over but nobody can ever forecast what the future holds.

My biggest disappointment was that we didn't get another game with Dublin. As Mayo showed, Dublin were vulnerable so Laois would have had a great chance of gaining revenge and after giving such an anaemic performance a few months earlier, they certainly wouldn't have lacked for motivation. But it didn't happen so we'll never know how a rematch would have turned out.

When I look back at my days in Laois, I regard them with a mixture of great affection and a fair sense of achievement but also with a feeling that we didn't achieve as much as we should. The first year was fantastic. Everybody was on the same wavelength, we were on a great adventure, we remained largely injury free and nobody questioned how I did anything.

It was never the same from there on. We were crucified with injuries. Influential lads like Joe Higgins, Tom Kelly, Kevin Fitzpatrick and Beano McDonald, the most naturally gifted forward in the county, all began to pick up injuries and it just seemed to spread. And then in the middle of it all, Colm Parkinson took off around the world for the summer. There were times when it became unbelievably frustrating but all I could do was get on with it.

I got great backing from the County Board officers but when we didn't retain the Leinster title in 2004 criticisms began to pop up from other quarters. Some people seemed to think that they could do the job better and, in time, some of the players began to absorb the negativity. That never happened in Kildare. We had good days, bad days and mixed days in Kildare but the players never asked questions. They got on with what they had to do and let me do the same with my end of the business.

Impatience set in far earlier than it should have in Laois. In hindsight, maybe it would have been better off if the Leinster final wasn't won in my first year. It became the benchmark and, amid all the backslapping and euphoria, sight was lost of the reality that there was absolutely no guarantee that Laois would get any better.

I'd have to say that I was disappointed with the way things progressed, especially how the players seemed to lose faith in me after 2004. It was noticeable in small ways but I tended to ignore them because I always had both eyes on the bigger picture which was winning the All-Ireland title.

Credit where it's due though, Laois is a remarkable county for producing under-age talent. They have possibly the best structure in the country but it hasn't happened by accident. In fact, other counties would do well to study the Laois model which gets players up to a high standard as juveniles so that by the time they reach minor level they're well able to adapt to the greater demands. There are a whole lot of unsung heroes involved at juvenile level in Laois – marvellous people who are driving Gaelic football in a very positive direction.

The trouble is that minor success tends to distort expectations in Laois. That doesn't happen in Kildare because there has been no recent history of achievement at under-age level. I'd have to say that if I compare my terms in both counties, Kildare were more unlucky not to have won an All-Ireland. Also, I'd admit that I found my time in Kildare – especially the second spell – more rewarding than any time in Laois.

Don't get me wrong, I had good times in Laois but it was never quite the same from the end of 2004. Unlike Kildare, they didn't seem to be quite able to take the bad days and began to look for scapegoats. More often than not, they looked in my direction which I could never understand.

For all that, I enjoyed most of my days there. I met lots of great people, had some marvellous experiences, enjoyed some success and left with my head held high. Another interesting chapter in the rich and varied tapestry of life.

Sham and Shamateurism

I read somewhere years ago where professors were defined as people whose job it is to tell students how to solve the problems of life which they themselves avoided by becoming professors in the first place. A touch harsh perhaps, but I often think of it when I hear full-time, well-paid GAA employees laying down the law about the absolute need to retain amateurism in the Association.

The sheer hypocrisy of the GAA's stance on amateurism is breathtaking. More than that, it's totally illogical and wouldn't stand up to any scrutiny in the Court of Fair Play.

It's as simple as this: we're either an amateur organisation or we're not. Either everybody has a chance to share in the cake or nobody gets to put a finger near it.

As it is, a certain number of people are doing nicely, thank you very much, while the real wealth creators – the players – have to scuffle for crumbs which very often are grudgingly dispensed. It's actually a form of slavery where the masters set the rules and the poor old workers are sent out to toil in the midday sun. And when they return in the evening, they're told to be happy with their lot. If it was good enough for your predecessors, it's good enough for you. Only it's damn well not.

Let's take All-Ireland final day. All the GAA's top brass are there in their best gear, busy no doubt organising the day and making sure everything runs to plan. It's part of their job for which they're well paid, but they're not the only ones making money from the occasion. Some of the stewards are paid, so too are the ground staff, the stile operators, the security people, programme sellers and the caterers in the bars and corporate boxes. And if a doping officer decides to drug-test a player, he or she is paid. I presume that some of the Gardaí on duty are on overtime so they're profiting too.

It's bonanza time for everybody except the lads who are down in the dressing room, worrying about how they will play in front of 82,500 people with the eyes of a critical and – yes – professional media monitoring their every move. Gate receipts from an All-Ireland final come in at around €4 million these days, yet all the players can expect is a measly contribution to a holiday fund. Even the County Boards involved receive only a small cut for expenses while the rest of the money goes into Central Council funds.

Now what exactly do the boys on Central Council do? Meet every few months to keep an eye on the overall situation while contributing very little to its development. As for coming up with initiatives on how the GAA can continue to develop in an increasingly competitive sporting world, don't ask Central Council to contribute anything. Some of the members are there so long that they think the position and the perks are theirs by right. Players and managers are judged every weekend but who decides whether a Central Council member is doing a good job? Who knows who they are?

I guarantee you that if you asked one hundred GAA supporters at any game around the country to name their county's Central Council delegate, ninety per cent of them would have no idea. The same goes for players, many of whom have probably never heard of Central Council.

Technically, a Central Council member can be voted out by County Convention but it rarely happens because clubs are too busy trying to survive without caring about national committees. Besides, the more able people concentrate on their own clubs rather than trying to climb up the greasy pole of county and national officialdom. I'm sure there are some good people on Central Council but in terms of overall impact on the GAA, I regard it as next to useless. Nothing personal, folks, it's just the way I feel.

They have taken to meeting in private session nowadays so we don't even get an account of how members perform, even on important issues. Why the secrecy? Why aren't the media allowed in? The media is the link between these bodies and the GAA membership, yet they're excluded from meetings. I have no idea why. As far as I'm concerned, Central Council is a secret society answerable to nobody which is totally unacceptable in an organisation that trumpets on about its democracy.

The real heroes in the GAA are the players and the hard-working volunteers in clubs all over the country. They make the GAA what it is, not Central Council – or any other council for that matter.

I fully accept that such a big organisation as the GAA needs to have a professional management structure. What I can't take is the contradictory policy where those who generate the money have no right to share in it while paid staff, at county, provincial or national level, can make a good living out of the efforts of amateurs.

I have no doubt that the dam will burst one of these days and the players will revolt because the current situation where the GAA takes in ever-increasing amounts of money but fails to appreciate the players' input can't last indefinitely. I'm amazed that the Gaelic Players' Association haven't been a lot more militant in this area.

They were treated with suspicion right from the start so they should live up to the image that the GAA authorities have of them. If you have a reputation for causing trouble, you might as well kick up a fuss because you'll be blamed anyway. If I were in the GPA, I'd be advocating that GAA doors got kicked a lot harder because the softly, softly approach won't work.

I'm not advocating pay for play on a weekly basis, but why not give inter-county squads even a small share of the gates as part of a genuine expenses package? Gate receipts for League and championship this year were around €40 million. On top of that, there was income from TV, sponsorship, advertising and various other commercial deals. The final figure wouldn't be far short of €50 million, every last cent of which was generated – directly or indirectly – by inter-county players.

If even twenty per cent went back to the players, it would generate a fund of €10 million which could be divided among them, depending on how far they progressed in the championship. Players who reach the All-Ireland final should get €25,000 a man which, for two panels of 24, would still cost just over €1 million each for hurling and football.

That still leaves nearly €8 million to be disbursed among the rest of the counties, depending on how far they progressed in the championship. It's a fair system in that the players who generate the most, ie those who remain longest in the championship, do best.

We're not talking about huge money here. Central Council took in nearly €45 million on its own last year. The four provincial councils also took in big money so if €10 million went back to the players, it would hardly break the bank but it would show that the GAA understood the need to react to the changed times we live in.

Player rewards aside, it's extraordinary how the GAA manages its money. Either provincial councils or Central Council collects and administers the huge sums earned by the championships while the counties involved, most of whom are struggling financially, receive relatively small team expenses. Monies will accrue later in the form of grants for grounds, coaching or whatever, but I feel strongly that counties should be paid directly from gate receipts for each match. The gate money should, in fact, be divided three ways between the two competing counties and the controlling body. That way, everybody gets to share in the pot.

It would also have a positive impact in terms of encouraging counties to devise ways to increase gates. As things stand, there is no incentive for counties to promote games, most of which don't attract full houses. So, we have a situation where the grounds have unused capacity, yet the competing counties have no incentive to increase the crowd. If they knew that they stood to get one-third of the gate, it would make sense for them to sell the games, increase the gate and boost their coffers. There might even be something extra for the players if counties were in a better financial position. It's simple and obvious, yet the GAA retains an outdated, centralised financial structure which wouldn't be tolerated by any business.

One of the arguments put forward for not financially rewarding players is that it would lead to jealousy among those further down the line and that the volunteer ethic which has underpinned the GAA since its foundation would disappear.

Wrong on both counts. Most ordinary club players are happy to be where they are. They put in a good effort, but nothing by comparison with the county players. They understand that, so I have no doubt that they would accept a situation where the star performers who are under enormous pressure got some financial reward. Rugby and soccer survive on that basis worldwide so why should it be any different in the GAA?

It's unacceptable, in these days of massive house prices, lengthy commuting and serious job pressures, that star GAA players who generate so much money can end up out of pocket. The GAA still refuses to compensate players who miss out on overtime or who are otherwise financially disadvantaged because they're putting so much effort into football or hurling.

Let's go back to All-Ireland final day. You could have a situation where a Garda working outside the grounds is on overtime, yet a Garda who is playing gets nothing even if he misses out on overtime because of his involvement in the final. How can that be justified? The wealth creator, not to mention the entertainment provider, gets nothing, yet others benefit from his hard work.

The GAA nearly ripped itself apart a few years ago while trying to decide whether or not to open Croke Park for soccer and rugby which had to be the craziest debate in the history of sport. It wasn't as if the IRFU and FAI were threatening to seize Croke Park. All they wanted was to use it while Lansdowne Road was being redeveloped, yet the stone age argument raged within the GAA as to whether they would hire their ground to other sporting organisations at a time of need. The alternative was to export Ireland's rugby and soccer internationals to Britain which would have been a national disgrace.

Thankfully, common sense prevailed and Croke Park was opened up and has turned into a high-yield cash cow which, if we're to believe the reports, is yielding more than €1.5 million per game. Bizarrely, the GAA plans to lock the gates of Croke Park again once Lansdowne Road is redeveloped, rather than declaring that they will continue to open for business for the big rugby and soccer occasions where a 55,000 capacity Lansdowne Road won't be big enough to cater for demand.

Imagine the situation in years to come if the GAA adhere to the daft notion of closing up Croke Park once Lansdowne Road is redeveloped. Rugby games against England and France would always pack Croke Park where the capacity is 28,000 more than Lansdowne Road. It would make neither sporting nor economic sense to play those games in Lansdowne Road as it would not only deny 28,000 people the opportunity to attend the game, it would also cut income for both the GAA and the IRFU.

It has been suggested that, once Lansdowne Road is redeveloped, the IRFU and FAI will have no interest in Croke Park. If that's the case, how will they explain to the rugby and soccer public who can't get tickets that they really don't care about them? By leaving themselves open for business, the GAA would win any PR battle that might arise in such a situation.

I would go further than merely leaving Croke Park open. There's absolutely no reason why the Munster rugby team can't play their high-interest games in the Limerick Gaelic Grounds. And if Connacht were going well, the occasional rugby boot appearing in Pearse Stadium wouldn't scar the GAA for life either. It's a matter of practicality and judgement.

The Limerick situation is unreal. The Gaelic Grounds can cater for nearly 50,000 people but how many times will it be full? The only time its capacity will be tested is for a Munster hurling final. With Thurles and Páirc Uí Chaoímh getting most of the Munster finals, Limerick will be lucky if they get one every four or five years. For the rest of the time, the capacity of the Gaelic Grounds is totally under-utilised so what would be wrong with renting it out to Munster rugby for the games where Thomond Park can't cater for the demand? The rent money could, for instance, be used to promote hurling in Limerick city which, according to what I hear, is badly needed.

The GAA would be using rugby money to help promote its own games which is the essence of good business. As it is, the GAA has a major asset in Limerick which is totally under-utilised. If proof were needed of the need to modernise thinking in a challenging sporting world, it came in 2006 when the Kerry v Galway National Football League final was fixed for Limerick a few hours after Munster and Leinster had met in the Heineken Cup semi-final in Lansdowne Road. Only 7,000 people turned out for the League final between two of the most attractive footballing sides simply because it was played in the wrong place at the wrong time.

The GAA has an awful lot to be proud of in terms of the infrastructure it has put in place all over the country. I was amazed to find, when I joined Wicklow, just how many clubs had excellent floodlights and other state of the art facilities. The same applies to lots of other counties. However, you can never stand still and when it comes to exploiting our major grounds, the GAA needs to be more imaginative.

There could never be any question of opening all GAA grounds to other sports. Most GAA club grounds are overworked as it is; besides there would be no financial gain in it. But when it comes to major centres such as Croke Park, the Limerick Gaelic Grounds and Pearse Stadium, Galway, there is absolutely no excuse for not using them to generate money by renting them out.

Exploiting grounds and rewarding players are only two of the serious issues that need to be addressed. I'm constantly amazed by the lack of marketing and promotion undertaken by the GAA. In fact, I fear that, unless this is addressed, gaelic games will come under enormous pressure from rugby over the next twenty years.

The days are gone when Irish rugby was happy to live out a sedate life in fee-paying secondary schools and other small pockets around the country. It was no threat to gaelic games then, but in the new, professional age it is developing rapidly as a global sport. In the old days, the only rugby we saw on TV were the internationals and the occasional Barbarians game. It's very different now.

There's rugby on TV several times a week in what has become virtually a 12-month season. People are familiar with players from New Zealand, Australia and South Africa and have a detailed knowledge of the home scene thanks to the progress made by the Irish team and the provinces.

Apart from the TV blitz, there are other reasons why the GAA needs to keep a close watch on the rugby scene. Unlike soccer, where the top Irishmen are all playing abroad, our rugby stars are at home which means that most weekends the public can go along and watch Brian O'Driscoll, Ronan O'Gara, Paul O'Connell and the rest of the boys in action.

That's helping to create an identity with the players. Leinster and Munster games in particular have become big social occasions, places to go on Friday and Saturday nights. It's all helping to increase an awareness of rugby which wasn't there before, especially among young people. Munster even has supporters from places like Waterville and other small villages which have no tradition of rugby. In time, that interest will build into something substantial and rugby will extend its base way beyond what would have been regarded as its main heartland.

Rugby has another appeal too in that it suits the Irish psyche. That explains why our international and provincial sides do so well from a relatively small pick, certainly by comparison with England and France. Rugby is a hard, manly game that suits Irish men and I have no doubt that it will get stronger and stronger in this country. Bear in mind that rugby union has been a professional game for little over a decade, yet it has made enormous strides. Where will it be in another twenty years?

It's up to the GAA authorities to ensure that rugby's advance is not at the expense of football and hurling but I see no evidence of a plan to cater for the inevitable challenge. As a professional sport, rugby has a natural appeal that gaelic games lack, certainly in their current form where the purse is zipped so tightly. Unlike soccer where a gifted young fella has to head for England in his teens to pursue his dream, his rugby equivalent can remain at home and continue his studies while also developing his rugby skills. The prospect of making a living from rugby is a powerful recruiting agent, especially by comparison with gaelic games where a top player can end up actually losing money because of his expertise.

I would also be concerned for the GAA by the knock-on impact of the successes in Irish rugby. When the current wave of rugby stars retire, I suspect that a great many of them will turn to coaching which will further strengthen the game. That's another area where the GAA has failed to exploit its own riches.

Take hurling. We all agree that it's an absolutely marvellous game, a national treasure that should be nurtured and protected. Most of all, there has to be a detailed plan in place to ensure that it continues to thrive in the traditionally strong counties while giving it a chance to grow in other areas.

The obvious way to do that it is to use the top stars to both sell and coach the game. If I were in any position of power in Croke Park, I'd ring up lads like DJ Carey, Henry Shefflin, Eoin Kelly, Ken McGrath and Joe Deane and offer them jobs as hurling coaches and despatch them into the weaker counties where they would work with schools and clubs. I'd make the package so attractive that they couldn't refuse. You can have a great coach who isn't known to youngsters and he won't have anything like the impact a Carey or a Shefflin would. We have so many star names in both hurling and football who could be employed by the GAA to coach youngsters but they're ignored. It's something I can never understand, especially at a time when it's difficult to organise coaching in a lot of primary schools because of the decline in the number of male teachers.

The GAA should have a coach visiting every single national school in the country to make sure that gaelic games remain very much on the agenda. Rugby is certainly spreading its wings in these areas so really the GAA has no choice but to get its act together. For God's sake, lads, hire the star names. Pay them well and send them out with a mission to promote gaelic games.

We've built the stadiums and now is the time to invest in the people and the games. The money is there and, even if it weren't, a few years renting Croke Park for rugby and soccer, not to mention for pop concerts, would create quite a war chest.

Another area where I believe the GAA is falling down is in how it uses television and radio. I don't believe that they are being used to their full potential, either in terms of coverage or in rights fees. Croke Park should have an experienced promotions unit to deal with this hugely specialised area which could be of enormous benefit to the GAA.

For years, the GAA let RTÉ television get away with providing a terrible service. When RTÉ covers games it does it well, but the problem was that for many years, there was virtually no gaelic games on TV between the end of September and St Patrick's Day. Why the GAA let RTÉ away with that is beyond me. Mind you, why RTÉ didn't show more games is also a mystery. It was a scandalous policy by the State broadcaster who should have been told bluntly that if they weren't prepared to provide coverage in winter, they could forget about the championships too. That would have concentrated the minds in Montrose.

Along came TG4 and, to their great credit, they spotted the gap in the market which they cleverly exploited through coverage of the club championships and National Leagues. The viewing figures were good and it didn't take long for Setanta to get in on the act too.

We all remember back in the 1980s when usually only the All-Ireland semi-finals and finals were covered 'live'. In fairness to RTÉ, that was a GAA decision and a daft one at that. They took the view that if more games were shown 'live', it would result in smaller crowds when, in fact, the reverse proved to be the case. Once the TV coverage was increased, more people tuned in, saw how much entertainment was on offer and opted to attend the games. It was a logical progression, yet for years the GAA stood stubbornly against it.

That's why they now need expert international advice on how best to use television to promote their games. The global nature of soccer and rugby means that they're being promoted all the time on the many channels now available in Ireland. The GAA is different. It has to rely on its own devices to sell itself, something it's not doing well enough at present.

Purely from a promotional and exposure viewpoint, it would be a good idea to stage one championship game each week other than on a Saturday or Sunday. Friday night would be ideal or, if they really wanted to try something new, why not opt for Wednesday night? Of course, that would involve players taking a day off work but it could be structured in such a way that different counties played the Wednesday night rota so I'm sure employers wouldn't cause a problem with one-off arrangements.

It would be different, though, when it came to compensating players for taking a day off work. We're back to the stupid regulation whereby the GAA won't pay lost wages. This is a classic example of muddled thinking. The promotional value of a midweek championship game would be enormous, yet it won't happen – for the foreseeable future anyway – because it would cause problems when players sought compensation. Instead, the GAA allows soccer to totally dictate the midweek TV schedules with rugby joining in from Friday and through the weekend.

Another shortcoming in GAA policy that drives me mad is the failure to appoint a commercial manager in every county. The job would entail dealing with all business aspects of running the organisation such as sponsorship, marketing, promotions and fundraising.

Basically, the person would be a full-time revenue generator and, provided he or she had the right expertise, I have no doubt it would prove hugely successful. It would be a no-lose situation as the appointment would be made on a performance-related basis. It would go some way to sorting out the nonsense that currently exists in relation to sponsorship of teams. Most counties are completely under-selling themselves, mainly because the people who are negotiating on their behalf are completely out of their depth in the commercial world.

I'll probably be criticised for being too hard on the GAA in the whole area of player payments, commercial activities, marketing and promotion but I'm doing it because I care. I have been a GAA man all my life, I love the organisation and the games but that doesn't mean that I have to park my critical faculties. I fear that we're spending too much time arguing over trivial issues and not facing up to the real challenges and tests that lie ahead.

The biggest of all is how players are looked after. It's impossible to see the situation continue whereby the GAA rakes in massive amounts of money, pays quite a large staff at various levels and then tells its players that there's no possibility of them ever getting any financial reward. It's a challenge that should be handled carefully, based on modern-day realities and not on an outdated philosophy that's selectively applied.

It's as simple as this – those who generate the wealth are entitled to share in it. It makes more sense to recognise that and plan accordingly rather than continuing to wallow in the hypocrisy of pretending that the GAA is an amateur organisation when it's actually not. How can it be when it pays so many people?

Peter Quinn is somebody I have great time for in the GAA because he's not afraid to speak his mind or to walk an unpopular line. So, when he says that the GAA's very survival is at risk unless it re-evaluates where exactly it's going, then it's time for others to take heed. As he said, the Roman Empire ruled the world for centuries and disappeared in twenty years. That's coming from a former GAA President, not a critic of the organisation.

The biggest mistake of all is to continue denying the players compensation for their ceaseless efforts. It's short-sighted, unnecessary and morally wrong. It can't last.

'Micko, You Let Me Down'

His eyes were cold, his stare severe and he spoke with a stern voice.

'Micko, you let me down.'

The emphasis on 'me' and 'down' was unmistakable. Clearly, he saw it as a personal affront that his invitation hadn't been accepted. Saying 'no' to one Charles J Haughey wasn't the done thing in the Ireland of the early 1980s, but I did it anyway and lived to tell the tale. The reason for his annoyance was that he wanted me to run in a general election for Fianna Fáil in south Kerry and wasn't pleased when I said no.

For years prior to that he would always send me a letter of congratulation after Kerry won an All-Ireland. It would be handwritten, humorous and usually make reference to the Dublin angle as we had beaten them a few times. I had visited his house in Kinsealy on several occasions and he often mentioned how he wanted me to run for the Dáil. At first I didn't know whether or not he was serious, but he raised it so regularly that I finally realised he meant business.

'Micko, there's a seat there for you. Say "yes" and the rest will be organised.'

I loved the certainty in everything he said. Nothing seemed a problem. If he said it would be 'organised' then it would.

'But what about local Fianna Fáil? Won't they kick up if I'm parachuted in as a candidate,' I asked.

'What do you mean "parachuted"? Who's more south Kerry than you?'

'I know, but I'm not involved in politics. They won't like it, you know, if I march in from nowhere.'

'That's not your problem. Just say you'll run and leave the rest to me.'

He was clearly very determined to get my name on the FF ticket because he would inquire from time to time when I was coming to Dublin and send a car to pick me up from the Burlington Hotel and whisk me out to Kinsealy. There, we would spend a while chatting.

He was easy company. We got on well and, in time, developed a warm relationship so when he cast his eye in the direction of south Kerry he obviously thought it would be good for Fianna Fáil to have me running there. My profile was high because of Kerry's success and he kept telling me that I was certain to win a seat if I ran.

There were even hints that, if I was elected, I would be made Minister for Sport at some stage in the future. Haughey got others to apply pressure on me too. On one occasion, I was driving over to Ballyvourney to pick up the lads from Coláiste Íosagáin when a senior FF official phoned the house. There were no mobile phones in those days so I couldn't be contacted, but Mary Carmel told him where I was headed.

So, when I drove into Coláiste Íosagáin two Mercedes were waiting for me. There was a by-election in Cork at the time and all the big Fianna Fáil guns were down to help the cause. Among them were Ministers Brian Lenihan and Gene Fitzgerald and Fianna Fáil General Secretary Frank Wall. I sat into one of the Mercs and they set about convincing me that my future lay in politics. They painted a very rosy picture which was hard to ignore, but I still harboured big doubts.

I had a passing interest in politics since I was a young lad, mainly because all belonging to me on both my father's and mother's side were republicans. Having fought in the 1916 Rising and the Civil War, my father had very strong views on political matters although he made it clear that he never wanted me to run for office.

We found ourselves in a most unusual position one time when he supported Jack Flynn, who held a seat for Fianna Fáil in south Kerry in the Forties and Fifties, while I backed Sinn Féin's John Joe Rice in the 1957 General Election. My father had fought with Jack in the Civil War while I knew John Joe well. I was involved with Sinn Féin and was helping out in this election by putting a few cars on the road to assist John Joe with his canvassing and also to bring people to the polling stations on election day.

He was elected but, together with the other Sinn Féin TDs, he wouldn't take his seat in the Dáil. It seemed a total waste of time to me to go to the trouble of running an election campaign, winning a seat and then refusing to enter the Dáil. Surely, if Sinn Féin wanted to bring about change at the time, it should have been done from inside the Dáil. A lot of people became disaffected with them because of their abstention policy.

Their TDs were elected mainly on local issues but, since they stayed outside the system, they couldn't do anything for their constituents so it was a sham really. I argued the case vigorously with John Joe, who was a really good man with deeply held convictions, but there was no move. So, when he stayed out of the Dáil, I lost interest in Sinn Féin and switched allegiance to Fianna Fáil.

Not that I was ever deeply involved with them. I was, what you might call, an enthusiastic supporter because I saw them as the main party that represented the real Ireland. Haughey would have known that. I knew his brother Jock quite well as he had played for Dublin and we came across each other quite a few times on the pitch.

I was always lukewarm over the prospect of running for the Dáil. For a start, I would be up against John O'Donoghue, the current Ceann Comhairle of the Dáil and a neighbour of mine from Caherciveen. John had failed to get elected in three general elections in the early Eighties which was probably why Haughey wanted me to have a go at winning a second seat which had been lost in 1981.

John had far more political ambition than me and I didn't want to have any unpleasantness with him or his family. I'd wrestle a bear over anything to do with football but I could take or leave politics. Still, the pressure kept coming from on high – well, Haughey mainly – and I finally agreed to give it serious consideration. In fact, it was all set up that I would be proposed and seconded at a convention in Killarney and I was told that I'd win a ballot if it came to that. And even if I didn't, Fianna Fáil head office would have added me to the ticket.

I went to the convention in a half-hearted mood and as I entered the hall I looked around and asked myself: 'Is this what you want? Do you really want to run for election and all it entails or are you allowing yourself to be pressurised into it? Are you doing this because you want to or because Charlie Haughey wants you to?'

There was only one answer. I wasn't committed to it nearly enough and all the hints about a ministerial appointment didn't mean a whole lot to me. Besides, I had my own Mercedes and, even if I didn't, I'd be happy in some other car.

Apart from the hassle of having to run an election campaign, I knew that if I got elected, I would have had to start dealing with all sorts of local issues. I'm not sure how I would have coped with people coming up to me asking to get roads tarred or bridges repaired. That suits some people, which is why they go into politics, but it wasn't me.

Withdrawing from the race came as a bit of shock to those who were set to propose and support me but I wouldn't change my mind. I knew it wouldn't go down well in Kinsealy but I wasn't going to have my life decided by anybody else or by Fianna Fáil's desire to win a second seat in south Kerry. John O'Donoghue ran again in 1987 and this time he won the seat and has been in the Dáil ever since.

Haughey didn't like being turned down and made it clear when I met him shortly afterwards. The letters also stopped from there on, and I didn't hear from him or see him again for years. However, on the night of the 1997 All-Ireland final, Páidí Ó Sé, who was a close friend of CJ, told me at the function in the Burlington Hotel that he was going out to Kinsealy the following morning. He insisted that I go with him, which I duly did, and we had a grand few hours out there. Haughey never mentioned my refusal to run all those years earlier, but then it wasn't important to either him or me anymore.

I doubt if many people refused an invitation from Haughey to run for Fianna Fáil but I was always my own man and would only do what I thought was right for me. Despite the controversies in which he found himself embroiled in later years, I always had great time for Haughey.

He had vision and courage, he got things done and he made things happen. Okay, so he bent some rules which nobody could condone but it was the culture of the time. That's not an excuse but it is an explanation. And when history judges him, I have no doubt that it will be favourable while also acknowledging that he had his faults. Ultimately, a politician has to be judged on whether he was good for the country and Haughey certainly scored in that regard in terms of the many business initiatives he devised which were hugely helpful to a struggling Irish economy.

I never regretted not going into politics. Some people said I would have been a natural at the job, although I'm not sure if that's a compliment or an insult! Anyway, it would have been virtually impossible to combine a football and a political career and, when it came down to it, there could only be one winner and it wasn't politics.

If I'm honest that was probably the biggest factor of all. Politics would have interfered with my job as Kerry manager – in fact I would probably have had to give it up – a bleak prospect which I couldn't entertain. Apart from winning three more All-Irelands with Kerry in 1984, '85 and '86, I would also have missed out on the fun and excitement I had with Kildare, Laois and Wicklow.

Besides, political life managed fine without me! Nowadays, I would take a very local view of politics and vote for the candidate who does most for our area. Unfortunately, Jimmy Deenihan isn't in my constituency because if he was, he'd get my vote every time, even if my leanings are towards Fianna Fáil. He's a good man and a good politician and the fact that he did so much for Kerry football would be a help too in securing my number one.

Despite staying out of formal politics, I have always maintained a keen interest in national affairs and I have to admit that I would be very concerned over the direction the country is taking. People never had more money, yet they never had bigger debt. The wild grab for more expensive houses, bigger cars, extra holidays has sucked society in a certain direction but nobody seems to know exactly where it's headed or who's in control. Nowadays, you will find lights on in houses at 5 am while there's darkness at 10 pm. The idea that some people have to be up before dawn to commute long distances to work and that they're so exhausted when they get home that they are in bed by 10 pm is worrying. Is that the direction the new, prosperous Ireland has taken? And if so, what sort of society is it creating?

Half the population is trapped in a cycle from which there seems to be no escape. The pressure is horrendous, especially on young people, and will inevitably lead to a far less contented society which is alarming.

When you see the traffic tailbacks heading into the big towns and cities every morning you have to ask why development has been allowed to proceed with so little proper planning. Why is everything based in the towns and cities? In another ten years, the countryside will be denuded completely while the urban areas will be bigger, crammed and far less comfortable.

The standard answer that this happens in every country is too simple. This is a small country so it should have been possible to plan things in such a way that a healthy balance was maintained between rural and urban living. As it is, cities and towns have too many people and not enough facilities, while the countryside is seriously under-populated.

Look around large areas of Kerry now and all you will see are houses that lie empty except at weekends. It's the same in counties like Cork, Clare, Galway, Mayo, Donegal and Wexford. People work mad hours all week so that they can buy houses in the country where they can escape to at weekends. Yet, in many cases, locals run into problems when they want to build one-off houses for themselves. What sort of an Ireland have we created for ourselves when young people can't get planning permission to build a house on a site given to them by their parents? It's total nonsense, yet it continues to happen.

We're told that the building of one-off houses, dotted around the countryside, is bad planning and that it makes more sense to have clusters of houses around towns. I don't go along with that. The countryside is more vibrant when there are people living there, as was the case down through the ages. Now, we're going for the model where everything is centralised in high density town and city living while the country areas are losing their people and their character.

It's a development that will have serious repercussions for the GAA into the future. Apart from the difficulty in having enough clubs to cater for large population centres where land for playing fields is scarce and expensive, there's the imbalance issue. The population of Dublin will be more than 1.5 million in another few years, yet they are represented by one county team. There was a proposal to have two Dublin teams, one from the northside, the other from from the southside, some years ago but it nearly led to a second Easter Rising as the County Board opposed it as if they were being asked to merge with Kildare and Meath. The idea was promptly binned but the underlying problem of how to cope with so many people under one Board still remains.

It calls for careful planning but, as of now, the GAA seems quite happy to muddle along, ignoring the reality that there has been a massive change in population trends right across the country over the past thirty years. The GAA aren't the only ones who haven't adapted to the ever-altering landscape.

It has happened on the economic front too where many great opportunities have been missed, ones that the country will come to regret in years to come. Take the fishing industry. We're an island race so fishing should be a massive industry in Ireland, certainly all along the west coast, yet it was never properly resourced by the State. It was obvious when we joined the EU that our fishermen would come under increased pressure, what with quotas and the challenges from the likes of France and Spain, but they never got the required support. As a result, the fishing industry is in serious trouble in this country which is an economic tragedy.

We didn't help the situation ourselves either because of the image that fish had as a food. I grew up in an Ireland where you didn't eat meat on a Friday; it turned into the day for fish. Because of the meat ban, fish was regarded as something of a punishment food to be tolerated once a week. As a result, Ireland never became a fish eating country to any great degree which is incredible when you think of where we're situated.

I make these points to highlight what I regard as a failure to exploit some of our natural resources and to plan properly for the future. We have allowed ourselves to become far too reliant on inward foreign investment. It has been very good for the country but we can't depend on multi-national companies doing business here forever. They'll go where market forces take them and, if there's cheaper labour in the Far East, they will have no compunction about moving out of Ireland as some have already done.

I'm not saying we can stand as an island race cut off from the rest of the world but we should be more self-reliant in certain areas. That's why the fishing industry should be booming, instead of which it's being squeezed to such a degree that people are leaving it in their droves.

Things have gone well for the country over the last decade but it would be stupid to assume that the boom will last. Hopefully it will, but we have to be prepared for every eventuality which is not the case at present. Selfishness and the 'must have now' mentality have taken over to such a degree that the country is unrecognisable from what it was. The economic upswing is fantastic, especially when you think of the hard times endured by so much of the population over the years but, as with any success, whether in business or on the pitch, it has to be managed. Unfortunately, some of the more unfortunate Celtic Tiger by-products are doing nothing to advance the standard of people's lives as opposed to their standard of living.

It's all part of a new trend in Ireland where we seem to have lost our identity and sense of place. We were never as affluent, yet probably never as selfish. The 'me' mentality is everywhere unlike in the old days when people got together to help each other out. Nowadays, people have to be paid for everything whereas in the past they got together as 'meitheals' and worked in small co-operatives for the general good. If a neighbour was in trouble, help arrived with no questions asked.

Times were harder but it was easier to find contentment. Nowadays, the search for happiness seems to be increasingly associated with alcohol and, in some cases, drugs.

While I never drank alcohol, I'm not against it either and ran many establishments where we sold lots of alcohol. However, a none too subtle change has taken place in recent years which is potentially very damaging to the fabric of our society.

I suspect that alcoholism will be a major problem in this country over the coming years. People don't go out for a drink in their local pub as much anymore. It was as much a social exercise as a desire to drink and was very much at the heart of local communities. That has changed to a large degree and now far more drink is being consumed at home, a development that could have devastating consequences.

Twenty years ago, wine was a minority drink in Ireland but it's everywhere nowadays. You pull into a filling station for petrol or a newspaper and when you go to pay, you have to pass the wine shelves. Walk around a supermarket and wine is laid out invitingly in almost every aisle. It seems to me that wherever you turn, the fruit of the grape is there to tempt you. And unfortunately, all the signs are that plenty of people are happy to be tempted.

It's a very aggressive marketing campaign which is clearly working as wine sales have rocketed. It's all being drunk at home which sets an example for young people who themselves will grow up to join that culture. People used to be offered a cup of tea when they dropped in on friends or neighbours, but now the wine bottle is out. Very often, it doesn't last long either.

I have no doubt that the increase in drinking at home will lead to a surge in alcoholism problems down the line and the worrying thing is that nobody is reacting to it. It's vital to have an education programme in place for youngsters (and maybe for adults too) which will redefine their approach to drink but right now the country is drowning in alcohol issues.

It's impacting on sport too as those involved with clubs know only too well. The top players look after themselves but you'll hear plenty of stories at club level of lads not turning up on Sunday morning because they were out the night before and are nursing serious hangovers.

If drink is becoming a national scourge, obesity is following closely and will also get worse unless it's addressed. The approach to healthy living has to be indoctrinated in children from as young as four or five years. If physical exercise was included in the schools' curriculum from the junior infant stage, then children would grow with it and accept it as part of their everyday lives.

I can't understand why successive governments have ignored such an obvious step towards a healthier society. One hour a day of physical exercise in all schools would not only lead to fitter youngsters, but would also get them into a good habit which, in many cases, would continue into later life.

Instead of making physical education a central part of school life, I have heard of instances where kids have been stopped running in the yard at lunch time because of insurance implications if they fall and hurt themselves. Can you credit that? We want our children to grow up with a positive approach to their fitness and general physical welfare, yet we stop them running around the school yards. It's a disgrace and a total betrayal of children. I'm a member of the Irish Sports Council and I keep bringing up the whole area of sport and recreation for kids because it's something I feel passionate about. The other members of the Council are probably sick listening to me but, in fairness, they all agree with the basic point. Now, it's a question of getting the government to act because frankly they are not discharging their responsibilities in this vital area.

Maybe I should have gone into politics after all, where I could have taken on some of those issues and exerted real influence. The trouble was that so many aspects of political life would have driven me crazy. I couldn't have seen myself sitting in the Dáil on a Tuesday or Thursday night listening to a debate on the committee stage of some dreary Bill, or doing John O'Donoghue's refereeing job as Ceann Comhairle. Well, certainly not when I could be in Killarney, Newbridge, Portlaoise or Aughrim training a team. And, if I'm honest, that's the real reason that a political career didn't appeal to me as it would have wrecked my football life. And that would have been about the most serious punishment I could have suffered.

No Compromise on
Ireland's Call

A t this stage of my life I have become philosophical about most
things. I don't get annoyed easily and I tend to let things pass
over my head. I also take people as I find them, I'll see more good
than bad points and I'll definitely give the benefit of the doubt
wherever I can.

I'm sorry to have to say that the same doesn't apply all across the
GAA world and certainly not in the corridors of power. I was never
paranoid but that doesn't mean that the GAA establishment wasn't
out to get me! In a sense, it did too and that showed just how petty
the system can be.

I would have loved to manage the Irish team in the International
Rules (or Compromise Rules as they were originally known) series
but I never got the opportunity. Instead, the honour headed in all
directions but Waterville. I have no doubt that the reason for
overlooking me was because I was viewed with a large degree of
mistrust by the GAA's ruling classes.

They were deeply suspicious over the manner in which Kerry
bent their idiotic rules on commercial deals back in the 1980s and
they have never been happy with my straight-talking style. So, when
it came to choosing an international manager, I wasn't just down
the list but off it altogether.

The closest they came to having me involved was when my fellow
countyman Seán Kelly, the then GAA President, asked me it I was
interested in becoming assistant to Pete McGrath in 2004..Pete is a
fine man and an excellent coach, as he proved with Down in their
All-Ireland successes of 1991 and 1994, but it was still an insult to
ask me to be his assistant.

I'm sure Kelly didn't mean it that way but if he thought about it to any extent it was obvious that I would have to say no. Maybe he reckoned that one Kerryman couldn't appoint another to the top international job but, if that was the case, he would have been better off not to mention it to me at all. Hadn't I done enough to be offered the job?

I was still managing Laois at the time which presumably came against me, although I don't know why it should. If Kevin Sheedy, full-time coach in Essendon, could manage Australia in 2005 and 2006, why couldn't a serving county manager do the same with Ireland? Besides, when Kevin Heffernan was appointed manager back in late 1985, he was still managing Dublin. He resigned in early 1986 but, as far as I'm aware, that had absolutely nothing to do with the Irish job.

I'm convinced that the real reason I was never appointed was because I wasn't liked in Croke Park. The elephant never forgets and the GAA had trunk loads of reasons why they didn't want me as international manager. Or at least they thought they had.

They made that abundantly clear when they appointed Heffernan as manager for the 1986 tour. Galway's Liam Sammon was his assistant. Don't get me wrong, I'm not saying I had a God-given right to the job ahead of Heffo but over the previous seven years, Kerry had beaten Dublin in four All-Ireland finals so I must have been doing something right.

When it came to appointing replacements for Heffo and Sammon, the GAA turned to Eugene McGee and Seán McCague. Again, my name didn't come up or, if it did, it was quickly shot down. The series with Australia was abandoned between 1990 and 1998 but when it resumed, I was still ignored and the manager's job passed from Colm O'Rourke to Brian McEniff to John O'Keeffe to Pete McGrath and finally to Seán Boylan. Johnno was manager while he was still training the Kerry team so there was no problem there, yet my involvement with Kerry, Kildare and Laois always seemed to count against me.

It did because the GAA wanted it to. Being passed over for the Irish manager's job might look like no big deal but I would have regarded it as a great honour to be appointed. Being involved with one's country at any level is a special privilege, one I would have savoured and appreciated. I would also have put in a huge effort – whether or not I was involved with a county team – but when the establishment says no, it means it.

Nonetheless, I'm entitled to ask why? Did they think I wasn't up to the job? If so, it says something about their judgement. I would have brought a lot of new ideas to the table and I'll tell you this – we would have been a damn sight better prepared than either the Irish team that was walloped in Australia in 2005 or the one that caved in against Australia the following November. I'm not criticising Seán Boylan who played the hand he was dealt but I'm amazed he didn't demand another one which involved keeping the squad together for a few weeks. They should have been in camp for a week before the first test and remained there until the night of the second game.

I could never understand why Boylan didn't insist on that. Instead, the team dispersed and went back to work until the following Thursday when they reassembled.

That had been the policy with the Irish team for previous 'home' series against Australia but it never made any sense. In fact, it was ridiculous. The Irish team, comprised totally of amateurs, returns to work in between the tests, while the visiting Australians, all of whom are accustomed to the professional life, spend the week gearing up for the second game. Even without their vengeful approach, the Australians are usually favourites to win because they are better prepared.

If I had been in charge, I would have demanded that the Irish team be together for at least two weeks. In cases where players suffered a loss of earnings, I would insist on having them reimbursed. With over 110,000 people attending the two tests, the coffers could afford to take a small hit!

Besides, there was never a problem looking after the Irish team for over three weeks when they travelled to Australia. Yet they weren't even kept together for the home series when it was abundantly clear that they needed time to work on tactics, not to mention getting proper rest for what was always going to be a fierce physical challenge.

The question of keeping the Irish team together for a week or more was raised by the media at the time and the response from the

GAA authorities was that players would find it hard to get time off work. Are they serious?

Is there an employer anywhere who would refuse to give a player two weeks off to represent his country? It's not as if it would be a regular occurrence since the series is played only once a year. Even then, there is quite often a big turnover of players from year to year so the same companies wouldn't be losing players all the time. Anyway, imagine the damage it would do to a company's image if they refused a player time off to play for his country. There would be very few employers who would make an issue of it, especially if the GAA paid the wages of the players involved.

As far as I'm concerned that's the crux of the matter and the real reason the GAA didn't want players staying together for two weeks. Compensating players for loss of wages is a very sensitive matter in the GAA. So sensitive, in fact, that the GAA feels the best way of coping is to ignore it altogether. If a player loses out on overtime because of his involvement with a county team, that's his problem. He won't be compensated even at a time when there's a record amount of money flowing into the GAA. That can't be right.

It's most unlikely now that I will ever get a chance to manage the Irish team because, apart from the GAA's obvious policy of ABM (Anybody But Micko), the future of the series is in doubt. The GAA decided to 'park' it after last year's bust-up in Croke Park and it's unclear when, or indeed if, it will be reactivated.

The GAA over-reacted to what happened last year. Granted, some of the rough stuff perpetrated by the Australians was totally unacceptable but the problem lay in the failure of the referees to implement the rules. Why didn't they send players off on straight red cards right from the start? That would have settled things down quickly.

It's bizarre that two associations like the GAA and the AFL, who created a game that the public and players love, have abandoned it because good discipline couldn't be maintained. As happens so often, the players will be the losers. They made it clear at the time that they wanted the series to continue but, surprise, surprise, their views were ignored. It was clear from some of the rather frothy comments coming out of the Australian camp between the two games last year that they were going to attempt to intimidate the

Irish team in the second test, but what did the GAA do? Nothing, it would appear.

At the very least they should have met the Australians and told them that 'open slather' (a term which everyone knew translated into pure mayhem) would not be accepted. The GAA should also have made a public statement in advance of the second test that they would not tolerate any nonsense from the visitors.

I sincerely hope that the series is relaunched because it's an excellent concept. If it is restarted, I'll still be watching from the stands as I don't suppose I'll ever get the call to manage the team! But then, I didn't get many other calls from the GAA either. I was on a Rules Revision Committee once where we made a number of recommendations, including the introduction of the direct pick-up, but none of them lasted the course. I coached an All-Stars team on a tour to America one year but I wasn't the manager. No, that honour went to Paddy Muldoon from Mayo.

I have no doubt that officialdom's suspicion of me arose from the manner in which Kerry challenged the daft regulation on playing gear, advertising and endorsements back in the Seventies and Eighties. Things had improved from my days as a player but for some strange reason the GAA were terrified that their amateur wall would come crashing down if they allowed the players to climb up on it and have a look out at the rest of the sporting world.

It was a classic defensive pose and sadly there was little vision as to how change should be managed. It was clear that in a developing Ireland, commercial companies would be keen to become involved with the GAA but the response was one of scepticism and suspicion, not to mention sheer bloody-mindedness especially when it related to players.

Kerry's All-Ireland successes in the Seventies and Eighties meant that we were regular travellers to the US for the games between the champions and the All-Stars. They were hugely enjoyable, offering the players some great experiences and, as someone who always loved to travel, I never missed out on those tours if at all possible.

Deep down, I had another hankering. In 1970, I had travelled to Australia and New Zealand with the Kerry team that won the All-Ireland. It was a daring venture, designed to show off Gaelic football to the Australians but it didn't work out on that front. The

Australians were only interested in their own game and it was clear that if the GAA wanted to link up with them formally, it would have to be on the basis of a mixture of Aussie Rules and Gaelic football.

Still, it was a wonderful experience. I loved Australia, especially Perth where I found the people to be so friendly that they could have been from Kerry. I made up my mind to go back to Australia if the chance ever arose which it did in 1981 when Kerry embarked on the trip of a lifetime. It was an expensive trip, taking in New York, San Francisco, Melbourne, Adelaide, Perth, Sydney and Hawaii, but we saw an opportunity to harness the commercial side of Kerry's success and reckoned we could raise the necessary finance.

We set out with a target of around £70,000 (nearly €90,000 in today's money) but ended up with a kitty of £110,000 (€140,000) which meant that the touring party's wallets were nicely padded as we jetted out of Shannon. We worked hard at raising the money and our success in that area showed beyond doubt that the appetite for Gaelic games in the commercial world was sharpening all the time.

Adidas came on board as substantial sponsors (they gave us £10,000 which was a lot of money back then) and that's where the friction began to arise. In return for that sponsorship, I promised Adidas that we would use their gear, even if wasn't allowed under archaic GAA rules which insisted that only Irish-made gear could be worn.

I could never fathom out how all that was policed and frankly I couldn't care less. Adidas were supporting us so we'd support them. The GAA knew the situation and didn't like it and began to apply pressure through the County Board and, in particular, the Chairman, the late Frank King.

Frank was an absolute gentleman but, when he started to feel the heat from Croke Park, he quite naturally took it up with me. He told us before the 1982 Munster final that the strip manufactured by O'Neills, who had the official gear franchise for the GAA, would have to be worn. I was caught in a bind. I didn't want to make life awkward for Frank but a deal had been done with Adidas and was not going to be reneged on.

People might say that I was over-stepping my authority, and maybe I was, but it was all being done for the good of the players. I had grown sick and tired of watching outsiders make money out of our players by selling team photos, calendars, Kerry mugs, pens, scarves and the rest. Because the team were so successful, a whole industry had grown up around them and, unless we took some control of it, we would have been completely ripped off by every opportunist with an eye to the half chance.

It wasn't as if the Kerry County Board were making anything out of it either. No, all this extra-curricular activity was in the hands of complete outsiders so we started to box clever. We messed up pre-match team pictures by leaving a few players out so that nobody would have the full line-up except ourselves. We would then take an official photo and sell it as part of our fundraising activities. We made £30,000 in one year alone from team shots, money that flowed into the holiday funds when otherwise it would have gone into the pockets of people who had nothing whatsoever to do with the team or even football.

That whole area is still in a fairly chaotic state today. Things have tightened up a bit but players are still being exploited and it seems to me that the authorities are more interested in controlling what lads can and cannot earn than they are in preventing outsiders from exploiting them.

Anyway, the whole gear controversy erupted into open mutiny in the summer of 1982. I told Frank King that we would be ignoring the directive from Croke Park regarding gear and that I would prefer to lose the All-Ireland rather than accept instructions which were blatantly anti-player. Okay, so maybe I was a bit of a dictator but it was all done on behalf of the players.

They couldn't take on Croke Park but by God, I could and I did. I wasn't on my own of course. The Supporters' Club were very strong on this issue, especially the Chairman, Tom McCarthy from Dingle, who did great fundraising for the squad and who believed very strongly that nobody should be allowed to exploit the players.

We wore the 'banned' Adidas jerseys in the Munster final and again in the All-Ireland semi-final against Armagh, but I knew that the real issue would blow up once we got to the final. The pressure on King grew to unbearable levels. The phone calls from Croke

Park became increasingly frequent and they weren't enquiring as to our wellbeing for the final. Basically, Frank was being told to assert the authority of the Kerry County Board and to fall into line with Croke Park policy, however unfair or misguided it was.

On the Thursday before the final against Offaly, we got word that, because of a clash of colours, we would have to wear our second registered colours, green with gold collars and cuffs. I have no doubt it was done to throw us off guard. O'Neills would have that strip readily available but Adidas wouldn't, so the GAA thought we were in trouble.

Earlier that week, the late Mick Dunne, RTÉ's GAA correspondent and a man I had great time for, showed us the pin stripe Adidas jersey that we were supposed to wear. He held it up for the TV cameras but it was in the original Kerry colours, not the second colours we were subsequently instructed to wear.

I was livid when I heard what the GAA had done. It was a sneaky way of trying to force us out of the Adidas gear but we weren't having it. I rang Michael O'Connell of Adidas on the Thursday night and asked him could they produce a set of jerseys in our second colours in time for Sunday.

He said it would be a very tight call but, fair play to him, he got onto it straight away. The new set were made in Donegal (so they were manufactured in Ireland after all!) and delivered to the Grand Hotel in Malahide where we were staying on the Saturday night. Another set came out from O'Neills but we were never going to wear them, certainly not in the final anyway.

Poor Frank King was in an awful position, trapped between the bigwigs from Croke Park instructing him to assert his authority on behalf of the Kerry County Board and a determined manager who wasn't prepared to accept anti-player regulations. On the day of the final, a senior official from Croke Park – I think it was the late Pat Quigley who was GAA public relations officer at the time – came into our dressing-room and inspected the jerseys, presumably expecting to spot the Adidas tag. There wasn't any to be found because we had cut them all off. We got around €20,000 from Adidas that year and the County Board was fined €500 for the so-called gear violation, so we made a nice profit.

More importantly, we had made a statement that we weren't going to be pushed around. When we lost the final, critics claimed that we allowed ourselves to be distracted by the whole gear issue which wasn't the case. The players were kept well shielded from it while all the controversy behind the scenes certainly didn't upset me. In fact, I thrived on it.

However, I have no doubt that it added another few pages to the 'Micko File' in Croke Park and when it came to choosing an Irish manager, my name wasn't anywhere in line. It wouldn't be the first or last time that we got into trouble over commercial deals.

The famous full-page Bendix washing machine advertisement which appeared in the Sunday papers on the morning of the 1985 All-Ireland final caused quite a stir too. It ran with the slogan 'Only Bendix Could Whitewash This Lot' and featured pictures of a group of Kerry players and me standing around a washing machine in various stages of undress after a training session.

All hell broke loose. Croke Park, already fuming over some of our earlier deals, deemed it to be in bad taste. The poor souls must have lived awful sheltered lives altogether. The Bendix deal was actually organised by the County Board and my view was that if we were going to get funds from it for a holiday, we would be more than prepared to stand near a washing machine for a few minutes to have a picture taken.

The deal was reputedly worth £5,000 (we didn't get full details because it was organised by the Board) which was ridiculously low. Had I been involved, I would have looked for at least £20,000 and even more later on because Bendix got a massive amount of publicity from the ensuing controversy.

The Bendix deal took an unfortunate turn some time later and this time it had nothing to do with GAA headquarters. We thought the £5,000 would go to our holiday fund but the Board seemed to think that, since they had organised the deal, they would control the funds. A team holiday was organised for the Canaries but not all of the lads could go so we demanded that they be provided with travel vouchers for use at a later date. The Board, possibly afraid of getting into more trouble with Croke Park, refused. It was one of the very few times I had a serious issue with the Board but I felt they were being unfair to the players. It was time to make a stand.

We were due to play Laois in a challenge game in Portlaoise in mid-May 1986 and we saw this as the perfect way to assert ourselves by threatening to pull out of the fixture. Such mutinous thoughts might have been seen as heresy by many Kerry people but there was a principle at stake.

When word got out that we were considering boycotting the game, we were crucified by sections of the media. We were accused of being too big for our boots, of losing touch with reality and of betraying the spirit of the GAA. And all because we wanted what was rightfully ours. In the end, an uneasy truce was brokered with the Board reluctantly agreeing to give holiday vouchers to the players who didn't travel to the Canaries. No doubt, my role in the affair was noted in Croke Park.

The clash with Laois wasn't any ordinary challenge game. Laois had won the League title for the first time in sixty years two weeks earlier so the county was buzzing. Nearly 10,000 people turned out in O'Moore Park to salute a team that they thought were on its way to even greater things.

The League trophy was shown off before the game which we thought rather amusing as it seemed a little bit over the top to be publicly celebrating a League win with such gusto so close to the championship. We had most of our All-Ireland team on duty but their minds were elsewhere and Laois hammered us. It was a bad result for them, even if they didn't know it at the time. They had won the League and beaten the All-Ireland champions in the space of a fortnight so some of them began to believe their own publicity. It wasn't the first time it would happen in Laois.

Meanwhile, over in Wicklow, Kevin O'Brien and his mates were watching with interest as the Laois hype machine went into overdrive. A month later, Wicklow pulled off a great coup, beating Laois in the Leinster quarter-final in Aughrim. It was a disastrous day for Laois, who had three players sent off. It wrecked the momentum Laois had built up over the previous year and they wouldn't reach another Leinster final for five years or win one for 17.

Losing a challenge game to Laois didn't bother us but the controversy that had surrounded our appearance wasn't good for anybody and should have been avoided. However, I have always held that it was of the County Board's making although, in fairness to them, they were probably coming under such scrutiny by Croke Park that they were afraid of making a mistake.

It was sad that, instead of noting how many opportunities were out there, the GAA took the narrow view that raising money for team funds and holidays was a stepping stone to some sort of professionalism. It was far from it. All we wanted to do was get as much as we could for the players. It was open and above board. We made sure, for instance, that all players were treated equally and that no elite clique prospered to the detriment of the others. Detailed accounts were kept and not a penny went astray.

The trouble was that we were ahead of our time and, as such, we were treated with deep suspicion. And since I was the figurehead at the top of what the GAA perceived as a threat to old values, they made damn sure that I was locked outside when it came to the International Rules job.

The GAA powerbrokers might not have liked the way I tested their regulations on commercial deals all those years ago but I don't think they could ever accuse me of doing anything out of order on a pitch or a sideline. I have always lived by a code of decency and fair play, yet I was damn near suspended in 2006 in the craziest of circumstances.

I was amazed to learn, a few weeks after Laois had beaten Offaly in the qualifiers, that I was to be charged with encroaching onto the pitch, not once but twice. Now, if it had been for the Tyrone game a few weeks earlier, I might have had a case to answer as I was really wired that day but things weren't nearly as tense against Offaly who were on a downer after losing the Leinster final.

We won handy and moved on quickly to planning for the quarter-final with Mayo, only to discover that the 'eye in the stand' had reported me for pitch encroachments. Even the times of the so-called misdemeanours were recorded and that gave me an out. We had a video of the game which showed exactly where I was on the sideline at the times I was supposed to be on the pitch, so I headed for the hearing in Croke Park looking forward to having my say.

There were all sorts of rumours that I was bringing a high-powered legal team with me to present my case but I had no intention whatsoever of doing that. Instead, I travelled with Dick

Miller, the Laois Chairman. It was my first time before a disciplinary committee and, in a strange sort of way, I was looking forward to it because I wanted to see how these things operated. I told the committee that they would be bang out of order if they banned me from the sideline, reminded them of my record as a player (never sent off) and manager (never in trouble before) and then handed them the video.

I was confident that if fair play prevailed, I would get off and thankfully it did and I was exonerated. So why was I called in at all? Did someone want to get me in what they thought was my final year as a manager? It was nonsense from start to finish but then a few years earlier, the GAA had pulled one of the most stupid stunts of all time when they fined Laois €1,400 after Joe Higgins' twin sons marched with the team in the pre-match parade for the 2003 Leinster final.

It made a lovely picture which was carried in several papers the following day, but the GAA decided it was against some regulation and promptly slapped a €700 fine on Laois for each of the two lads. I think Laois got off on some technicality but the damage was done from the GAA's public relations viewpoint because it showed them to be petty over a small thing on what was a special day for Laois who won the Leinster title for the first time in 57 years. The pettiness didn't surprise me because I have seen plenty of examples of it over the years, not least in the steadfast refusal to give me a crack at the International Rules job. But then, I had taken on the system and was never forgiven for it.

Pitch Fever: Season by Season

1954: Highlight: Munster minor title

Anyone see my Munster medal? I scored 1-6 in the semi-final replay against Waterford but was down to number 18 for the final against Cork. I was down even further for the All-Ireland semi-final and wasn't even an official substitute for the final against Dublin which Kerry lost by a point. For some reason which nobody ever explained, I never got my Munster medal. Has anybody got it?

1955: Highlight: 1st Kerry county senior title

A county senior medal with South Kerry at the age of 18. Happy days. I kicked the levelling point against North Kerry and we won the replay. North and South Kerry would have had very little in common at that time. We felt like second class citizens in the south, believing that we had to be twice as good as the rest to get a run with Kerry. We weren't far out either.

1956: Highlights: Munster junior medal; senior Kerry debut; 2nd Kerry title

I was at midfield with Ned Fitzgerald (Maurice's father) against Waterford in the Munster junior final but lost the All-Ireland semi-final replay by a point to Monaghan. I was as stiff as a board after getting my training all wrong. I never got into the game and was replaced but seven weeks later I got the call-up for the seniors. Me – a county man! Dateline – 21 October 1956.
Venue: Austin Stack Park, Tralee.
Competition: NFL.
Opposition: Carlow.

Position: Right half-back.
Opponent: Brendan Hayden.
Result: Carlow 0-9 Kerry 0-6.
Verdict: 'Newcomer Mick O'Dwyer was not a success at right half-back,' wrote John Barrett in *The Kerryman*. Thanks, John!

1957: Highlight: 1st Munster senior championship game

All players recall their first senior championship debut and I certainly remember mine, even if it's for the wrong reasons. Kerry have rarely been beaten by Waterford but my championship debut day, 2 June 1957, was one such occasion as we lost by a point in a game that got plenty of publicity at the time and again in 2007, the 50th anniversary of one of the great upsets in GAA history. Mind you, Waterford deserved their victory against a Kerry team that was a shambles for all sorts of crazy reasons. And to crown it all, my performance didn't impress *The Kerryman* which was less than complimentary of my efforts.

1958: Highlight: 1st Munster senior medal

The first of my 12 Munster senior championships arrived courtesy of an easy win over Cork in the Athletic Grounds. It rescued a year that looked to be heading for disaster when we lost a League game to Kildare by 3-10 to 1-0 in Naas. Even then, we were lucky to get a goal. My first championship game in Croke Park ended in defeat in the All-Ireland semi-final where we lost to Derry by a point.

1959: Highlights: 1st All-Ireland senior medal, 2nd Munster medal, 1st NFL medal, 3rd Kerry county title

The first of my four All-Ireland final wins and the closest I ever came to marking Kevin Heffernan. He was at left full-forward on the Dublin team that lost to Kerry in the All-Ireland semi-final while I started at left full-back before moving to my favoured left half-back slot. I can't recall our paths crossing very much that day. We beat Galway surprisingly easily in the final. We gained revenge on Derry for the previous year's All-Ireland semi-final defeat when we beat them by a goal in the League final. I broke into Munster's Railway Cup team for the first time but we lost to Leinster in the final. I won a third county title with South Kerry which was actually for the 1958 season but the final wasn't played until spring 1959 after a boardroom battle between us and Kerins O'Rahillys. The title meant nothing to me because O'Rahillys had beaten us in the semi-final and we only got back in on an objection which was no way to win anything.

1960: Highlight: 3rd Munster senior medal

The Munster title was poor consolation in a year when we lost the All-Ireland final to a Down team that brought a new dimension to Gaelic football. Fitter, sharper, better organised and with a definite hint of cynicism when it came to taking out opponents, Down won the All-Ireland for the first time, beating Kerry by eight points in the final, the biggest defeat ever suffered by the Kingdom up to then.

1961: Highlights: 4th Munster medal, 2nd NFL medal

More misery at the hands of Down. They beat us by six points in the All-Ireland semi-final. They were ahead of us in all facets, most of all in a tactical sense. We demolished Derry in the League final but by the end of the year, there was no doubt that the balance of power had swung north to Paddy Doherty and Co.

1962: Highlights: 2nd All-Ireland medal, 5th Munster medal

Kerry have always been experts at picking up All-Irelands in seasons where the standard is fairly moderate. Tradition kicks in and Kerry walk away with the prize. 1962 definitely fell into that category. Cavan walloped Down in the Ulster final but then lost to Roscommon in the All-Ireland semi-final. The final really was one of the worst on record, not that it bothered us as we won by six points. Besides, the record books only show who won titles, not the quality of football they produced.

1963: Highlights: 6th Munster medal, 3rd NFL medal

We finally got the better of Down, beating them by a point in the Home League final in a game that very nearly cost me my big toe. We went on to retain the Munster title and were odds-on favourites to beat Galway in the All-Ireland semi-final but were shocked by a young team that would go on to torment us over the next few years. What was it about Galway? They caused me untold trouble over the years.

1964: Highlight: 7th Munster medal

Broken legs, crushed dreams, Kerry in decline. Cork weren't really putting it up to us in Munster in those years while Cavan caved in completely in the All-Ireland semi-final. However, Galway were a different proposition in the final, beating us by five points. I switched from defence to attack that year but made no impression after suffering serious leg injuries early in the year.

1965: Highlight: 8th Munster medal

We grew to hate the sight of Galway who beat us in both the League ('Home') and All-Ireland finals. The All-Ireland was my worst ever game for Kerry. I wasn't fully fit after injuring my ankle and I can assure you that playing against Noel Tierney, Seán Meade and Co was not recommended unless you were in the whole of your health.

1966: Highlight: Became a Kerry selector

A long list of injuries had taken their toll. I wasn't playing well which frustrated me so much that, after a big defeat by Cavan in a League game in February, I quit the county team at the age of 29. However, I was still involved, this time as a selector having topped the poll on 53 votes at the County Convention in January. Selectors were elected rather than appointed back then.

1967: Highlight: Topped the selectors' poll again

It was a bleak time for Kerry football. Cork won the Munster title again while even the League was going against Kerry whose level of performance had dipped to such a degree that Wicklow were unlucky not to beat us in Tralee. I was still officially retired but again topped the poll in the selectors' vote.

1968: Highlight: 9th Munster medal

My injury sheet was clear and the bug had bitten again so I returned to the county panel. We broke Cork's run in Munster which was very important. However, after being lucky enough to beat Longford in the All-Ireland semi-final, Down returned to haunt us again (what was it about Down and Galway in the 1960s?), beating us more comprehensively in the All-Ireland final than the two-point margin suggested.

1969: Highlights: 3rd All-Ireland medal, 10th Munster medal, 4th NFL medal, Texaco Footballer of the Year, country's top scorer

My best year as a player. I was the country's top scorer in a season where everything went right as we beat Offaly and New York in the League finals ('Home' and 'Away'), Cork in the Munster final and Offaly in the All-Ireland final. There's no better feeling than when you're in good condition, the games are going your way and you're playing well. Being chosen as the Texaco Footballer of the Year at the age of 33 was a real thrill. Hell, I had quit three years earlier.

1970: Highlights: 4th All-Ireland medal, 11th Munster medal, country's top scorer

I won the last of my four All-Ireland medals as Kerry completed our first two-in-a-row since 1940. Nobody could have envisaged then that the next four seasons would prove so problematical for us. We beat Meath in what was the first eighty-minute final and I again topped the year's scoring lists.

1971: Highlights: 5th NFL medal, player/manager, country's top scorer

A League medal barely registered on our achievement scale after Cork beat us by 11 points in the Munster final. I was player/manager for the closing stages of the League which we won by beating Mayo. I topped the scoring lists for the third year in a row but it made no impression on the All-Star selectors in what was the inaugural year of the scheme. They decided Andy McCallin (Antrim) and Séamus Leydon (Galway) to be better choices as corner-forwards.

1972: Highlights: 12th Munster medal, 6th NFL medal, 1st Railway Cup medal

I finally filled a vacancy in my collection when I won my first – and only – Railway Cup medal when Munster beat Leinster in a final replay. I had played on three losing final teams prior to that. For some reason, Kerry players didn't seem to give a hoot about the Railway Cup up to then. I punched the levelling point in the All-Ireland final against Offaly but Willie Bryan destroyed us in the replay and we lost by nine points, Kerry's highest ever losing margin on the big day.

1973: Highlight: 7th NFL medal

Another League medal (we beat Offaly by four points in the final) meant very little to me or Kerry. The target was to make amends for the 1972 All-Ireland final replay defeat but we came nowhere near achieving it and were smashed by Cork in the Athletic Grounds in what was my last Munster final.

1974: Highlight: 8th NFL medal

My eighth and last League medal was secured as a substitute when Kerry beat Roscommon in a replayed final on the same day as Dublin began their All-Ireland run by beating Wexford in a first round Leinster championship game. I wore the Kerry jersey for the final time on 19 May, coming on as a substitute against Sligo in a challenge game in Killorglin. I scored three points and the selectors wanted me to play in the NFL final replay against Roscommon a week later but I declined. Had I played, I would have continued for the championship. By then I would have been 38 years old. My instincts told me it was time to go.

1975: Highlights: Manager: 1st All-Ireland senior and U-21, 1st Munster senior and U-21, 1st Railway Cup titles

This manager lark is easy. Dublin and Cork were supposed to be the top two sides in the country but we beat them by seven and ten points respectively. We also crushed Tipperary and Sligo, going through all four championship games without conceding a single goal. Let the good times roll with this young side, many of whom were also aboard the successful U-21 team.

1976: Highlights: 2nd Munster senior and U-21 titles; 2nd All-Ireland U-21, 2nd Railway Cup title

Reality check. When you're perched on the highest peak, you have to keep a constant lookout for those who are massing below. We didn't. The good life beckoned and too many of the team supped more regularly than was wise. We should have been beaten by Cork in the Munster final but survived. Not so against Dublin who were a side possessed after losing to us a year earlier. They beat us well in the All-Ireland final, delivering a harsh dose of reality to all of us.

1977: Highlights: 3rd Munster senior and U-21 titles; 1st NFL and 2nd All-Ireland U-21 titles; 3rd Railway Cup title

A decent title haul but not enough, it seems. Get Micko out – he doesn't know what he's at. The All-Ireland semi-final defeat by Dublin presented a threat to my survival as manager. Many in Kerry wanted me out but, thankfully, County Chairman Gerald McKenna didn't and he got his way. A third successive U-21 All-Ireland win almost went unnoticed in Kerry.

1978: Highlights: 2nd All-Ireland, 4th Munster Senior and U-21, 4th Railway Cup titles

The start of a glorious run where we won four successive All-Ireland titles and remained unbeaten for 19 successive championship games. We scored a total of 15-63 in four championship games in 1978, including 5-11 against Dublin in the All-Ireland final. It was the highest score ever conceded by Dublin in the final.

1979: Highlights: 3rd All-Ireland, 5th Munster Senior titles

Clare, Cork, Monaghan and Dublin felt the force of our awesome power in what was probably our best year. There were times when it looked as if we had two solutions for every problem. At no stage in the championship did we feel threatened en route to a 25th All-Ireland title.

1980: Highlights: 4th All-Ireland, 6th Munster Senior titles

Roscommon blew their All-Ireland prospects by adopting the wrong tactics in the final. They came with a negative game plan which should have been revised when they went five points up early on. Had they been more positive, they could well have beaten us as we were quite vulnerable that day. It was Roscommon's best chance to win an All-Ireland for years.

1981: Highlights: 5th All-Ireland, 7th Munster Senior titles; 5th Railway Cup title

We landed the four-in-a-row, thus emulating the Kerry team of 1929–32 and Wexford in 1915–18. Offaly pushed us harder in the final than the seven-point winning margin would suggest, giving them renewed hope if we were to meet in another final which we did a year later.

1982: Highlights: 8th Munster, 2nd NFL title; 6th Railway Cup title

We should have known! We had last won the League title in 1977, only to be beaten by Dublin in the All-Ireland semi-final. The 1982 League title was the forerunner to an even bigger disappointment this year as Séamus Darby pounced for probably the most talked about goal of all time, wrecking our dream of becoming the first team to win the five-in-a-row.

1983: Empty sideboard

First Séamus Darby, now Tadhg Murphy. What is it with Kerry and last minute goals? Murphy's late goal for Cork ended our season in the Munster final and also ended an eight-year dominance over our great rivals.

1984: Highlights: 6th All-Ireland, 9th Munster, 3rd NFL titles; Manager of the Year

Triple success in the GAA's centenary year. Okay, we missed out on the Centenary Cup but the other three did nicely, thank you. We beat Galway in the League final, Cork in the Munster final and

Dublin in the All-Ireland final. A good season's work. There was another nice honour for me when I was chosen as Manager of the Year which brought recognition for Kerry's achievements in the wider world of sport.

1985: Highlights: 7th All-Ireland, 10th Munster, 1st Open Draw titles

Just as in 1978–79, we beat Dublin in the All-Ireland final for the second successive year. It was Kevin Heffernan's last season as Dublin manager, thus concluding a great rivalry between us, while it also marked the end of Brian Mullins' great playing career. Monaghan gave us our biggest test in the championship, drawing an All-Ireland semi-final before losing the replay.

1986: Highlights: 8th All-Ireland, 11th Munster, Kerryman of the Year

Another three-in-a-row; an eighth All-Ireland and 11th Munster title in 12 seasons. Recovering from a seven-point deficit against Tyrone in the second half of the All-Ireland final was a remarkable achievement. Would we have recovered if Kevin McCabe had goaled from a penalty to put Tyrone nine points clear early in the second half? Of course we would!

1987: Highlights: What highlights?

Beaten in the League final by Dublin, who were clearly a whole lot more determined to win than we were. Never mind, we'll be okay in the championship. Not this time. A Larry Tompkins point earned a draw for Cork in the Munster final and they swamped us completely in the replay in Killarney. The circus was over, even if we didn't quite recognise it at the time. I should have quit but such was my faith in that squad that I couldn't accept that it would be downhill from there on.

1988: The shadows lengthen

Cork beat us by a point in the Munster final. It was the first time for 14 years that we had lost to them in successive championships. The critics began to circle, claiming that I had remained too loyal to the old guard. Perhaps I had, but loyalty had always been a cornerstone of our dressing room so it wasn't easy to discard players who had achieved so much. Besides, where were the ready-made replacements? Subsequent events would prove that they weren't there.

1989: The end of the line

Back to the well one last time, only to find there was hardly a drop left. Cork played poorly in the Munster final but still won by three points on a day when I definitely knew I had stayed on too long. Bad enough to lose twice in a row to Cork but three times? I don't think it had ever happened to Kerry before. It was time to get out, so a week after the Munster final I announced my retirement.

1990: Kildare calling – and they won't go away

When Kildare come knocking they were told I wasn't at home. So they knocked again. And again. In the end, Michael Osborne and his posse of persuaders got me to agree to help set up new structures in Kildare. I'll give you six months, I told them. I stayed for four seasons. And that was only my first stint.

1991: Bright dawns, dark afternoons

There's a theory that the first season very often offers a new manager the best prospect of success. It's disproven as often as it's proven but there's no doubt that Kildare could well have won their first National League title that year. We lost the final by two points to Dublin after conceding a freakishly soft goal. Then Stefan White's last minute goal for Louth downed us at the first hurdle in the Leinster championship. It was clear there were going to be no shortcuts to success. If only I could have called on Larry Tompkins and Shea Fahy down in Cork.

1992: Dublin and that giant thumb

Dublin had suffered so much under Kerry in the 1978–85 era that they were taking great delight in keeping Kildare under their big, firm thumb. They didn't have to press very hard in the Leinster final which they had won by half-time. Of course, that was a very good Dublin team but the cynics preferred to dwell on my perceived failure to turn Kildare around. Not that it ever bothered me what anybody thought.

1993: Losing ground, gaining critics

We were lucky to beat Wicklow in the Leinster championship after trailing by nine points at half-time but Dublin were certainly getting me back for all those defeats they suffered during my days with Kerry. They beat Kildare again in the Leinster final and, to be honest, we didn't appear to be getting any closer to them in a real sense. It was getting very, very frustrating.

1994: Dodging the hangman

Another championship defeat by Dublin, this time in a replayed Leinster first round game. The critics were massing in Kildare since the previous year and it would have taken a Leinster title to scatter them When we lost to Dublin again, I didn't hang around to wait for a public execution. A few hours after the game I phoned Kildare Chairman Jack Wall and told him I was quitting.

1995: Golf, fishing, Waterville and hurling on the ditch

My first full year away from the inter-county scene for a very long time was most enjoyable, even if I did miss the thrill of the big days. I went back to working with Waterville while all the time keeping a close eye on Kildare results. They lost to Louth in the first round of the Leinster championship and this time, I couldn't be blamed.

1996: Kildare on the line again

Another poor championship season left Kildare looking for a new manager and, much to my surprise, they were back on the line again. Even those who wanted me out in 1994 welcomed me back.

It would have been easy to remind them of some of the cutting remarks that had been passed two years earlier but I was never one to harbour grudges. Besides, I believed in the Kildare players. Once more into the breach.

1997: A tingling sense of expectation

When 13-man Kildare dug in for one of the most courageous performances ever produced by a Lilywhite team in beating Laois, I knew I had made the right decision to return. All the more so when they raised their game ever higher in three wonderful Leinster semi-final clashes with Meath which ended in a two point defeat. Had we beaten Meath, I'm convinced we would have won the All-Ireland. Still, I felt the team was nearly ready for a really big push.

1998: Highlight: Kildare's first Leinster title since 1956

Sunday, 2 August. Glenn Ryan became the first Kildare man to receive the Leinster trophy for 42 years. It was as emotional for me as for the Kildare players as I had invested so much time and energy in them over two stints since 1990. Besides, it was a vindication for my son Karl who played a major part in the success after being scandalously ignored for years in Kerry. Kildare beat Dublin, Meath and Kerry, the three previous All-Ireland champions, to reach the final only to lose to Galway who, just as they had done in the Sixties, came back to haunt me.

1999: The season after optimism

I never drank alcohol so I don't know what a hangover feels like but its sporting equivalent descended on Kildare that year. Whipped by Dublin in the League quarter-final, we were just as flat in the Leinster championship losing in the first round to Offaly by four points. Frankly, we were flattered by the relatively narrow margin.

2000: Highlight: Beating Dublin in the Leinster final replay

Whatever the county and whatever the competition, there's always a special satisfaction in beating Dublin in a final. It was all the sweeter for Kildare who looked all washed up when trailing by six points at half-time in the Leinster final replay. Two quick goals sorted that out and Dublin wilted badly, scoring just one point in the second half. Kildare's All-Ireland ambitions soared but, once again, Galway were waiting to thwart them – and me. What did I ever do to deserve such bad luck against Galway?

2001: The beginning of the end

I could sense that the team's edge was beginning to blunt. Meath beat us fairly easily in Leinster and, although there was another chance in what was the first 'back door' season, Kildare didn't switch on to it and lost to Sligo rather tamely in Croke Park. Poor showings in the qualifiers would become something of a norm for Kildare in the following years. The qualifiers looked made for counties like Kildare but they have never quite adapted to them.

2002: White door closes, blue door opens

The Kildare adventure ended with a Leinster final defeat by Dublin, followed by a weak display against Kerry in the qualifiers. It was time to slip out of Kildare and return to the quiet life. And then along came Laois to intercept me on way back home to Waterville. I couldn't say no to a new challenge, now could I?

2003: Highlight: Laois's first Leinster title since 1946

A fairytale season for Laois. I got a wonderful response from the players right from the start and, after reaching the League final where we lost to Tyrone, it was clear they were ready for the championship step-up. They brought the Leinster title back to Laois for the first time in 57 years, a prize that appeared to be totally unattainable a year earlier when they capitulated like lambs against Meath in the All-Ireland qualifiers.

2004: The case of the missing two-in-a-row

Westmeath were the nation's favourites as Páidí Ó Sé led them to the Leinster title for the first time after beating us in a replay. Unquestionably, it was a lost opportunity for Laois to win the two-in-a-row. There were no discernible signs of over-confidence in our camp but sometimes they don't show and that's when they're at their most dangerous. I suspect they were there though, which shouldn't have been the case as Westmeath had a good record against Laois at under-age levels in previous years.

2005: Anybody see our lucky charm?

We were ravaged by injuries after 2003. So much so that it took up a lot of our time trying to figure out how to plug the gaps. The curse of the one-sided semi-final also struck. We beat Kildare so easily in the Leinster semi-final that I worried it might turn out to be our final. It did. We weren't nearly as effective against Dublin; nor did we enjoy any luck either in general play or in refereeing decisions and went down by a point. One title from three Leinster final appearances was a poor return for that Laois squad.

2006: Once more through the revolving door

I should have left Laois sooner but there was certainly no way I was staying on after a disastrous Leinster semi-final performance against Dublin, followed by another wasted opportunity against Mayo in the All-Ireland quarter-final. In between, we had got back to the basics that stood to us so well in 2003 as we battled through the qualifiers, but my time had come so whatever happened, my days with Laois were always going to be over when that championship ended. And then along came Wicklow and convinced me to start all over again.

2007: Good growth in the Garden County; Tommy Murphy Cup win

Wicklow games 'live' on TV for three successive O'Byrne Cup weekends in January. Hype mixed with hope for the League but we hadn't enough time to put in the amount of work I would have liked and we just missed out on a top four finish in our group. We should have beaten Louth in the Leinster championship but lost a second replay. Wicklow needed something to mark a year of growth and it came in the most dramatic circumstances when Tommy Gill kicked the winning goal in the last second of stoppage time in the Tommy Murphy Cup final against Antrim. Wicklow had finally managed to win a senior championship game in Croke Park. It made the year for a great footballing county.